No Harm

Ethical Principles for a Free Market

T. Patrick Burke

PARAGON HOUSE
New York, New York

First edition, 1994

Published in the United States by

Paragon House
401 Fifth Avenue
New York, New York 10016
Copyright © 1993 by Paragon House

Library of Congress Cataloging-in-Publication Data

Burke, T. Patrick
    No Harm : ethical principles for a free market / T. Patrick Burke. — 1st ed.
        p.   cm.
    Includes bibliographical references and index.
    ISBN 1-55778-618-6
    1. Free enterprise—Moral and ethical aspects.   2. Economic policy—Moral and ethical aspects.   3. Economics—Moral and ethical aspects.   4. Distributive justice.   5. Libertarianism—Moral and ethical aspects.   I. Title
HB95.B87   1993
174—dc20   93-12444
                                                                         CIP

Manufactured in the United States of America
Typesetting by AeroType, Inc.

Figures from ECONOMICS, 8/E by Richard G. Lipsey et al.
Copyright©1987 by Richard G. Lipsey, Peter O. Steiner and Douglas D. Purvis.
Reprinted by permission of HarperCollins Publishers Inc.

This book is dedicated to
Marnie (Frances Margaret) Burke,
who gave the author so much support,
and is now struggling for her life.

Punishment is punishment only when it is deserved. We pay the penalty because we owe it, and for no other reason; and if punishment is inflicted for any reason whatever than because it is merited by wrong, it is a gross immorality, a crying injustice, an abominable crime, and not what it pretends to be.

F. H. Bradley, *Ethical Studies*, 2nd edition, pp. 26–27

Contents

Primum non nocere.
Ancient adage in the spirit of Hippocrates.

Iuris praecepta sunt haec:
honeste vivere, alterum non laedere, suum cuique tribuere.
Justinian, *Institutes,* Book I, Title I.

Acknowledgements

My first thanks go to the foundations that overcame their sensible doubts and rashly decided to take a risk on an unknown author. The Earhart Foundation, under its president, David Kennedy, and program director, Antony Sullivan, have been outstandingly generous in their support over several years, and it is due more to them than to anyone else that the book is eventually seeing the light of day. The Lilly Endowment, through the good offices of Gordon St. Angelo, also provided substantial aid. The Center for Libertarian Studies, under the leadership of Joseph Peden, furnished the initial grant which enabled the project to get started. The Heritage Foundation, at the instigation of Richard Larry, helped with travel funds.

Several friends were willing to put their own projects aside in order to read the manuscript and give me detailed comments on it: my colleagues at Temple University, John Hasnas, who helped greatly with legal aspects of the argument; Michael Leeds, who took on himself the burden of seeing to it that my grasp of economics improved; Leonard Swidler, Sidney Axinn, and Daniel Bachman; Michael Kerlin of La Salle University, Philadelphia; Tibor Machan of Auburn University, and Fred Miller of Bowling Green State University, Ohio. Eric Cox, attorney in private practice, also helped with some of the legal material.

Thanks must also go to various groups that subjected themselves to listening to my papers on portions of the argument: the Philosophy Department at La Salle, the Philosophy Department II at Sydney University under David Armstrong, which raised some especially good questions, and then published one of my papers; the Religious Studies

Department there also, under Eric Sharpe; the Faculty of Theology of Hamburg University, Germany; the Evangelische Akademie in Hamburg; and the American Association for the Philosophic Study of Society.

Several of my graduate students also gave me comments on the manuscript, especially Richard Rinard, Annette Holmann, Andreas Rickerl, Fred Goos, and Nancy Smith. Being confronted with it in class they could scarcely escape, but bore up with fortitude.

Gustav Gumpert, of Smithkline Beecham, gave me helpful advice about the focus of the project when it was just beginning.

Despite all this help, needless to say, no one but myself should be blamed for the work's inadequacies.

Introduction

AMERICA'S CONDITION

After a struggle lasting some fifty years, a struggle waged whether by force of arms or by more peaceful means in almost every corner of the globe, the United States in the final decade of the twentieth century is witnessing the acknowledged triumph of the principles for which it has historically stood. In nation after nation dictatorship is in the process of being replaced by democracy, repression by freedom, and the stultification of planned economies by the dynamism of markets. With the collapse of communism in Eastern and Central Europe, the disintegration of the Soviet Union, and the abandonment of central planning even in China, America has become in many respects the model against which every nation must measure itself.

At the same time, however, the United States finds itself facing a host of formidable problems at home. Its economic power, which is the foundation of its military and political significance, has suffered a long-term decline relative to that of other nations, as shown especially in the weakness of its manufacturing industry, which has been saved in large part only by devaluing its dollar to less than half what it was thirty years ago. After four years the country is still struggling to emerge from a brutal recession which sent unprecedented numbers of businesses into bankruptcy, and rapidly increased unemployment. Its savings and loan system has been threatened with collapse, leading to an extremely expensive rescue by the federal government. Its system of public education, which consumes vast amounts of tax funds, is pervasively disappointing in its results. Its inner cities have turned into crime-ridden slums, haunted by the homeless. Its black underclass is mired in poverty, drugs, and alcohol, and black family life is to a large extent in ruins. If the now-defunct Soviet Union could be compared to a giant with powerful muscles but a diseased and feeble heart, does not a similar image apply to the United States?

Many commentators on these problems, in the newspapers and television, in university lecture rooms, and in the halls of government, appear to see these problems for the most part as having little to do with one another. Each problem is analyzed for its own particular causes. The cause of America's industrial difficulties lies in the low savings rate and the high cost of capital, perhaps, or in the management style of American corporations, or the inadequate education of the work force. The recession is the inevitable result of the profligacy of the eighties, the extravagances of the high-flying Reagan era and its supply-side economics. The savings and loan crisis is the result of inept or criminal management and of deregulation. The crisis in education is the result of poor school management or inadequate approaches to teaching. The decay of the cities and of the black underclass is the result of generations of racial discrimination. Homelessness is the product of the greed of landlords and developers. The drug problem is the outgrowth of a self-indulgent society. If there is any one theme that links all these evils, it is perhaps selfishness and greed, a moral decay which is nothing more than can be expected from capitalism. As for the victory over communism, that is essentially the triumph of a human longing for democracy, it provides no comfort for capitalism, and has little to teach nations which are already democratic.

Other commentators, however, see a very different picture. According to this other picture, all of these developments are indeed linked, not by the selfishness and greed of individuals, but by the theme of the excessive and inappropriate use of governmental power. In this view, the difficulties experienced by American manufacturing have been caused especially by the high cost of labor, which is chiefly the result of laws and regulations: laws imposing collective bargaining, laws mandating manifold benefits for employees, and laws which tell employers whom they must hire and whom they can discharge.[1] According to this view the recession resulted largely, if not entirely, from misguided attempts by the federal government to manipulate economic forces such as taxes, interest rates, currency exchange rates, credit availability, and the money supply.[2] The crisis in the savings and loan industry was the combined result of the collapse of the real estate market, brought about largely by the 1986 Tax Act, together with an unnecessary system of government deposit insurance, which at the expense of the taxpayer has protected savings executives from the normal market consequences of bad investments.[3]

The education crisis, in this view, is the result of the monopoly which government has over education, leading to an effective absence of competition between schools, and to the subordination of genuinely educational goals to a variety of politically motivated programs.[4] The social problems of homelessness, poverty, and the destruction of the black family, in this interpretation, are largely the paradoxical but predictable result of tax-supported welfare programs.[5] According to this view the factors which are causing the decline of American society are fundamentally analogous to those which brought the Soviet Union to its knees. There socialism, here not socialism in the full sense of the word, no doubt, but something which proves to have some astonishing similarities to it when examined dispassionately. Like Gulliver, who awoke from sleep to find himself unable to move because held to the ground by a thousand fine threads, American society in this view is being disabled and incapacitated by the thousands of laws and regulations which now impose forcible restrictions on individual initiative.

THE MARKET SYSTEM

It is clear now to everyone willing to consider the matter dispassionately that the market system presents the best means for ensuring economic progress: the best both economically and morally. Economically, because the market system has demonstrated that it has an unrivalled power to produce goods and services, and to produce them cheaply and in abundance. As a result of this fecundity the standard of living of even the lowest income groups in the West at the present time surpasses in many respects that of the highest income groups of earlier generations: for example, in such fields as medicine, transportation, and communications. Small countries with very limited resources, such as Hong Kong, Singapore, Taiwan, and South Korea, which not so long ago were on the bottom rung of the economic ladder, have been able, by relying chiefly on the market, in one generation to attain a material standard of living equivalent to that of the West. By contrast, those countries that have relied on governmental control of their economies for any length of time have suffered economic disaster, so that now even the most basic necessities of life are often unavailable.

If the market system has shown itself more successful economically, it has also shown itself more acceptable morally, since it represents less of an infringement on individual liberty and is more compatible with democracy and human rights. Central planning can evidently be maintained as a system only by dictatorial means, and those nations that have insisted on it have had to deny to their people systematically what the developed world considers the most elementary human rights, such as freedom of speech, freedom of the press, and freedom of association. The demand for political democracy and the demand for a market system go hand in hand.

The acknowledged power of the market system is reflected in the fact that at the present time there are numerous movements towards the expansion of it in the West and across the Pacific, for example in the dismantling of international trade barriers within the framework of the General Agreement on Trade and Tariffs, and the ongoing economic unification of Western Europe; and in the privatization of government services, especially in Great Britain in this decade.

However, the demonstrated superiority of the market over government control of the economy does not mean that a majority of people even in the West support the market unconditionally. Many still harbor serious doubts and suspicions about numerous aspects of market activity. Everyone is familiar with the market, everyone knows how easy it is to make a mistake when buying or selling, how easy it is to be gulled by an unscrupulous seller into buying low quality at a high price, how easy it is to be taken advantage of by an unconscionable employer. In business dealings the possibility of fraud lurks almost always in the wings. And while some business transactions are relatively insignificant, on others our very life depends. For most people, making a living in the market is not easy.

These difficulties carry over into a widespread distaste for the market as such, so that even where force and fraud are not in question, suspicion and aversion are common. The motive which animates the world of business is the desire for profit, which is a form of self-concern, and which appears to many to be indistinguishable from greed and to be the opposite of the concern for others which a mature sense of ethics enjoins. The desire for profit leads often to a crass commercialism which places little value on the criteria of good taste. The operation of the market may produce extensive changes, so that familiar products and accustomed ways of doing things, which some might prefer, are no longer available. From the viewpoint of justice, the market is acceptable to many only when the participants are relatively equal, or at least not excessively unequal, in their economic power. If one party enjoys a large advantage over the other, the market can no longer be relied upon to be fair, and corrective action by the government is necessary. It is generally taken for granted that, quite apart from questions of force and fraud, it is possible for one person to harm another by buying from him or selling to him if he is in difficult circumstances.

In consequence every Western nation has many laws designed to protect people from their exchange partners in economic transactions. Employees are typically considered to be in a weak position in relation to their employers, especially in the case of large firms, since if an employee loses his job he loses his livelihood, while the employer may suffer only a temporary inconvenience. So it seems to many people only right and necessary that employees should receive special protection. As a result trade unions receive special monopoly privileges by law, and numerous other laws require or forbid employers to enter into various kind of agreements with their employees in regard to salaries, working conditions and employee benefits. In some countries the government takes it on itself to fix wage levels and working conditions for entire industries.

Similarly in the area of consumer protection, many laws exist to ensure that businesses do not take unfair advantage of their customers, for example the laws concerning product quality and labeling, or those which restrict the sale of certain goods. Large sectors of the economy, such as banking, the stock market, communications, and the airlines, are subject to special regulatory bodies which exercise constant supervision of their day-to-day activities. One area of special importance, that of primary and secondary education, is to all intents and purposes a governmental monopoly, which effectively eliminates competition. Since 1986 alone, Congress has enacted eleven major pieces of legislation to regulate business.[6] By the end of 1991 the *U.S. Federal Register* contained 67,715 pages of economic regulations, and that does not include the many regulations imposed by state and local governments.

Not content with the current restrictions on the market, some people wish to limit it even more severely. Many environmentalists view the market system as intrinsically hostile to preservation of the environment and take it for granted that only collectivist solutions can be effective in solving environmental problems. Religious, artistic, educational, and journalistic circles, and in general the members of what has been called the "New Class" at the present time tend to share the common distrust of the free market and to demand more extensive governmental controls on the market as necessary requirements of social justice and humanity. In Eastern Europe the leaders of the newly democratic nations almost with one voice have stated that the kind of system they have it in mind to erect will not follow a free market model, but will be patterned rather after the protectionist "social-market economy" of nations such as Sweden or Germany.[7] Although socialism is clearly an economic failure, then, and although even the prestige it has long enjoyed as a moral ideal is now badly tarnished, a substantial amount of government regulation of the economy is still generally taken for granted as a moral necessity by opinion-makers.

MODERN LIBERALISM

Socialism is a system in which the government reserves to itself the production and distribution of goods and services.[8] It causes economic decline because it destroys the one incentive that leads most people to produce: the possibility of individual profit. It eliminates profit intentionally, because it considers it evil.

The system that has developed in the United States and other Western nations at the close of the twentieth century is one which leaves large areas of the market in place, but utilizes government to manipulate aspects of the market for the purpose of protecting various groups in the society from its dangers, and especially from inequality and unfairness. Workers, consumers, producers, and the disadvantaged, all at various times and in various ways are viewed, by both the Left and the Right, as needing protection from the ravages which an untrammeled market is believed to cause. A modest profit is allowable, but not beyond a certain point: "windfall" profits may be disallowed, and "profiteering" is not a term of approval. A name often given to this system is *modern liberalism*, because it has the appearance of being liberal, in the sense of generous to those who are in difficult or unequal circumstances. To see why it causes economic decline, we must study what are known to economists as the *opportunity costs* of regulation.

It's an obvious truth that if money is spent on one thing, the same money cannot be spent on something else. If I spend ten dollars on dinner, I cannot spend those same ten dollars on a book. The result of this is that every benefit has a cost. This does not cease to be true when the government mandates the benefit. Suppose that a lawnmower sells for $200, and the government mandates, as some states do, that it have a safety switch added to turn it off in case it escapes control while in use. The safety switch costs, say, $30. If a million lawnmowers are sold, that's a total cost of $30,000,000. Where does this sum of money come from? It comes from other benefits. It represents so much food, or clothing, or medical care, which people would have spent it on, but now cannot.

When government mandates the safety switch, it assumes (if it thinks about the matter at all) that the switch will be a greater benefit overall to the society than the other benefits that people now must lose as a result of it. How does the government know this? The answer is, it doesn't. There is no way it could possibly find this out, because there is no way of finding out what other benefits people would have spent that money on. On the contrary, there is good reason to believe that the benefit of the switch is *less* than the benefits it deprives people of. For obviously that is what the society believes, otherwise there would have been no need to make a law. The judgement of the market is the judgement of the society, and in the judgement of the market other things were preferable to the safety switch, taking its cost into account, otherwise the demand for the switch would have made it profitable for the manufacturer to add the device himself voluntarily.

This analysis will hold good if everybody who previously intended to buy a lawnmower still buys one, despite the additional cost. But some people will not buy one, because it now costs too much. They will get their old one repaired and keep using that. The new law has the effect of restricting the market. The size of the market (that is, the number and size of sales) decreases, and economic activity declines. But the prosperity of a society depends directly on the size of its market, as Adam Smith showed. Suppose that 50,000 people out of the million decide not to buy a new mower because of the additional cost. That means that $10,000,000 worth of sales do not take place. That would have paid the wages of 333 workers at $30,000 per year. Society has just lost 333 jobs. No doubt some of that will be taken up by extra jobs for repairmen, but perhaps not a large proportion of it.

We will see more about this in Chapter 4, in discussing the idea of economic value. The economic value of the switch is less than its cost, for the only meaningful measure of economic value is what satisfies the desires of individual buyers. There is no objective standard of what is good for a society economically apart from what individuals wish. There is no privileged standpoint from which it could be possible to say that some item is economically good for people even though they do not desire it. We can say, then, that almost by definition, if it is necessary to pass a law to achieve some economic benefit, then that benefit has less economic value than would otherwise have been achieved.

In 1981, in order to protect American automobile manufacturers with their many thousands of workers, Chrysler being near bankruptcy, the U.S. government negotiated "voluntary" quotas on Japanese car imports. What effect did these restrictions have? According to researchers at the Brookings Institution, they made it possible for the Japanese automakers to raise their prices by about $2,500 a car. This in turn made it possible for American manufacturers to add about $1,000 to their prices. The total cost of these increases to car-buyers by the time Washington lifted the quotas in 1985 came to about $14 billion. How many jobs did they save? The researchers calculate that the overall effect was a loss of 30,000 jobs! The car companies took advantage of the profits resulting from the higher prices to reduce the number of cars they produced by 300,000.[9] In addition, the quotas led to the U.S. car companies becoming ever more uncompetitive. Subsequently, in order to protect the jobs of manufacturing workers in general in the United States against imports, the value of the dollar itself relative to the yen was forced down by the U.S. Treasury. But this has had the effect of lowering the market value of everything in America, so that U.S. real estate and U.S. corporations can now be bought at bargain prices by foreign investors. This is not an atypical example of the effects of government regulation of the economy. At the same time, this is the result of only one economic regulation.

No doubt it is a serious problem that the Japanese government gives special help to its manufacturers and exporters. But there is a better way for the United States to respond than by imposing import restrictions, as we shall see in Chapter 3.

The net effect of economic regulation is to increase the price of goods and services, reduce employment, reduce production, retard innovation, lower the overall standard of living, and make it more difficult for the nation to compete against other nations. It is important to see that the same kinds of effects will ensue if the government makes any law regulating the manufacture, sale or purchase of lawnmowers, or of anything else. For economic legislation only *prevents* economic activity – by penalizing it; it does not in the overall create or stimulate it. When legislation is used to stimulate some specific kind of economic activity, which it can certainly do with subsidies and the like, it achieves this effect only by preventing other activity which the market would have judged more valuable. According to an estimate of the Center for the Study of American Business at Washington University in St. Louis, regulation in 1976 decreased the Gross National Product by $66 billion, or 3.6 percent.[10] If we consider that the increase in GNP is usually only about 2 percent per year, this is not a small amount. In the intervening years the burden of regulation has become noticeably heavier.

For reasons such as these, and because of bitter experience with the disastrous effects of planned economies, it seems safe to say that the purely economic argument for a free market has largely been won around the globe. Although the new administration in Washington seems to believe that the economy can be helped by regulation, that confidence is no longer as common as it once was. The chief arguments advanced at the present time against economic freedom, and the main reasons brought forward for economic legislation and regulation, are now almost invariably based, not on economic grounds, that regulation will lead to greater overall prosperity, but on moral grounds, or at least grounds which appear to many people to be moral, namely, considerations of fairness and social justice, the need to protect the weak and to prevent exploitation, that is, to prevent harm.

Despite the magnitude of the issues at stake, and despite the strong economic arguments in favor of complete market freedom, and the enormous losses which economic regulation often imposes on individuals and nations, it has usually not been felt that this philosophy needs to be supported by any very explicit arguments. For the most part these laws have been enacted without any extensive debate; their moral rightness has been taken for granted as something obvious, which any right-minded person must see.[11]

The economic collapse of socialism, which became clearly apparent in 1989, has convinced millions of doubters overnight that socialism is not the noble ideal that many had thought it to be. About modern liberalism, however, few doubts have been raised among its devotees. On the contrary, just at the time when the rest of the world is undergoing conversion to the market, to the system of which America is the symbol, the government of the United States has taken pride in enacting further laws to restrict the market, such as the Americans with Disabilities Act of 1990, and the Family Leave bill of 1993. There are weighty objections to such laws both on strictly economic grounds and above all, as we shall see, on ethical grounds. But the objections are dismissed by large numbers of American commentators as heartless.

THE IDEA OF A FREE MARKET

The thesis of this book is that social justice requires market freedom. The usual name for the point of view espoused here is *classical liberalism*, liberalism in the original sense in which the term was used in the nineteenth century, as distinct from modern liberalism, and part of the aim of the book will be to argue that a classical liberal economy is genuinely liberal, while what is called modern liberalism is not genuinely liberal.

Since the idea of a free market is widely misunderstood, it is perhaps advisable to explain it briefly at this point. The idea of a free market as used in this book is essentially a *legal* concept: whether a market is free is a question of what laws there are. The reason for this is that it is law which regulates the use of physical force: every law is a law only because it is backed up by the threat of a physical penalty.[12] Some readers may perhaps wish to question whether physical force is so distinctive a factor in removing freedom; but we shall hope to persuade them that it is. A free market, in the sense intended in this book, means that there are no special laws regulating market activity – buying, selling, and lending, giving and taking employment, trading or refusing to trade – over and above the ordinary laws which prohibit crime and civil injury. It is taken for granted in these pages that there will be laws prohibiting crime, that is, the deliberate infliction of harm on others, as well as laws providing remedies for civil or unintended injury, and so prohibiting the use of force and fraud in market transactions. It is also taken for granted that there will be laws defining what constitutes property, for example patent rights. It is not the case, then, that in a free market anything goes, that people would be entitled to rob, cheat, defraud, blackmail or otherwise injure one another with impunity. A free market, as it is understood here, does not mean that there is no government. It means that in economic matters the government does not go beyond forbidding actions which cause harm. We shall ask later what kinds of action cause harm.

But, it might be objected, is it not strictly speaking an infringement on people's freedom to forbid them by law to use force or fraud? And is not the concept of a free market as outlined here, then, a contradiction, or at the least a paradox?

No doubt it is a restriction of an individual's freedom, to forbid him to use force on others, but it is not a restriction on the freedom of the market, the freedom of exchange. For an exchange to take place it is necessary to have two parties acting jointly, and if the exchange is to be free, the action of each party entering into the exchange must be freely undertaken, that is, it must be free from force and fraud. By eliminating the freedom to use force, the law protects the freedom to exchange.

PUNISHMENT

The central focus of this book is on *punishment*. Its thesis is that to use legislation and governmental regulation to achieve economic goals is to employ the weapon of punishment on people who do not *deserve* be punished. There must be punishment for force and fraud, because these truly cause harm; but in the absence of force and fraud the law should not punish either party to a contract because of any terms of the contract, for these do not cause harm. Nor should it punish those who refuse to do business with others, no matter what their reasons, for that also does not cause harm. Government, however, invariably acts only by causing or threatening harm.

If it is the case that we do not cause harm to people by trading with them, in the absence of force and fraud, *no matter what* the terms of the trade; and if we likewise do not harm them by refusing to trade with them for whatever reason; if government, whenever it acts, does so only by causing or threatening harm; and if those who have not caused harm have a right not to be harmed; then it follows that people ought not to be restricted by government in their economic activity so long as they abstain from force and fraud. For to impose governmental restrictions on trade for the purpose of protecting people from their trading partners or their competitors, or in order to compel them to trade, is to harm people who have caused no harm, and that offends against the most fundamental of ethical principles. This is the chief thesis of the book.

Although material from economics, law, and other fields is used, this is a book of philosophy. The questions facing our society are funda-mental questions about the most basic principles we have, and they will not be settled by anything less than a broad agreement in philosophy. They will not be settled by economic theories, because our economic theories, and even our selection of significant economic facts to judge our theories by, depend on our philosophy. They will not be settled by experience or history, because our interpretation of our experience and history depend on our philosophy, as the reactions of many modern liberals to the collapse of the Soviet Union has made fascinatingly clear. If we wish to solve the problems of our society, it is to our philosophical theories and assumptions that we must look.

It needs perhaps to be stressed here that what is offered in this book does not pretend to be a complete or comprehensive ethical system. It has nothing to say, for example, about the motivations which should animate our lives, about the goals that we ought to strive for, or about the means that would lead most faithfully to those goals. It neither criticizes nor approves the ways that individuals live their lives. It does not attempt to spell out what a humane society would be like in any positive, concrete detail, beyond the fact that it requires economic freedom. It does not by any means imply the absurd idea it is often taken to imply, that the whole of human existence in society can be reduced to market or business relationships. It is focused on a single, narrow question, namely, *what laws there ought to be*.

The relationship between free markets and capitalism calls perhaps for some comment on this score. If we accept Peter Berger's definition, capitalism is the production of goods for sale in the market rather than for consumption by the producer.[13] The argument of this book is that in the absence of force and fraud, and so long as there are no harmful externalities, the production of goods for sale in the market is invariably beneficial, should not be penalized, and therefore should not be regulated or impeded by law. Protectionism, in this view, is an ethical as well as an economic mistake. Yet capitalism is not identical with economic freedom, and is compatible in practice with a high degree of protectionism. Many successful proponents of capitalism have been ardent protectionists. While an argument for market freedom is an argument for capitalism, then, the reverse is not necessarily the case.[14]

TAKING ACCOUNT OF OBJECTIONS

Free markets have been the subject of violent controversy. Is it possible to have a rational discussion of this topic? I believe it is not impossible, though the possibility hinges on a condition that our human nature finds difficult. The condition is that each side recognizes the possibility that it may be mistaken. Whether we hold a position rationally is a question of the extent to which we are prepared to take account of the objections to our views.

The natural sciences, which have been so astonishingly successful in adding to human knowledge, must be our models in this regard. In physics and chemistry it is not sufficient for the scientist to lay out the arguments in favor of his theory, although that of course is indispensable. What is distinctive about the scientist is that he must be willing to put his theory to the test, not sit back and wait for others to show that it is mistaken, but himself take the initiative to discover the difficulties it is subject to. It is well-known that when Einstein published his General Theory of Relativity he indicated at the same time some pieces of evidence which could disprove it. If his theory was correct, he said, then a ray of light from a distant star passing by the sun on its way to the earth would be deflected by a small but definite amount. If this did not occur, then his theory was mistaken.[15] As it happened, his theory passed the test with flying colors.

In the humanities and the social sciences, by contrast, this willingness to seek out the possible weaknesses in one's own position is not always evident. Freud does not say, "Perhaps my theory of the superego and the id is fundamentally bilge. Here are the arguments against it, and we must be sure that we have sound answers to them before we can be confident that the theory is correct." Marx does not seem to have lain awake at night, tossing and turning in his bed, worrying whether his theory of exploitation might not possibly, after all, be totally groundless and mistaken.

Yet in the absence of an active concern to avoid error, an opinion which is put forward, however novel, ingenious or interesting it may be, and no matter in how much detail it may be elaborated, remains at best merely a set of possible considerations and cannot genuinely commend itself as a reasonable belief. In the absence of an active concern to avoid error, it is all too easy to settle for mere plausibility as the criterion to judge by. But plausibility is often relative to the individual's desires. Such is our human nature that if we find an idea which we like, that is frequently sufficient to persuade us that it is correct. Of course, we may like a theory because it appears to have great explanatory power. But that by itself is not enough to demonstrate that it is true. A paranoid may be capable of devising a very full explanation for all the behavior he encounters. And no doubt we may find it difficult to give a theory up if there are no alternative explanations available. But that by itself is also not enough to show that the theory genuinely warrants our assent.

In philosophy and the social sciences, of course, the kind of decisive empirical tests which the natural sciences can use are for the most part unavailable.[16] The support for a theory, and the objections against it, often come from other sources than hard experience. Sometimes the presuppositions on which an objection is based may be so remote that it is difficult even to comprehend it. The possible objections to a theory may be endless. A consequence of this is that in these fields fashion and whim often play a significant role in shaping opinion.[17] Yet the difficulty of establishing theories decisively in these fields does not mean that the theorist is released from the task of viewing his own theories in a critical light. Rather it makes that task all the more necessary.

By the same token, those who raise objections also have a responsibility, namely, to seek a genuine answer. Just as it is easy when we like a position to search out only the arguments in its favor and pass over its difficulties in silence, so when we dislike a viewpoint, it is attractive to raise whatever objections we can, not so much with a view to finding an answer, but in order to discredit the position we dislike. This presupposes that the position is mistaken, and perhaps it is, but then again, perhaps it may prove in the end to have more to be said for it than we imagine.

The views which are put forward in this book were not adopted simply as a matter of blind faith. They run counter to opinions I held for many years.[18] When the ideas set out in this book first occurred to me, I assumed that there must be cogent answers to them, and I spent a considerable time trying to find those answers. It was only when the search proved unsatisfactory that I began to explore the ideas themselves more fully.

Following my own prescription, in writing this book I have tried to discover and take account of every distinct objection that can be raised against the views argued for here. Despite that, I have no doubt that I have implemented my prescription only very imperfectly. It remains highly likely that some significant difficulties have been missed, and I do not doubt there are many objections which I have failed to grasp as profoundly as those who advance them would like.

In particular, it is easy for supporters of free markets, being human, to make devastating mistakes in the practical implementation of free-market policies. A policy may be correct in principle, but human society is immensely complex, and any significant change may produce utterly unexpected and unforeseeable results. What in the long run is right and necessary may cause havoc in the short term if introduced too quickly or too slowly, too broadly or too narrowly in society. In addition to theoretical insight, the implementation of free-market policies requires a great degree of practical wisdom.

1

The Liberal Society

THE EMERGENCE OF RELIGIOUS FREEDOM

Across the street from Boston Common, in front of the State House, stands the statue of a Quaker woman, Mary Dyer, who was hanged there in 1660. The only crime she had committed was that of being a Quaker in a Puritan society. Her statue, generously erected by the Puritans' descendants, is a silent testimony to a revolution of thought and feeling which divides what we may call the modern world from everything which preceded it as effectively as the Himalayas divide India from China. She was hanged because to the world of the Middle Ages and for some time afterwards it seemed a self-evident truth that a society could only afford to have one religion.

If we were to try to explain this assumption in terms understandable to a person living at the present time, we might perhaps say something like this. It is religion which lays the foundation for society. Religious beliefs provide the cognitive foundation for society because they provide the interpretation of the cosmos within which the society has its being, and religious values establish the foundation for the values of the society because they provide the overarching goals of human life, and so the ultimate framework and guidelines of social existence. Religious beliefs and values have a direct and profound effect not only on a society's understanding of itself, and on its goals, but also on the socially acceptable means to those goals, and on social relationships altogether. A society only exists in virtue of shared meanings, and therefore the unity of society, that is, its existence as a unified realm under a single government, demands religious unity. A society which allowed freedom of religion to individuals would be undermining its own basic reality, and the result would be anarchy and chaos. The religion of the State must therefore be maintained collectively: a society is entitled to use the force of arms to make sure that the religious unity necessary to its survival is preserved.[1]

At the time of the founding of the United States, however, a historic change took place. Several of the colonies had their own religious traditions: Massachusetts was Puritan and Congregationalist, Pennsylvania was Quaker, Virginia and the Carolinas were Anglican. But during the eighteenth century a more tolerant spirit had taken hold, probably under the impact of the Enlightenment, and the colonies had each loosened many of their restrictions on other forms of religion than their own. Furthermore, if they were going to found one nation together, they could scarcely afford to put one another to death for religious differences. The members of the First Congress therefore agreed, and enshrined it in the First Amendment to the Constitution, that the new federal government "shall make no law respecting an establishment of religion, or prohibiting the free exercise thereof. . . ." The United States was to have *freedom of religion*. The actual implementation of this provision in the sense in which we understand it today took some time.[2] But by this one act, arguably, more than by any other, the new nation crossed the watershed into the modern world.[3] Today the principle of freedom of religion is generally accepted as an integral part of a democratic constitution.

In the ancient world and in the Middle Ages men feared that freedom of religion would lead both to the death of religion and also to the death of society. In point of fact, however, as we now know, it has led to neither. The reality is rather the opposite. Freedom of religion has been an immense boon to religion. Perhaps in no other society has religion enjoyed the voluntary support of the people to the extent that it has done in the United States. In comparison with the citizens of other Western countries, a high percentage of Americans attend church and synagogue and describe themselves as believing in God.

By the same token freedom of religion, far from weakening the State and civil society, has strengthened them. Experience has supported what Roger Williams wrote, "The Church is like unto a corporation, society, or company of East India or Turkey merchants, or any other society or company in London, which may wholly break up and dissolve into pieces and nothing, and yet the peace of the city not be in the least measure impaired or disturbed."[4] Because of the freedom it allows, the United States has traditionally enjoyed the enthusiastic support of the vast majority of its religiously inclined citizens. In churches and synagogues typically the American flag flies, a thing which surprises visitors, and which would be ludicrous or offensive in most other countries. Because of the religious freedom it permits, the talents of its people have been available to their society no matter what their religious convictions, and it seems reasonable to think that it is partly as a result of this that the United States has experienced the remarkable outpouring of human energy which it has.

The historical developments which led to freedom of religion also brought about the more general freedom of speech and of association. The traditional societies of the ancient world and the Middle Ages knew nothing of free speech. Any statements which could be taken in a political or politico-religious sense were dangerous, as Socrates, Jesus, Galileo, Giordano Bruno, and hosts of others had cause to know. In Great Britain it was a criminal offense until 1695 to publish any printed matter without first obtaining a license,[5] and even in 1776 there was no legal guarantee of freedom of speech or of the press. In Austria it was still prohibited in 1805 to possess any book in the Hebrew language.[6] Similarly in traditional societies there was no such thing as a right of association. Roman law, which remained the basis of European law, viewed any association among subjects as a potential conspiracy against the state, and the only way to legitimize an association was to obtain a special license for it from the government.[7]

How could mankind make such an enormous mistake, for such a very long time? What was wrong with the ancient arguments, which were accepted for millennia apparently without question? Why do we believe that freedom of religion is indispensable to our society, instead of the monstrous threat it was believed to be?

One reason that has sometimes been given for freedom of religion is that it is impossible to prove scientifically that one religion is the true one. Religious beliefs are not the kind of thing that can be established by demonstrative proof. They are a matter of faith, and faith is something which must be left up to the individual. While this may be an important consideration in the twentieth century, however, it is an argument of more recent date than the First Amendment. The authors of the Amendment were for the most part supporters of religion, as is evidenced amongst other things by the fact that some weeks before they approved the Amendment they reenacted the Northwest Ordinance, which stated that religion is necessary to good government and the happiness of mankind. Besides, even if it could be proven that one particular set of religious beliefs was correct and true, the principle of freedom of religion would still stand. It is generally conceded that the Law of Fixed Proportions in chemistry has been proven true, yet no one suggests that, in case there should be skeptics about it, they should be burned at the stake. Typically Americans believe not only in freedom of religion, but in freedom of opinion and expression in general.

RESPECT FOR THE INDIVIDUAL

The fundamental reason for this belief in freedom is the growth of a greater respect for the individual human person, over against the putative claims of authority and society. A human person is and should be an autonomous being. Adults have the power to govern themselves, and that power should be respected by others. The power to govern oneself belongs essentially to the being and the well-being of every sane adult. And so an adult, it is felt, has the right to determine the course of his own life. So far as society is concerned, the crucial thing is that he should cause no harm to others. So long as he does no harm to others, he is entitled to hold whatever opinions he wishes and follow whatever practices he wishes. "If a Roman Catholic believe that to be really the body of Christ which another man calls bread, he does no injury thereby to his neighbour. If a Jew do not believe the New Testament to be the Word of God, he does not thereby alter anything in men's civil rights," argues Locke.[8] An individual has the right to develop his potentialities to the fullest, in the direction which he himself chooses. To compel him by the threat of imprisonment or death to subscribe to some common faith would be a grave injustice, an unjustifiable encroachment on the liberty of the individual.[9] Views such as these are a hallmark of the liberal society.

The liberal society has been supported with arguments drawn from a variety of philosophical positions. Among the soundest of these, in the opinion of the present writer, is the view that points to the key role of freedom of the will. In this view, adult human beings are autonomous because they have the unique power of making voluntary choices. They are not machines, not even very sophisticated ones. They have the mysterious ability to initiate action, and therefore to be responsible for their own behavior. They can act ethically or unethically, selfishly or generously, prudently or foolishly: that is, they are answerable for what they do, there are moral standards by which their behavior can be judged. This places them in a category quite apart from any other beings we are familiar with. It bestows on them human dignity, and it entitles each one of them to profound respect. In the language of some philosophers, a person is not an object, but a subject.

Locke is clear about this also:

> No way whatsoever that I shall walk in against the dictates of my conscience will ever bring me to the mansions of the blessed. I may grow rich by an art that I take not delight in; I may be cured of some disease by remedies that I have not faith in; but I cannot be saved by a religion that I distrust and by a worship that I abhor. It is in vain for an unbeliever to take up the outward show of another man's profession. Faith only and inward sincerity are the

things that procure acceptance with God. . . . If they believe, they will come of their own accord, if they believe not, their coming will nothing avail them. . . . men cannot be forced to be saved whether they will or no. And therefore, when all is done, they must be left to their own consciences.[10]

This power to be responsible for one's actions is so integral to the being of a person that no amount of good, no quantity of wealth or power which might be conferred on a person from outside could be satisfactory if it abolished that self-responsibility. This realization, consciously or implicitly, which can be summed up under the term "individualism," has been a cornerstone of the liberal society.

Because they are responsible for their own behavior, persons cannot effectually be commanded what to believe. They have the power to make up their own minds, and in a certain sense there is no other way they can believe anything. If they wish, of course, they can take someone else's word, but that does not relieve them of their responsibility: they are still responsible for the fact that they have decided to take someone else's word, instead of finding out for themselves. Since people can make up their own minds, it is degrading to them to try to coerce them into believing anything. Belief cannot be forced. People must be free to decide their beliefs for themselves. A large number of people in the West accept this view and have shown that they are willing to respect this freedom.

This same respect for the individual has led in the course of the twentieth century to a more liberal view of family and sexual morality. Divorce was once prohibited as immoral, as something which would undermine indispensable social relationships (as it is to this day in, say, the Republic of Ireland). Now, even though serious questions remain about its effect on children, it is widely felt that adults should have the right to determine their own fate. Homosexuality once incurred the death penalty. Now, while many people do not condone it from a moral viewpoint, there is a widespread feeling against imposing legal penalties on homosexuals.

To speak in very general terms, traditional societies are typically authoritarian. They tend to accept one way of understanding the world as unquestionably right, and to impose it upon the entire society either by law or at least by opinion. The whole complex of values generally acknowledged in the society are taken to be objectively valid and clearly evident to anyone of good will, so that there is little room for dispute about them, and even minute deviations from them may be punished severely. There is a relatively tight set of customs which indicate what kinds of behavior are acceptable, and anyone who does not follow those customs is likely to find himself in deep trouble.

A liberal society, by contrast, is a tolerant society. It accepts that there are many ways of understanding the world, any one of which may prove to be right or partly right, and it is willing to allow a free competition between opinions vying for acceptance. It acknowledges that no human being is infallible, everyone can make mistakes, and truth can be found sometimes in the most unlikely places. It understands that many values are subjective, and opinions about them can vary legitimately from individual to individual; that it is often extremely difficult to tell what is true and what is false, what is good and what is bad. A liberal society takes a generous view of diversity of behavior and is willing to a large extent to put up with people who have bizarre ways of doing things. In any society, of course, there must be standards which rule out some kinds of conduct as unacceptable, but the liberal society is inclined to draw the limits of the unacceptable fairly loosely, leaving as much as possible to the judgement of the individual. It is inclined to estimate individuals on their merits, rather than in the light of the qualities typically associated with their group. By the same token a liberal society does not in principle look disdainfully at other cultures but is open to the possibility that it may be able to learn something interesting or useful from them.

In short, the emergence of the modern world was marked by an increased respect for the individual human person, together with a growing realization that coercion, the use of physical force on an individual, is incompatible with that respect, and that therefore the burden of the law, which always acts by means of coercion, should be kept to a minimum and should only be imposed with the consent of those subject to it.

To the critical eye of the authoritarian society, the liberal society looks anarchic and immoral. But underneath the storms of diversity which it may experience, it rests on a bedrock of moral principle, the one unquestionably sound principle of social order, that no one is to cause harm to his neighbor. In regard to infractions of this principle a liberal society cannot afford to be tolerant. It may proceed only very reluctantly to take action, it may take a long time to make up its mind that an activity is truly harmful, and having made up its mind, it may subsequently change it in the light of further debate; even where it is clear that harm has been done it may acknowledge many sorts of palliating circumstances in difficult cases. But in the end its verdict must be that harm cannot be tolerated. It is the liberal society which has been the champion of human rights.

THE BENEFITS OF TOLERANCE

The tolerance and humanity which are the hallmark of the liberal society, together with its insistence on certain key ethical standards, has produced some astonishing benefits for mankind during the brief period of some three hundred years in which it has been tried. One of these benefits is science. Physics, chemistry, and biology have added immeasurably to our knowledge of the world we live in. The conditions of human life have been transformed by their discoveries. Why is it that they developed in the modern Western world, and not in traditional societies, even those, such as the Chinese, the Indian, and the Islamic, which in some repects were once more culturally developed? It has not been an accident. Science arises because, amongst other things, a free competition of ideas is allowed. Those ideas that can establish themselves by experiment and evidence are adopted, those that cannot are put aside. The rise of science was an outgrowth of the development of the liberal society, beginning in the sixteenth and seventeenth centuries.[11]

John Gray, a noted student of liberalism, has recently maintained that this argument cannot be used to support liberalism, since the growth of science is not necessarily a good thing. The value of knowledge, he holds, depends on what it is used for, and he points to the weapons of mass destruction that have followed the development of science.[12]

No doubt it is possible that in certain circumstances knowledge may be more harmful than ignorance. We shall argue in a later chapter (though without developing the argument at any length) that nothing can be counted on to be good always and absolutely except refraining from causing harm. All positive values are good only in principle, all things else being equal, and in any particular situation all else may not be equal. In principle, knowledge is better than ignorance, but in a particular case it may turn out that the person with knowledge causes more harm to himself or to others. But this possibility by itself is not an adequate account of value. There is a reason, deriving from the very nature of knowledge, why knowledge is better in principle, and why therefore under most normal circumstances knowledge will also be better in practice, namely that it is through knowledge that we adjust our actions to reality. It will be the exceptional case, rather than the rule, that ignorance is more beneficial. Furthermore, it is surely necessary to make a distinction between a thing and the uses to which it may be put. A good thing may be put to a bad use. Knowledge is one thing, and the use that may be made of it is another. The one does not necessarily follow from the other. All things else being equal, a form of society which fosters the growth of knowledge will be more beneficial to mankind than one that does not.

The liberal society is itself the best guarantee that knowledge will not be abused. As several authors have pointed out, it has rarely if ever happened that democratically governed societies have gone to war with one another. The weapons of mass destruction have been developed either by dictatorships, or, if by democratic societies, only in response to the threat of aggression by dictatorships, and with immense regret.

Gray argues further against the liberal society that the progress of knowledge is not sufficiently explained by the competition of ideas, by constant mutual criticism, but may sometimes rather require an illiberal dogmatism. The liberal society may not always be the best place, then, for the development of science, he maintains.[13]

It would be better to say that the progress of science sometimes requires determination and dogged confidence in one's own theories, for these are not incompatible with criticism, as dogmatism is. But even if we accept Gray's point, there is a great deal of difference between the dogmatism of an individual who is merely certain that he is right, and the dogmatism of a government which will not allow any doctrine to be taught but the party line, under penalty of imprisonment or worse. The individual dogmatist can still change his mind, but no such change is possible under a dogmatic government without overturning the political order. Whether or not scientific knowledge may be advanced by occasional dogmatism, however, it certainly needs constant testing and criticism. The historical fact is that scientific knowledge has grown only to the extent that there has been this testing and criticism. This requires a free competition of ideas, and it is only in the liberal society that this competition has been allowed to take place.

Science of itself is simply a quest for knowledge. The transformation of that knowledge into actual achievement, into concrete goods and services of benefit to human beings, is not automatic but requires great expenditures of energy. Again, however, it is in the liberal societies of the West that the economic and technological developments which produced those goods and services first took place. It is in the liberal societies of the West that bacterial diseases have been largely vanquished, that the age-old specter of famine has been banished, that life expectancy has doubled and trebled. If we compare the standard of living of a modern American with that of a European at the close of the Middle Ages, or with that of the majority of inhabitants of what is now called the Third World, it is clear that the liberal society has produced an improvement in the material conditions of human life that is nothing short of astounding.

Liberal societies are more effective than authoritarian societies in satisfying human needs, in the first place because the satisfaction of human needs is more important to them. In most authoritarian societies the satisfaction of the needs of the individual is not a matter of paramount importance. In order to take people's needs seriously, it is necessary first of all to have a profound respect for the individual human person, regardless of his or her social status or class. Furthermore, human beings are individuals, and diverse, and their needs are constantly changing. An authoritarian society tends to have a rigid view of what people's needs are, and what can be done to respond to them. Instead of allowing people to say what they need, it largely contents itself with deciding for them what their needs ought to be. A society which allows the freedom to experiment (even though that must also be the freedom to fail) can bring its resources to bear on genuine needs with immeasurably greater efficacy.

Not only has the liberal society produced immense scientific and economic benefits, it has also and perhaps above all brought great political benefits: it is to the liberal society that we owe the establishment of representative government as an effectual system. The idea of democracy is enshrined in two principles: majority rule, and human rights. Both of these, but especially human rights, are antipathetic to authoritarianism. The democratic system is based on the principle that every human being is of equal moral value and should be of equal legal importance. At the present time we witness attempts to develop democratic forms of government in many different countries around the globe, because it has become evident to even the least tutored that it fares better economically with people in democratically governed countries. But unhappily many of these attempts have been less than successful, because the basic attitudes of these societies are authoritarian, and the governmental practices which prevail in them fail to give the individual the guarantee of freedom and respect which is indispensable to a democracy.

LIBERALISM AND PUNISHMENT

The liberal respect for the individual shows itself in a notable way in a heightened sensitivity to the implications of punishment. Punishment is not something that liberals are fond of. The liberal attitude towards punishment is typically that it is at best an evil necessity. One of the greatest triumphs of the liberal movement has been the reform of the criminal justice system.

In England in 1820, some two hundred and twenty-two offenses were punishable by death. These included the theft of five shillings' worth of goods from a shop, the making of false entries in a marriage license, counterfeiting, horse- and sheep-stealing, smuggling, and rioting. Over the next forty years, as the result of a groundswell of liberal opinion inspired by the Italian writer Beccaria, and led by such men as John Howard, Jeremy Bentham, Sir Samuel Romilly and Sir Robert Peel, these were reduced to three: murder, treason and piracy.[14]

For crimes not penalized by death, the tradition of punishment inherited from the Middle Ages both in Britain and America was one not of imprisonment but of corporal punishment, using methods which today most civilized people would find appalling: flogging, mutilation, branding, the stocks and pillory, confinement in irons, the chain gang, the ducking stool. In the course of the eighteenth and nineteenth centuries, largely through the influence of the Pennsylvania Society of Friends, these came to be replaced by the vastly more humane system of imprisonment with labor.[15]

Liberal values have manifested themselves not only in changes in the punishment of crime, but also in the improvement of methods of ascertaining guilt. Perhaps the most notable achievement in this regard has been the abolition of torture as an accepted and legal means of securing confessions.[16]

It has been a consistent feature of liberal opinion from its earliest appearance to desire to humanize, to mitigate and reduce, the punitive element in society. So true is this that some liberals have even advocated the abolition of punishment altogether, and its replacement by psychological treatment.

A RESTRICTED CONCEPTION OF SOCIAL HARM

The humanity of the liberal society, as compared with authoritarian societies, has stemmed, paradoxically, from its willingness to adopt a restricted conception of harm, especially of social harm. If the idea of harm is taken very broadly a liberal society becomes impossible, because from some perspective or other almost any human action or state of affairs can be considered socially harmful. During the Middle Ages Europeans in general thought that religious dissent was harmful to society. The Puritans thought that anything that was immoral or even unspiritual was harmful to society—and included dancing on their list of immoralities. What could be more obviously harmful to a society than public criticism of those who hold the reins of government, which must inevitably tend to undermine due respect for it, and so weaken the foundation of the society? But the liberal society recognized that the appearance of harm here is deceptive, and that on the contrary the freedom to criticize the government, while it may occasionally result in unwise policies if used excessively, in the long run is immensely beneficial to society because it makes it possible for citizens to participate in the process of government, which thus becomes stronger, as well as because it makes it more likely that mistakes on the part of government will be corrected.

American society, however, like other Western societies, is both liberal and authoritarian, that is, its liberal revolution was never more than partial and incomplete. The liberal vision was ever only possessed and understood by a relatively small number of people, who by good fortune were enabled to implement it to a limited extent, especially in

Britain and its former colonies. In regard to manners and in the realm of personal interaction Americans in general tend to have more liberal attitudes than many other peoples. The U.S. Constitution enshrines the essence of liberalism in the Bill of Rights. But in regard to other legislation authoritarian attitudes have remained strong. The descendants of the Puritans, even when they lost their faith in divine revelation, often retained the conviction that they knew what was best for society, and were determined to impose that where they could, as the temperance and "blue" laws of many states showed in the nineteenth century, and federal Prohibition in the twentieth.[17] Also, those who immigrated to the United States from more authoritarian societies typically brought with them the very patterns of thought and feeling which had fashioned the societies from which they were anxious to escape. But the tradition of liberalism has won one decisive victory after another over the remnants of medieval authoritarianism.

A sensitive conscience, and the experience of mankind, tell us that a society can be humane only to the extent that it is free from the excessive use of coercion and punishment. It has been the great achievement of the liberal tradition to have understood that, to have fought for humanity and for freedom, and actually to have succeeded in bringing about a large measure of freedom in some significant areas of human life.

ECONOMIC FREEDOM

There is one area, however, where this is not the case. There is one domain, and that a vitally important one, where liberal-minded people have abandoned the liberal vision on which they otherwise have prided themselves and have betrayed their own best insights and their highest values. This is the realm of the economic. In the twentieth century those who have been the champions of freedom of speech, of freedom of conscience, of freedom of association, of freedom of religion, and of the right of privacy have not been the champions of economic freedom. On the contrary, they have become the chief supporters of governmental regulation of economic life. Those who have been the opponents and the humanizers of punishment in other domains of social existence have vastly extended its range in matters concerned with the world of business. In regard to the activity of the market they have reverted to the repressive, authoritarian and punitive conceptions of the Middle Ages. In doing so they have placed themselves in a state of fundamental self-contradiction.

To be sure, this has not happened without a reason, and a reason which in its own way should receive the respect of every humane person.

They have felt a sense of moral revulsion at inequality, they have been affronted by the sight of poverty, of unemployment, of factories where workers are paid low wages and work in unpleasant or unhealthy conditions, of discrimination against minorities and women. They have been repelled by what they conceive of as the greed which animates capitalism.

In short, they have felt many of the same feelings of moral revulsion which an ancient Roman experienced on encountering Christians, which Christians used to feel when they had to deal with Jews and Muslims, which Catholics and Protestants once felt for one another, and which the New England Puritans felt when they encountered a Quaker. Only the focus of moral concern has shifted from the religious to the economic. Like their religious predecessors, modern liberals have concluded that their feelings of moral revulsion should be enforced by the penalties of the law.

The result has been a profound transformation in liberal goals. During the eighteenth century and most of the nineteenth, the goal of liberal-minded people was above all to increase the domain of individual freedom from the long arm of government, that is, from the use of force and the imposition of punishment. This goal is still retained in some noneconomic matters, for example in the insistence on the right to privacy. But beginning in the latter half of the nineteenth century, under the impress of the working conditions in the factories, and perhaps even more as a result of the experience of the Great Depression, and then the Civil Rights movement, this goal came to be replaced, in matters touching on economic activity, by the goal of giving more societal power to those who have less. The overriding aim of those who now consider themselves liberals is typically no longer freedom, but equality. In the words of an earlier writer, "Liberty without equality is a name of noble sound and squalid meaning."[18] If not full equality in a thoroughgoing egalitarian sense, at least sufficient to guarantee basic needs. Inequalities are presumptively inhumane and harmful. In the process the idea of freedom has been typically reinterpreted to mean equality, or the possession of a certain quantity of economic means. Freedom now in the concrete according to this view means chiefly freedom from want, freedom from exploitation, freedom from discrimination. The ideal of minimizing force and punishment has gone. Classical liberalism has given way to modern liberalism.

That there are inherent difficulties in understanding the concept of freedom in this new sense can be seen if the attempt is made to apply it to freedom of religion. Freedom of religion as traditionally understood means that government does not penalize people for practicing a particular religion, but leaves them free to believe or not believe in whatever religion they wish. If economic freedom means freedom from want, then by analogy religious freedom should mean freedom from irreligion, perhaps freedom from atheism. But a freedom from irreligion enforced by the threat of prison would clearly be the opposite of what freedom of religion means, for it would imply that the law should enforce religion. Could freedom of religion mean, perhaps, a legislated guarantee of the positive opportunity to practice one's religion, for example that everyone should be provided with a church and a minister within reasonable distance? But what of Jews, Muslims, Buddhists, and agnostics? As yet no one has suggested that religious freedom should be understood in this sense.

Something similar seems to be true of political freedom. Political freedom as traditionally understood means that, amongst other things, people are not punished by government because of membership in some political party, but are free to organize or join whatever parties they wish. If economic freedom means a governmental guarantee of freedom from want, then by analogy political freedom should mean a governmental guarantee of adequate political parties. But of course political parties are private organizations created by the initiative of individuals; and a system in which parties were set up by government, or in which government judged their adequacy, would clearly be just the opposite of politically free. Again, no one seems to have suggested that political freedom should be understood in this sense.

Economic freedom in the original or classical liberal sense does not mean having some amount of economic power, or having equal economic power with others. It means that the government does not *punish* people for their economic or business activities. Liberal freedom in its classical meaning is not freedom from want, but freedom from the police power of the state, a freedom which guarantees to each person the right to use whatever means seems best to him to obtain a livelihood so long as he causes no harm to others. To the classical liberal equality is not the same thing as freedom, and an enforced equality is the very opposite of freedom. An enforced equality is not liberal, but authoritarian, just as the enforcement of Prohibition was not liberal but authoritarian, no matter how admirable the intentions were which animated it, or how large the voting majority which supported it.[19]

True economic freedom, in the sense of freedom that used to be important to liberals, would mean that people were legally free to enter into whatever contracts they wished, and to conduct whatever business transactions they liked, so long as they caused no harm to others. It would mean the sacredness of contract, that in the absence of force and fraud no one would be punished because of the terms of a contract, and that all contracts not the product of force and fraud were binding.[20] It would mean that people were free to keep the fruits of their labor, apart from a moderate tax to support the essential functions of government. It would mean that no one would be coerced into providing goods or services he did not want to provide. It would mean that the law would not impose any economic arrangements, or punish any economic arrangements, any more than it imposes or punishes religious arrangements.

The modern liberal has kept the name of "liberal." This was possible because of ambiguities in the meaning of the word. "Liberal" can mean "generous" as well as "valuing freedom," and in journalistic usage it often refers to proponents of change, irrespective of their actual position, so that even a communist can now be termed a liberal.[21] And the modern liberal truly believes in being generous, which is a very great virtue. In advocating governmental policies he is not typically intent upon his own gain. He is willing to take less so that others can have more. He is willing to give up his own position so that it can go to the underprivileged, he is willing to pay higher taxes so that the poor can receive welfare, he is willing to downplay the achievements of his own society in order to make sure that the achievements of other societies are not overlooked.

But in order to accomplish these things he is also willing to use force. Not content with being generous himself, he will compel others to be generous also. He refuses to rely on the voluntary efforts of individuals and on the power of persuasion and reason to bring about improvements in economic conditions, but he turns to legislation, that is, to the police and the prison, to handcuffs, the truncheon and the gun, and even in some cases the execution chamber, against individuals who cannot be demonstrated to have caused any harm. And with this fatal step he joins the ranks of all the other tyrants and oppressors of the human race.

JOHN STUART MILL

This degeneration of the liberal mind can be seen already in its paragon, John Stuart Mill. It was Mill who, to his great credit, formulated the fundamental principle of the liberal society, the principle of No Harm, namely that people ought to be free to do as they wish, so long as they cause no harm to others: ". . . the only purpose for which power can be rightfully exercised over any member of a civilized community, against his will, is to prevent harm to others. . . . The only freedom which deserves the name, is that of pursuing our own good in our own way, so long as we do not attempt to deprive others of theirs, or impede their efforts to obtain it. Each is the proper guardian of his own health, whether bodily, or mental and spiritual." Yet just in the course of explaining and developing this great principle, he muddles it up with two far-reaching fallacies which have played a significant role in the rise of modern liberalism. We will explore one of these in Chapter 4. For the moment we will focus briefly on the other.

This fallacy consists in the confusion of physical force with other kinds of pressure. Mill believes that the battle against political or governmental oppression has been essentially won, not only by the triumph of the system of representative government, but especially by the widespread recognition that even in a representative system it is possible for the majority to tyrannize over a minority. But, he continues, it is possible to have a social tyranny, a tyranny of opinion, which is more oppressive than a political tyranny. His ground for asserting this is that an opinion which is held by a majority, instead of remaining external to the individual, as law does, may become internalized, may be accepted almost unwittingly, in such a way that the person scarcely recognizes that he is becoming subject to an external power. Society can practice "a social tyranny more formidable than many kinds of political oppression, since, though not usually upheld by such extreme penalties, it leaves fewer means of escape, penetrating much more deeply into the details of life, and enslaving the soul itself."[22] In other words, what people think of us can restrict our freedom more than putting us in jail! It is on this basis that he goes on to make the principal argument of his book, that society should refrain from exerting social pressure on individuals to conform to its opinions.

Now there can be no doubt that an opinion which is widely held can exercise a great deal of pressure on an individual. But the question is whether that pressure, so long as it remains merely the pressure of opinion and is not translated into the use of force, can effectively remove a person's freedom.[23] In what sense can a majority opinion "leave fewer means of escape" than imprisonment does? The possibilities of escape open to a person in prison are usually felt to be somewhat limited. Perhaps Mill is thinking merely that the threat of imprisonment leaves more avenues of escape than an opinion does. But think of what a person has to do to escape from the police, compared with what he has to do to escape internally from an opinion. To escape from the police it is necessary to lead a hunted existence, to move to another locality, to change one's appearance, in short to alter one's entire physical and emotional way of living. To escape from an opinion all that is necessary is to exercise one's critical judgement, or to use one's imagination. No doubt if I have already accepted an opinion widely held in my society, I may find it difficult to be critical of it. But this difficulty should not be exaggerated. People succeed in doing it all the time. In the end it is a person's own responsibility, what opinions he accepts and what he does not accept.

In what sense is it possible for a mere opinion to "enter much more deeply into the details of life" than political oppression can? Law can transform the most elemental details of life. The Soviet law abolishing private property eliminated one of the commonest motivations that animate human beings and has plunged that nation into desperate shortages of the basic necessities of life. Is there any opinion which would enter into the details of life more deeply than the political oppression which sent millions to the Nazi gas chambers?

What can it mean that an opinion "enslaves the soul?" This can happen only when the individual abandons his own critical judgement. The term "enslavement" here has a fine rhetorical ring to it, but it is an exaggeration of the true situation. It is always within a person's power to change his mind. No doubt there may be many situations where that is unlikely, but the mere fact that it does not happen does not mean that it is impossible.

But perhaps it is not simply a matter of rejecting a common opinion, in a theoretical fashion, but of desiring to live in a way that incurs the severe disapproval of my neighbors. Again, no doubt that can be very difficult. But given a choice between incurring social disapproval and incurring imprisonment, how many people would be likely to prefer the latter? Social disapproval still leaves me the possibility of moving to another district or country where conditions are more agreeable to me; imprisonment removes that possibility.

Mill has succumbed to what appears to be a constant temptation of the liberal mind, to blur the dividing line between physical force and other kinds of pressure, a dividing line which it is essential for the maintenance of society to keep clearly in view. In its desire to be generous to others, and to make allowances for them, to avoid holding them responsible for harm that they experience, the liberal mind is easily led to exaggerate the extent to which persons are the passive victims of external influence. The mere fact that a particular influence is successful in inducing a person to do something, however, does not mean that he was not free to reject that influence. Pressure should not be confused with coercion.

THE EMERGENCE OF THE MODERN ECONOMY

During the Middle Ages there was little economic freedom. The great majority of workers were coercively obligated to supply their goods and services, and prices were set not by unimpeded negotiation between buyer and seller, but by law and custom. [24] The large majority of workers worked as agricultural laborers on manors and were prohibited by law from changing their occupation. The manorial system was a command economy, that is, it was at the same time both an economic and a political unit, and its economy was politically controlled. The lord of the manor was both government and employer, inextricably. As markets began to develop, the political authorities moved to keep them strictly under control. Commercial exchanges were for the most part allowed to take place only one day a week, for example, the market day, so that the lord could be sure of obtaining his revenue from them. Goods imported from foreign countries could be sold typically only once a year, at the fair, for the same reason. Goods could be sold only at the "just price," fixed by custom.

One consequence of this politicization of the economy was poverty. Such a system largely discouraged its workers from producing more than was necessary for bare self-sufficiency. And above all, it was rigid, making no allowances for the ever-changing patterns of need and production. As a result, famine was a constantly recurring experience during the Middle Ages.

This led repeatedly to massive desperation. The history of the Middle Ages is a history of peasant uprisings, continually put down by force and continually repeated, showing "a state of social exasperation which has been surpassed in bitterness by few subsequent movements."[25]

In the seventeenth and eighteenth centuries, as a more liberal society began to emerge, the political restrictions on production, prices, occupation, and trade were gradually dismantled, as they were on speech and religion, until during the nineteenth and early twentieth centuries something approximating to economic freedom was enjoyed to a considerable extent. This was the period which saw the emergence of science, and industry, and democratic government. It was also the period when the living standard of the poorest sections of society improved far more than during any comparable period of which we have knowledge.

As John Gray, the critic of liberalism quoted above, has conceded, ". . . for those who came afterwards, the century from the Napoleonic Wars to the outbreak of the Great War was a century of almost uninterrupted liberal progress and achievement. That century encompassed the largest and most continuous growth in wealth in human history against a background of stable prices and freedom from major wars; an unprecedented enhancement of popular living standards side by side with a colossal expansion in population; and a steady increase in popular literacy, numeracy and culture."[26]

The poverty of the manors and farms and of the workers in the cottage industries had been extreme, but dispersed, and largely invisible to the intellectuals, who lived in the towns. The poverty of the new factory workers was less, but it was concentrated, urban, and more visible. As the nineteenth century wore on, many who had been concerned for the promotion of a free and humane society turned to government to solve by legislation what they thought was the new problem of poverty and economic inequality.

THE ORIGINS OF REGULATION

The general attitude of Americans toward business at the time of the Revolution was optimistic. With hard work and a measure of good fortune wealth could be created for everyone. Growth and expansion were the chief concern. The dominant theme was the release of energy. As the nineteenth century wore on, however, this New-World optimism was replaced by a more Old-World pessimism, possibly as a result of the large European immigration. "By 1900, if one can speak about so slippery a thing as dominant public opinion, that opinion saw a narrowing sky, a dead frontier, life as a struggle for position, competition as a zero-sum game, the economy as a pie to be divided, not a ladder stretching out beyond the horizon. By 1900 the theme was: hold the line."[27]

There had always been some regulation of economic activity at the local and state level, responding to local problems. It was minuscule in extent, however, and varied from state to state, allowing competition between states for the most viable policy. Federal regulation, which of course eliminates that competition, grew most dramatically during the two world wars. In peacetime it has taken place, speaking very roughly and with much oversimplification, in three stages or waves. The first wave followed the great expansion of business that occurred after the Civil War. It grew chiefly out of fear of the large monopolistic corporations which were then becoming prominent, first the railroads, on which many people came to depend for their livelihood, and then the "trusts," the industrial combinations such as Standard Oil, which united forty-one firms engaged in different aspects of the petroleum industry. In point of historical fact monopolistic enterprises were constantly being formed from the time of the Revolution, but without government support they were inherently unstable and were constantly falling apart under the pressure of competition. This instability was largely lost sight of by the populace, however. The Interstate Commerce Commission was created in 1887 to regulate the railroads, and the Sherman Anti-Trust Act was passed in 1890.[28]

Ironically, this was also the time when occupational licensing blossomed. Plumbers, barbers, horseshoers, midwives, coal miners, veterinarians, physicians, dentists, chiropractors, ticket agents, undertakers, embalmers, funeral directors, and others were all henceforth required to obtain the approval of government before they could earn a living. The public rationale given for these measures was usually the obligation of government to safeguard the public health and safety. But a large part of the real motivation was the monopolistic desire of those already in these professions to exclude further competition. Boards or commissions were set up, composed of existing members of the profession in question, who would pass judgement on the fitness of others to be their competitors.[29]

The second wave of regulation was prompted by the experience of the Great Depression. Subsequent research has made it probable that the causes of the Depression, or at least of its great severity and duration, consisted primarily in certain governmental measures, especially the action of the Federal Reserve in raising interest rates, which decreased the money supply just when it needed to be expanded, and the passage by Congress of the Smoot-Hawley tariff bill, which had a catastrophic effect on international trade. At the time, however, this was not well understood, and the Depression was blamed on business. The response of President Franklin Roosevelt's government was the New Deal, which was hostile not only to monopolies, but to business and capital as such. Many regulatory laws were passed, and many administrative agencies created. Perhaps the event which had the widest effect was the conferring of monopoly powers on trade unions, in the National Labor Relations Act of 1935. In addition, programs were created for unemployment insurance, old-age pensions, and public housing.

A third wave of regulation has been instigated by the Civil Rights movement of the 1950s and 1960s, issuing in the Civil Rights Acts of 1964 and 1965 and various other measures since then. The immediate intention of this legislation was, of course, to bring about a greater equality in the status of blacks, and then subsequently of women and other groups. The means by which it sought to achieve this purpose consisted largely in far-reaching regulation of business, controlling who could be hired and discharged, who could be accepted as a tenant, a customer, or a student; to whom houses could be sold; the design of commercial and apartment buildings, and suchlike. The impetus for equality has also led among other things to an explosion of liability awards by the courts. The success of this legal activity in bringing about a greater equality is currently being debated, however, since it appears that during this time equality has declined in some significant respects rather than increased.

It would no doubt be an exaggeration, but only a slight one, to say that the modern liberal view is that whenever a noticeable problem arises in society, it is the task of government to remedy it. The answer to every difficulty is to pass a law.[30] As a result, what began as a trickle of economic legislation in the nineteenth century has become, in the course of the twentieth century, a flood; for once the policy has been established that government has authority over the economic decisions of individuals, there is in principle no limit to that authority. Almost all of the laws which restrict trade and commerce are passed in the name of a notion of "fairness," which is now thought to be as essential to society as religious unity was in the Middle Ages. In the economic sphere the liberal respect for the individual person and his freedom has been essentially abandoned. In its place an ideology of equality and the "community" has been erected, according to which the liberal respect for the individual human person is nothing better than selfishness. The individual owes what he achieves to the community, it is felt, and so the community has the right to use force on him in order to eliminate inequalities.[31]

The reader may think that at least the example with which this chapter opens, of Mary Dyer who was hanged for her religious beliefs, has no application in the realm of governmental control of the market at the present day. We may fine or imprison people, but we do not hang them for infringing on market restrictions. Unfortunately, however, even this cannot be taken for granted. On the one hand, the U.S. Food and Drug Administration, though of course it does not deliberately execute anyone, is prepared to allow large numbers of people to die who might otherwise have been saved through the use of many medicines that have not yet passed its rigorous and expensive testing requirements. The legal requirement that the FDA approve drugs not only as safe but also as effective before they can be used has not only created a notorious drug lag in the United States in relation to other countries more willing to allow its citizens to take risks, but it also results in unnecessary deaths.[32]

A more direct instance of what may be in store for us was given in 1986, when two Australians were hanged in Malaysia for possession of narcotics. This penalty was widely condemned as barbaric; but there were also not a few voices in the United States which approved of it wholeheartedly and urged that the death penalty be similarly instituted here for selling narcotics, a demand which was repeated in the context of the presidential election campaign in 1988, and was supported by members of the Bush administration. Recently U. S. military force has been used against narcotics producers and distributors in Colombia. This for something which earlier in this century was not an offense of any kind against the law!

The magnitude of this reversal is breathtaking. It is as if Churchill, fighting the Nazis, had decided the Jews were an impediment and should be eliminated. It is as if Washington, fighting for independence, had proposed making America a colony of France. Or as if Lincoln, fighting against slavery, had proposed that the rebellious Southerners should be made slaves.

CONSISTENCY

The fact is, unpalatable though it may be to many, that economic freedom is of one piece with freedom of thought and expression, freedom of association, academic freedom, freedom of conscience and freedom of religion. It is deeply inconsistent to cherish some of these and repudiate the others. If we believe in the value of individual human persons and their right not to be subjected to the coercive power of government in their thoughts and opinions, in their friendships and associations, in their teaching, research and publications, in their conscience and in their religion, then we should be prepared to follow the logic of our position and hold also that they should be free from coercion in their economic activities. This applies not only to consumers, but also to producers, not only to buyers, but also to sellers.

The fact that these various liberties are linked, and stand or fall together, is demonstrated by the fact that restrictions on economic liberty result in restrictions on these other kinds of liberty as well. It might have been expected that this would pose a serious problem for people who think of themselves as liberals, but this has not been generally the case. Spurred on by the zeal for economic equality, they have been preeminently the ones who have clamored for these restrictions.

The First Amendment of the U.S. Constitution guarantees "the right of the people peaceably to assemble." This is one expression of the historic liberal conviction that freedom of association is a basic human right, and one without which democracy cannot function. Historically, as we pointed out above, this viewpoint represented a giant step forward from the paranoid anxiety which led earlier civilizations to consider assemblies of citizens automatically as conspiracies against the state. But in recent years people who think of themselves as liberals have been willing and even eager to demolish the freedom of association for the sake of economic equality. In 1987 the Lions Club of California was found by the courts to be guilty of sexual discrimination because of its policy of not admitting female members and was faced with severe fines if it did not alter that policy. Since then the same fate has been imposed on numerous other clubs and organizations which restrict membership to males, or to white males (and recently in Pennsylvania also to one restricted to females[33]). This seems to be a clear violation of the right of free association. Yet scarcely a voice has been raised in protest by those who consider themselves liberals; on the contrary, they have been the chief agitators for these penalties, because they have come to regard the matter as one of fairness or social justice. On the other hand, when trade unions are criticized, though they enjoy monopoly privileges by law and are by no means simply free associations, those who have inherited the mantle of liberalism now rush to defend them as guaranteed by the right of free association. Strangely, no one has yet suggested that political discrimination should be outlawed—for example, voting for a candidate because that candidate is white or black or male or female or young or elderly—though presumably such discrimination must have a social significance at least equal to that of economic discrimination.

Perhaps an attempt may be made to defend the actions of the courts by making a distinction between political assemblies and commercial ones. The First Amendment guarantee would apply then only to those gatherings or organizations which clearly possess a political purpose. But such a distinction is impossible to maintain, for any commercial organization may undertake to influence legislation, and it will thereby automatically become political.

Again, the First Amendment to the U.S. Constitution prescribes that "Congress shall make no law . . . abridging the freedom of speech, or of the press," a straightforward concept, one would have thought, and one representing a goal that liberal-minded people fought for against the orthodoxies of church and state. But this did not prevent the Federal Communications Commission from authorizing the Fairness Doctrine, or Congress from passing the Equal Time Rule. The Fairness Doctrine requires broadcasters to devote a portion of their broadcast time to the coverage of public issues, and also requires them to provide an opportunity for the presentation of contrasting points of view. The Equal Time rule provides that if a broadcasting station permits one legally qualified candidate for public office to use its facilities, it must afford equal opportunity to all other such legally qualified candidates for the same office. In the spring of 1980, for example, a federal court ruled that all three major television networks violated the law when they refused to sell time to the Carter–Mondale Presidential Committee.[34]

These regulations seem to be a clear infringement of First Amendment rights, yet the modern liberal community has not seen fit to object to them, indeed enthusiastically supports them, preferring to assume that the electromagnetic wave spectrum is somehow owned by the U.S. Federal Government—a mystery which has never been satisfactorily explained, for it was not the U.S. government which discovered the existence of electromagnetic waves, or which invented the apparatus necessary to utilize them. When, more recently, the Federal Communications Commission decided that the Fairness Doctrine was, after all, not very fair, immediately a "liberal" group in Congress rushed to propose enshrining it in an explicit statute.

Meanwhile, the Supreme Court has decided that there is a sharp distinction between political speech, which in their view is protected by the Constitution, and commercial speech, which is not. Yet this sharp distinction, like the one mentioned above between political and commercial associations, is impossible to maintain. Commercial speech which dissents from government policy, for example from the policy of those governmental bodies which regulate or subsidize commercial activities, such as the Federal Reserve or the National Institutes of Health, is political speech, and is liable to be penalized as political speech.[35]

A further example of how modern liberalism contradicts its own best insights is provided by the policy of Affirmative Action. One of the most generous of liberal intuitions has been the realization that individuals should be judged so far as possible on their own merits, rather than in the light of qualities that mark the group they stem from. The son should not be punished for the sins of the father. For this reason the Founding Fathers rejected the proposal to create an aristocracy in the new nation. But the policy of Affirmative Action as it is widely understood and practiced requires precisely that individuals *not* be judged on their own merits, but that special legal privileges be given to certain *groups*—different groups now, to be sure, but groups all the same. The doctrine of group rights has emerged. In an increasing number of institutions in the United States, membership in some favored ethnic or gender group is now a prerequisite for employment. Examinations originally intended to test according to a common standard the abilities of those who sit for them have been restructured so that members of an ethnic or gender group are tested only against other members of the same group, so that groups possessing weak abilities receive special privileges. Yet there is an inherent conflict between the concept of group rights and the concept of human rights. Human rights are rights possessed by all human beings, and they exclude favoritism, while group rights are a form of favoritism. It is no surprise, then, to find that institutions which attempt to espouse both experience dilemmas. The university, for example, has historically stood for the principle of free speech, because it has recognized that the growth of knowledge requires unhindered communication. Yet on numerous campuses the doctrine of group rights has now led to policies forbidding statements which are insensitive to the feelings of certain groups, even if the statements should be true.[36]

The concern of modern liberals about poverty and equality presents indeed something of a paradox. On the one hand it seems beyond doubt that as a group they are genuinely concerned about poverty and equality. Yet if a person is genuinely concerned about poverty and truly desires to see it eradicated, then he will surely make an effort to discover which system in point of fact actually and as a matter of historical reality has done the most to eliminate poverty, and he will give his support to that. Now there is a good a priori case that a free market will come closer than any other system to eliminating poverty because it minimizes prices and maximizes employment. And if we take the historical evidence overall, it seems to provide strong support for this view. By contrast there are good theoretical and historical reasons for believing that redistributive schemes make everyone poorer in the long run, including those who are already poor. There is good reason to believe that Adam Smith was right:

> Little else is requisite to carry a state to the highest degree of opulence from the lowest barbarism, but peace, easy taxes and a tolerable administration of justice: all the rest being brought about by the natural course of things."[37]

This would at least be a serious question, to be investigated with some thoroughness: Do redistributive schemes actually help or hinder those in need or not? How do they compare with free markets in point of fact? Yet few of those who consider themselves liberals now seem prepared to investigate seriously with an impartial mind whether this might be the case, as the generally defensive response to Charles Murray's book *Losing Ground* has illustrated.

The situation is similar with equality. A person who is genuinely concerned to foster a more equal society would surely make a factual investigation to discover which system actually has done the most to bring equality about. The economic evidence seems sufficiently clear that in a totally free market income and wealth will be distributed more equally than in any redistributive system. All things else being equal, the gap between the highest income and lowest income groups will be smaller in free market societies than in redistributive societies for a number of reasons, especially because the lower prices and higher employment which accompany free markets benefit the poor proportionately more than the rich, and because redistributive schemes unavoidably lend themselves to various kinds of exploitation by special interest groups. A person who was truly interested in seeing a more equal world would at least feel obligated to inquire in an objective spirit whether this is or is not actually the case. But again, those who consider themselves liberals now seem for the most part to be ashamed to explore with an impartial mind whether free markets do or do not maximize equality. It appears to be simply an article of faith that they do not. Indeed, the very idea of an unbiased investigation into the facts of the case is now often dismissed as ideology, bourgeois or male, depending on the perspective of the author.[38]

The widespread support, among people who otherwise are liberals, for governmental regulation and control of economic activity derives from a number of broad philosophical assumptions about what happens in market relationships, especially in regard to what causes harm and what does not cause harm. Our aim in what follows is to propose an alternative and more truly liberal view of the nature of the market, and of the idea of justice.

2

The Principle of Mutual Benefit

A State, I said, arises, as I conceive, out of the needs of mankind; no one is self-sufficing, but all of us have many wants. Can any other origin of a State be imagined?

There can be no other.

Then, as we have many wants, and many persons are needed to supply them, one takes a helper for one purpose and another for another; and when these partners and helpers are gathered together in one habitation the body of inhabitants is termed a State.

True, he said.

And they exchange with one another, and one gives, and another receives, under the idea that the exchange will be for their good.

True, he said.

> Plato, *The Republic*, Book II
> Trans. Jowett

Until 1989 about 80 women did sewing at home for the firm of Overly-Raker, of McConnellsburg, Pennsylvania. Then the state government forced them out of their jobs, applying a 1937 law which forbids home work. Pennsylvania Deputy Secretary of Labor, Patricia Halpin-Murphy, who was responsible for the decision to enforce the law, defended her action by claiming that the workers were being exploited, for that conception obviously provided the grounds for the law. The company transferred the work to China and Mexico.[1]

In 1990 a further dozen workers who knitted sweaters at home on machines belonging to the French Creek Sheep and Wool Company of

Elverson, Pennsylvania, were also forced out of their jobs by the state government. The decision, which was applauded by the International Ladies Garment Workers Union, "benefited absolutely nobody," said the firm's president, Eric Flaxenburg. "The women cried. Some had young children. Some had invalids depending on them. We lost a lot of good workers, and the country lost production."[2]

Since Karl Marx developed it in the nineteenth century, the notion of exploitation has become almost universally accepted, even in the least communist of countries, the United States. It has provided the chief reason for the mass of legislation now governing business activity. Yet it has essentially as much reality as banshees and unicorns: it is a myth.

"Exploitation" means that two people may reach an agreement knowingly and deliberately, not as the result of any force or fraud, and yet one of them can be punished by the law for causing harm to the other. This makes no sense: it is a sheer absurdity.

PUNISHMENT

All laws inflict punishment. A law is not just a harmless piece of advice, a benign educational tool, or an innocuous guideline one is free to follow or not. Every law is a law only by the fact that it threatens some physical punishment. To make a law is to threaten to punish by the use of physical force, by means of the police, handcuffs, the truncheon, and the gun. It is to threaten prison, or the confiscation of one's property, and possibly death. A fine is no exception to this, for if a person refuses to pay the fine he will be carried off by force to jail. Whatever the form of punishment, laws punish. (It is true that there are some laws which provide exemption from punishment, but they are parasitic upon the laws that punish.)

WHO OUGHT TO BE PUNISHED?

This fact raises some questions of fundamental urgency. The first is: Who ought to be punished? The only just answer to this question can be: those who *deserve* punishment. A law which punishes people who do not deserve punishment is universally felt to be unjust and intolerable. As the British philosopher F. H. Bradley wrote:

> Punishment is punishment only when it is deserved. We pay the penalty because we owe it, and for no other reason; and if punishment is inflicted for any other reason whatever than because it is merited by wrong, it is a

gross immorality, a crying injustice, an abominable crime, and not what it pretends to be.[3]

WHO DESERVES PUNISHMENT?

The second question follows from this: Who deserves punishment?

As we shall see more fully in Chapter 7, there can be only one answer to this question: those who have *caused harm*. In order to deserve punishment, it is not enough that we would like a person to do something, and he doesn't do it. It is not enough that we dislike him or his behavior. He must cause *harm*. And it is not enough that he merely be loosely associated in a noncausal way with some harm, but he must actually be the *cause* of that harm or an accessory to it, that is, someone who helps in the causing of it, whether before or after. (Threatening harm is a form of causing harm, though not precisely the harm that is threatened.)

This idea is summed up in the concept of a crime. While the term "crime" can have a purely legal meaning, namely whatever contravenes the criminal law, that meaning derives its force from a prior moral meaning, signifying a deliberate act that causes harm.

THE CONCEPT OF AN EXCHANGE

All business transactions, all buying and selling, lending and borrowing, and giving and taking employment are exchanges. In common parlance an exchange means an exchange without money changing hands. Where money changes hands, we usually use other words such as purchase or sale. But to understand the basic nature of business transactions it is irrelevant whether one of the items exchanged is money.

An exchange in this technical sense is a mutually conditioned promise. An exchange has the form that two parties say, each to the other: I will give you a certain item if you will give me a certain other item in return. If Brown buys a book from Green, that is an exchange: Brown promises to give Green the money on condition that Green gives him the book, and Green promises to give Brown the book on condition that Brown gives him the money. Any purchase or sale is an exchange in this broader, technical sense, and so is any lending and borrowing, and any giving and taking of employment. To give a person a job is to buy his labor, to promise to pay him money in exchange for his labor; and to take a job is to sell one's labor, to promise to give one's labor in exchange for money.

It may help clarity if we point out some things that are not exchanges. Paying taxes is not an exchange, even though we hope for something in return, because government does not oblige itself to perform any specific act. Making a donation to a charity is not an exchange, or giving someone a gift. Bestowing or receiving an inheritance is not an exchange.

In addition, we shall frequently speak of *market exchanges*. By a market exchange is meant here any exchange which is not the product of force or fraud or mistake,[4] and which is carried out by sane, conscious adults: therefore, not by children, or by people who are drunk or drugged. We shall see the reasons for these qualifications later.

The idea of "exploitation" as it is commonly used in this connection implies that a person who is exploited is harmed in some way. If it should turn out that the action considered exploitative actually conferred on balance a benefit on him, there would be no point in objecting to it.

Our thesis can be restated, then: It does not make sense to believe that a person may cause harm to another by engaging in a market exchange with him. It does not make sense to believe that even when there is no question of force or fraud, a seller may cause harm to a buyer by selling him something which he requests to buy, and an employer may cause harm to an employee by giving him a job which he applies for.

WHY EXCHANGES TAKE PLACE

The fundamental question which needs to be asked, but which is often not asked, is: *Why* do exchanges take place? *There is only one reason why people engage in exchanges, and that is in order to benefit from them.* Unless a person believes that he will benefit from the exchange, he will not engage in it. This applies to both parties. *Both* must believe that they will benefit, otherwise no exchange will take place. It cannot be the case that only one party believes he will benefit. We shall call this the Principle of Mutual Benefit. Although it was apparently already clear to Plato, and lies at the heart of Adam Smith's analysis, its significance for the ethical assessment of market activity has largely been overlooked.[5]

Of course it is always possible for a human being to be mistaken, and it is often difficult to know what will in the long run really benefit us, so it is always possible that the person making an exchange may be doing something which he will later regret. We will return to this point later. However, at the time he makes the exchange he must believe he will benefit. This is the basis on which all market transactions take place. But if this is true, then persons who engage in market transactions not only do something which they consider beneficial to themselves, they also *neces-*

sarily act in a way that the other considers beneficial to himself.[6] The buyer not only benefits himself, but also the seller, and the seller benefits not only himself, but also the buyer. This benefit to the other takes place automatically, as it were, without any special intention, and without any special government commands or controls. It is a condition of the market that both sides must benefit.

SOCIAL BENEFITS

What does the individual do with the benefit, the profit, he has received from a transaction? If he does not consume it, if for example it consists in money, it becomes available directly for other transactions, which again benefit not only himself, but also the others with whom he does business. If he consumes it, if for example it consists in food, it helps to ensure that the person himself continues to exist, and is therefore available to make further transactions. In this way every exchange, every business agreement, spreads its beneficial effects out over the society like an expanding wave, benefiting more and more people. What looks initially, to the casual observer, like a purely private transaction, with a significance restricted to the two parties involved, shows itself upon examination as a social or public benefit. *The entire society benefits from every successful business agreement.*

This benefit to the other party, and so eventually to the entire society, is what Adam Smith refers to with his celebrated notion of an "invisible hand" which leads every buyer and seller "to promote an end which was no part of his original intention."[7] Latter-day social thinkers have sometimes derided this phrase, as if it were somehow magic, a piece of verbal legerdemain that conjured up social benefits out of nowhere; but this betrays a failure to understand what happens in an exchange, and in the series of exchanges which constitutes a market.

NOT A ZERO SUM

A zero sum event is one in which there is no overall net gain or loss, so that if one side gains, the other must lose. Football and tennis matches are zero sum events, and so is an election. In zero sum events there is a winner and a loser. Can a market exchange be a zero sum event? Many people appear to believe so, because business transactions are often described in terms of winners and losers.

The interests of buyer and seller, or of employer and employee, are of course partly different. Each would like to obtain as much as he can out of the exchange. Given that the exchange takes place, the bargaining over the price appears to be a zero sum event: what one gains the other loses. Similarly, competition between different buyers or between different sellers appears to be a zero sum event: if a customer spends his money buying the week's groceries at Acme, then he doesn't buy them at Pathmark. These facts give the superficial observer the impression that the market is a battlefield, in which there are winners and losers. But this impression, while true in some respects, is profoundly false in others.

An exchange in its totality is not a zero sum event. It takes place because buyer and seller reach an agreement, and at the point where they reach their agreement, each one benefits. To repeat, that is the only reason why anyone engages in an exchange at all. So although the interests of buyer and seller are partly different, they are not entirely different. They are not opposed in the way that two sides in a war are opposed, as if only one side could win and the other must lose. *If the exchange takes place, both sides win*. Wise business persons recognize this, and make it their concern to see to it that the other side get at least the minimum out of the exchange that will satisfy them. For if one side come to feel that they are not truly going to benefit from it, then the transaction will not go through.

A SMALL BENEFIT IS STILL A BENEFIT

According to current U.S. law, an employer who pays a worker only $3 an hour is subject to severe penalties, even though the worker knowingly and willingly applies for the job at that rate. American manufacturers with plants in Mexico are sometimes criticized for paying their workers there only, say, 40 cents an hour, and this is described as exploitation. Yet the mere fact that a benefit is small does not prevent it from being a benefit. A wage of $1 an hour may not be a large wage, but if a person decides he will be better off working for that wage than not working at all, then in his eyes it constitutes a benefit, not a loss, despite its smallness. Smallness, of course, is relative, and something which appears small to an outside observer may be anything but small in the estimation of the person who receives it. The decision is up to the individual, and his judgement ought to be respected. He will not make the transaction if he does not think it is worth making. Although 40 cents an hour may be a small wage by U.S. standards, it is not necessarily small by Mexican standards, and in fact may be quite generous in comparison with what is otherwise available in Mexico. If the Mexican worker thought that it was too small he would not be working in that factory.

AN UNEQUAL BENEFIT IS STILL A BENEFIT

Trade unions, as we shall see in more detail later, are given special enforcement privileges by law in order to make up for the inequality of bargaining power between a single individual employee and a large and powerful firm. A firm which refuses to bargain with a union, or which pays an employee a salary less than that provided for by the union contract, even if he would willingly work for it (for it might save him from losing his job entirely, if his labor would otherwise be priced out of the market), breaks the law and can be penalized heavily. Yet the mere fact that a benefit is unequal does not prevent it from being a benefit. If Smith makes a profit of $100 for every hour he employs Brown, while Brown only makes a profit of $10, it still remains true that Brown is making a profit. Even if other employees doing the same kind of work as Brown make a profit of $30, it still remains true that Brown's $10 is a benefit. Otherwise he would not be working there.

The Americans with Disabilities Act of 1990 requires that apartment and business buildings be henceforth constructed with special ramps and passageways to provide unhindered access to the disabled, and owners who do not provide such facilities will be subject to severe penalties. The grounds for this are to ensure that the disabled are treated equally with the rest of the population. Yet disabled people have rented apartments successfully in the past because they realized that they genuinely benefited from them, even if the benefits they received were less in a certain sense than those received by others. A lesser benefit is still a benefit.

A RELATIVE BENEFIT IS STILL A BENEFIT

Not only is a lesser benefit still a benefit, but also a merely relative benefit is still a benefit. A relative benefit is the lesser of two evils, something that taken by itself, in isolation, would be undesirable or disagreeable to the individual, and may even constitute a loss in comparison with his earlier condition, but is better than the only available alternative, which is still more undesirable or disagreeable. Suppose that I suffer from a fatal illness, and a remedy is discovered which will make me feel moderately nauseous for some time, but will cure the disease. I have only two alternatives, either to endure the prospect of death, or to stay alive while experiencing a feeling of nausea. Of course I would much rather not feel nauseous, but I would like dying even less. It is clear here that I have benefited, even though the benefit is not as great as I might have desired.

Or suppose that I buy some item, say stock in a company, at a certain price, hoping of course that the price will rise, but instead it falls. Fearing that it will fall still further, I sell. Since I sell it at a lower price than I paid for it, I suffer a loss. Nonetheless it is true that I sell the stock in order to benefit, because I am better off losing a smaller amount of money than a larger amount. If I did not believe I would benefit, in this relative sense, I would not sell the stock.

It is obvious that in a transaction like this no one has caused me harm. The person who sold me the stock has not caused me harm, for perhaps if I had held onto it longer I would have made a handsome profit; neither has the person to whom I sell it caused me harm, for he has no obligation to buy it; on the contrary, I should be grateful to him for buying it, for if he had not bought it, I would perhaps have had to sell it to someone else at an even lower price.

However, failure to understand the concept of a relative benefit leads many people to imagine that there are exceptions to this rule, namely, as we mentioned, in the case of persons who are in a weak position, who are not well educated, who are in difficulties, who are "compelled," as we say, "by circumstances" to engage in some exchange.

Let's consider the case of a man who has been trying unsuccessfully for a long time to find a job, has used up all his unemployment benefits, and is in danger of starving. An employer, learning of his desperate situation, takes advantage of it to offer him a job at a low wage which no one else would take because it is so disagreeable and dangerous. According to the common view the employer is exploiting him, treating him unfairly, causing him harm. In the words of a recent commentator, it is "morally ugly."[8] But if it harms him to take the job, why does he take it? What is the explanation for this bizarre behavior? "Because he has no alternative, he cannot help taking it, he is forced by his situation." Let us examine both of these assumptions, that he is being harmed, and that he is not acting freely.

THE MEANING OF HARM

In order to cause a person harm by some action two conditions must be fulfilled. One is that he must be worse off after the action than he was before it. Unless there has been some *deterioration* in his condition, it makes no sense to say that he has been harmed. The second is that the action in question must have *caused* the harm, that is, *produced* it. If there was harm but it was produced by some other development, it will also make no sense to say that the action of the other person was the cause of it. We will examine this second condition, the idea of causation, in more detail in Chapter 5. For the moment we will concentrate on the first.

Is it really the case that the worker just described is in a worse condition after he has accepted the job? Before he took the job he had no income, now he has an income. Before he took the job he was in danger of starvation, now he is not. Surely it is crystal clear that his condition is better than it was, not worse. Admittedly, his condition is not ideal, he would much rather not be doing this job, if there were some better alternative. But there is no better alternative, and he would rather be doing this than starving, which is why he takes the job.

We can easily test whether the job is truly a benefit. Will he be better off if we make a law forbidding him to accept it? Obviously not, for in that case he will be reduced to his former condition of being in danger of starvation. (Many people believe, however, that while that may be true in the short term, in the long term things can be different. We will examine that view below.)

THE QUESTION OF THE BASELINE

We just observed that for a person to be harmed by some action, his condition after that action must be worse than it was before. But is this the right comparison to make? Some people assume that we should compare his situation after taking the job at the low wage, not with his situation just before he took the job, but with what his situation would be under different circumstances, "what might normally have been expected," or with "the normal course of events." This typically depends on what is customary, what "generally happens" in such cases. The worker in our example will have "a right" to whatever is the "general practice," and so will have a right to the usual wage for such work.[9] Since the wage in the case we have been discussing is low, by comparison with what is customary, the employer is harming the worker, not benefiting him. In the course of developing his ideas on this subject, one author considers the possibility of making the comparison with the condition of the person before the action in question began, but when this is applied to particular cases he finds, as we do, that it leads to the conclusion that the person is benefited rather than harmed. But this conclusion, he says, is "counter-intuitive," that is, it goes against his presuppositions, and therefore the baseline must be mistaken![10]

This view that people have a right to whatever level of help is customary in their society assumes a static society, in which wages and prices, and the general standard of help that people provide for one another, remain fixed. It makes no allowance for the possibility that these may be improved, and it has the effect of penalizing those who improve them. Suppose that in a particular society it is customary to pay factory workers $1 an hour. An entrepreneur, however, in order to attract more labor, introduces the practice of paying them $2 an hour, and this becomes the custom. If he subsequently falls on hard times, and in order to stay in business must go back to paying them $1 an hour, he will now be convicted of harming his employees and will be liable to punishment. Similarly, if people have not been accustomed to helping one another in distress in that society, and then someone introduces customs which are more helpful, then anyone who regresses to the earlier level, including the one who introduced the better customs, will now be, not giving a lesser benefit, but causing harm, by the same actions that previously were helpful. But this seems patently unfair. It will pay everyone in such a society to keep their standards of altruism minimal.

A FALSE ALTERNATIVE

Proponents of the exploitation theory typically do not seek the abolition of the factory offering the low wage. Instead they want laws that will force the owner to pay a higher wage. But this is not the alternative that properly follows from their view. If it is true that a factory owner harms job applicants by offering jobs at low wages, then the job applicants should be benefited by abolishing the factory altogether. That is what follows from the theory. Since people are genuinely harmed by being robbed, they are benefited by a law that abolishes robbery altogether. In order to benefit robbery victims, it is not necessary to allow the robbery to continue, only fixing the amount of it at some convenient lesser sum.

HARM MUST BE DEMONSTRABLE

When the accusation is made that one person is causing harm to another, the usual implication is that the person causing the harm ought to suffer punishment. This is the effect of all laws regulating economic activity, since every law is associated with a threat of punishment. Punishment is a very serious matter, and it is not unreasonable to require that harm be demonstrated before such a law is passed, as it would have to be in a court of law. When a person is accused of robbery, it is not sufficient to assume on the basis of some general and abstract theory that he is guilty, but it has to be shown beyond all reasonable doubt that the victim suffered harm, and that the accused caused the harm. Similarly, when a legislature is contemplating passing a law which will punish certain people for doing a particular action, such as paying a low wage, on the grounds that they are causing harm to someone, such as their employees, it is only reasonable to insist that they not merely assume that harm has been caused, on the basis of some general and abstract idea, but that they demonstrate that the action they are intending to forbid actually causes harm. This requires in the first place that the harm be identified. But in the absence of force and fraud it is impossible to identify any harm in economic transactions.

NOT A FREE EXCHANGE?

It is often maintained that the actions of a person in economic distress are not free. An individual who is in danger of starvation, and who accepts a job at a low wage or with long hours or dangerous conditions is often said to be doing so because he has no alternative. He "cannot help it," but is "compelled by circumstances."

In the opinion of the present writer this question is largely a red herring. It is thought to be a significant question only because it is assumed that people in distress who accept tough conditions are being harmed. It is supposed to provide an explanation for what otherwise, on this interpretation, would be bizarre and incomprehensible behavior. Given that they are causing harm to themselves, what could explain such a paradoxical action, since presumably they are not masochists? The answer is made that they have no alternative, they are compelled to take the job. It is assumed that this explanation renders comprehensible an action which otherwise would make no sense. Where it is clear that a person is benefiting from an action, however, there is no urgent need to ask whether he does so freely. A penniless beggar given a lottery ticket which turned out to win him a million dollars would be under heavy economic and psychological pressure to accept the prize, but there would be little practical point in questioning whether his acceptance was truly free.

Nonetheless since the thesis is maintained so frequently that persons acting under economic pressure are not free, let us examine the assertion in its own right. It is surely clear that it is an exaggeration to say, as is frequently said, that they have no alternative. After all, it would be possible for the person who is in danger of starving to refuse the job, even though at great hardship to himself. If he discovered that his prospective employer was a terrorist who was going to use his services to carry out an assassination, or if he discovered that the employer had previously done grievous harm to one of his children: in such cases we can certainly imagine that he would be able to refuse to do the job, even if that were to cost him extreme hardship.

But, we shall be told, the question is whether he has any *reasonable* alternative. In the two cases just mentioned the alternative of not taking the job would become reasonable, but otherwise it would not be. It is not necessary that he should find it strictly speaking impossible to reject the job. If it were very difficult for him to do so, that would be sufficient to make it an unfree action. It is analogous, we are often told, to the use of force. If a gangster puts a gun to a person's head and demands money, it may well be true that strictly speaking the person can refuse; but still we say that in giving up his wallet he is not acting freely, or voluntarily, because he is under duress. It would not be reasonable to lose his life in order to keep his wallet. A recent writer, engaging in what he calls a theological critique of capitalism, goes so far as to assert that capitalists murder laborers, simply by employing them economically (his reasoning is that the laborers' lives are shortened by the fact that they receive a lower income than others[11]), which certainly implies that they are not acting freely, and are being harmed.

But does the fact that people have no reasonable alternative mean that they do not act freely? Aristotle investigates this question using the example of sailors who throw goods overboard in a storm in order to lighten the boat. Is this a voluntary action? he asks. He answers that the point might be debated. If we considered the action only in itself or in the abstract, that is, in isolation from the actual circumstances, then we would not normally describe it as voluntary, for if we only take into account the action itself, who would be so foolish as to throw goods overboard if he were not compelled to? But if we consider the action in actuality or in the concrete, he says, taking into account the purpose the sailors wish to achieve, namely saving the boat and their lives, it is voluntary, because it is *worthy of choice*; and this in his view is the right answer.[12]

Granted that the person who is acting under severe economic pressure is not acting with full or ideal freedom, that does not mean that he is not acting with sufficient freedom for his action to be genuinely free. To ask whether a person is acting freely is tantamount to asking whether he is responsible for his action. The fact that he is under severe economic pressure is by no means enough to relieve him of responsibility for his actions. This is borne out by the treatment of crime in the courts. If the worker we mentioned above, needing money to avoid starvation, should instead decide to rob his next-door neighbor of $1,000, could he plead that he was forced to commit the robbery, and it was not a free act? No doubt it is possible that the jury might be very sympathetic with him, and might agree that he had extenuating circumstances, so that he should not receive the most severe sentence. But it is not likely that he would be let off scot-free. Presumably the verdict would be that though his action was not perfectly or ideally free, it was still sufficiently free to qualify as a free act, and that he ought to be punished and make reparation. Typically courts are by no means sympathetic with debtors who embezzle their employers' funds in order to pay their gambling debts, for example, even though such people may experience a severe degree of economic need.

It is true that responsibility varies according to the action done, as well as according to the pressure there is on the person to do it. It has been pointed out that the courts typically apply different standards of voluntariness to contracts and crimes, so that sometimes a situation which would be taken as coercive if it leads to the signing of a contract, on the grounds that it leaves the person no reasonable alternative, is not taken as coercive if it leads to the commission of a crime.[13] The same court that would find Brown guilty of theft for stealing the $1,000 even though he was in urgent need, might well declare that his employment contract was invalid because he was in the same urgent need. This approach has been defended on the grounds that the question at stake in regard to coercion is whether an individual is responsible for what he does. It would take a lot of pressure to relieve a person of the responsibility for the commission of a serious crime, as we saw in the Nuremberg trials and in the Eichmann case, but it would take less pressure to relieve him of responsibility for breaking a contract, or taking a job at a low wage.[14]

Such an approach makes sense when it's a question of threats to cause harm. Compare two cases, one where Smith threatens to burn Jones's house down unless he breaks a contract with Brown, and another where he makes the same threat unless Jones kills Brown. We can well imagine that a court would consider the threat sufficient to relieve Jones of responsibility for breaking the contract, but not for committing the murder.

But where a market transaction is subject only to economic pressure the situation is very different. Suppose that the captain of a ship fails to take the measures necessary to keep his ship from sinking; could he plead that he had no obligation to do so, on the grounds that at the time he took the job he was in danger of starvation, and so his contract with the ship's owners was invalid? Or suppose that a family put their house up for sale, because they needed the money urgently for a life-saving operation; could they reclaim the house five years later on the grounds that the contract of sale was invalid, since they were experiencing severe economic pressure at the time? That would certainly not be in accord with the common law tradition of justice.

In other words, being "forced by circumstances" to enter into an exchange is a figure of speech, and is not the equivalent of being forced to do so by another person.

Even if we were to accept the idea that a person can be genuinely and not merely figuratively forced by circumstances to enter into a contract, however, that would not settle the question, for the role of the other person in the two cases is different. Consider a case where a gangster threatens to burn Smith's house down unless Smith signs a contract to work for him for a pittance. Here the role of the gangster is that he violates Smith's liberty, and it is clear that he deserves punishment. Then consider the case where Smith is destitute, and an employer offers him a job at a very low wage. Even if we said that circumstances compel Smith to accept the offer, the employer does not violate Smith's liberty, but on the contrary offers him a remedy, however partial, for his distress, and has done nothing to deserve punishment. Yet the minimum wage law will punish him.

MEANS VS. FREEDOM FROM PUNISHMENT

By the same token there is a significant difference between being prevented by circumstances from doing something, and being prevented by other people. This is approximately the difference between *possessing the means* to do something, i.e., having the ability to do it, and *not being threatened with punishment* for doing it. It is one thing to be incapable of playing the piano because I never took lessons, or because there is no piano, and it is another to be threatened with death or dismemberment by an irate neighbor if, though I possess the necessary skill, I attempt to use it to play a piece by Schönberg. Usually we would say that in the one case I was unable to play the piano, while in the other case I was not free to. Whatever words we use, it is clear that there is a fundamental difference between these two cases.[15]

This is the same as the difference between being prevented by lack of money or other economic resources from doing something, and being prevented by the law from doing it; between being unable to work because I cannot find a job, and being precluded from working because the law forbids it. Some maintain that this is not in practice a significant difference, that being legally free to work is of no benefit if there are no jobs available. But this is a mistake. If I am legally free to work, then my ingenuity at finding other skills to use, my willingness to make an effort, my determination not to be easily defeated, my readiness to make sacrifices such as leaving home, are called into play, and the possibility cannot be excluded in advance that these may enable me to find a means of earning a living, as many others in such circumstances have done before me. If I am free to earn a living, I may well be able to obtain the ability. But if I am prevented from working by a law, for example the state laws which prevent working in the home, or the Soviet law, still on the books at the time of writing, which has the effect of prohibiting private individuals from employing anyone,[16] then it is no longer a matter of my economic resourcefulness, my ingenuity in finding or creating a means of earning a living: the only resourcefulness that is relevant is my ability to escape being caught by the police. This is a very fundamental difference, and there is wisdom in marking it by a use of language which distinguishes between *ability* and *freedom*.

DOES FREEDOM MEAN HAVING A RANGE OF OPTIONS?

In a recent work on the idea of freedom, a work which makes an especially careful attempt to defend the morality of extensive government intervention in the market, the assertion is made that freedom consists, not in the absence of coercion, but in the ability to make choices from among a range of options. This is a common opinion. The absence of coercion is a precondition of freedom, the author concedes, but in order to have genuine freedom certain positive conditions are needed in addition. One of these positive conditions is the possession of a certain amount of material goods, and if that is lacking, the individual is not free. A consequence of this is that a working man who is in a situation where he has to choose between working in a factory for long hours in poor conditions or starving, is being subjected to coercion: ". . . if one person presents another with a choice between performing a certain action or losing his life, that is a paradigm case of coercion, not freedom."[17]

In other words, if a man is starving and another man offers him an income in return for certain work which will help relieve his starvation, then the second man, although he is increasing the range of options open to the first, which is precisely the author's definition of freedom, is decreasing the first's freedom!

The author seems to sense that he has a problem here, and goes on to concede that perhaps the factory-owner does not impose such a choice on the working man, but then asserts that it is imposed by "human social arrangements." In other words, if it were not for human social arrangements, the working man would not be in danger of starving! This is a very large claim. Until the arrival of capitalism, famine was a recurring part of life in all societies. (The author makes no attempt to support his claim, however, beyond remarking that the poverty of the urban proletariat is a consequence of "rural dispossession." This assumes, however, that rural workers before the industrial revolution were not poor or in danger of starving, which is rather the opposite of the historical truth.) In the meantime, however, it is not the "human social arrangements" that get penalized for paying what the opinion-makers consider a low wage, but the hapless employer.

THE ANALOGY WITH PHYSICAL FORCE

The opinion is frequently voiced that paying a person a low wage, or a low price for some item, when that person is in a difficult position, is analogous to using physical force, such as putting a gun to his head. One reason given for this view is that the outcome may well be the same: if the money is needed for some lifesaving reason, he may die.

But the fact that two sequences of events have the same outcome does not by any means imply that they are morally equivalent. Both the farmer and the bank robber carry out actions designed to increase their livelihood, but it does not follow from that that they are morally equivalent. To show that there is some analogy between buying from an impoverished person at a low price and threatening him with injury, it would be necessary to show that the actions themselves are morally equivalent. Is giving someone $2,000 instead of $5,000 for a car he is desperately anxious to sell, or employing him for $1 an hour instead of $3, analogous to inflicting a bodily injury on him? There is one very big difference between these two cases: the person who receives $2,000 is not receiving nothing, much less a bullet in the head, he is receiving $2,000. True, $2,000 may not be as much as he wants or needs, but it is not an injury. On the contrary, it is a substantial enough sum to justify him in his own eyes in depriving himself of the car in order to obtain it. But perhaps he is being robbed because he is receiving only $2,000 for an object the true value of which is $5,000? But this presupposes, mistakenly, that economic value is an objective reality capable of being measured independently of the agreement between buyer and seller. As we shall see in the next chapter, true economic value exists only to the extent that there are a buyer and a seller who reach an actual agreement on a price. What is called market value does not represent any actual agreement between a buyer and a seller, but is only a putative or presumed value, representing typically what other similar items have sold for recently, and so what we believe would be obtainable in the near future for this item if there is no sudden change in conditions.

THE CASE OF KUWAIT

The difference between market transactions and the use of force has been clearly brought out recently by the case of Kuwait. Saddam Hussein invaded Kuwait because in his opinion Kuwait was selling too much oil, thereby driving the international price of oil down. The OPEC ministers had reached a nominal agreement on oil production, but like all cartels they have experienced great difficulty in maintaining their unity. As oil prices fell over the last few years Arab nations which had been rich experienced a severe loss of income, and many increased their production further in order to increase their income. Kuwait was one of these. Saddam Hussein was concerned, because he wanted the OPEC pricing strategy carried out.

What is striking here is the agreement on the part of so many nations that that is not a sufficient reason to invade another country. In other words, there has been general agreement that there is a world of difference between economic competition and physical warfare, and that Kuwait has a right to sell as much oil as it wants, at whatever price it wishes, without suffering aggression, and the United States and other countries should have the right to buy that oil. Oil was indeed relevant to the U.S. action in the Persian Gulf, as Mr. Bush remarked, but the reason was not merely utilitarian, that we wanted to buy cheap oil; it was that Kuwait must have the freedom to sell its oil as it desires. What was at stake in the Persian Gulf was economic freedom. This fact is brought out by the contrast between the recent situation and that in 1974, when the OPEC nations increased the price of oil by several hundred percent, yet no one even suggested that military action should be taken against them.

COERCIVE OFFERS?

We stated above that in the case where it is clear that a person is receiving a benefit, there is little practical point in asking whether he does so freely. However, this has not prevented some philosophers from pursuing this question, and some have indeed maintained that it is possible not only for a threat of harm but also for an offer of a benefit to be coercive.[18] Suppose that Smith finds Jones about to drown, and offers to throw him a life-preserver on condition that he promises afterwards to pay a thousand dollars for the service: is Jones's promise free or not? A number of writers take the position that it is not free, because to forego the benefit would be to suffer intolerable harm.[19]

Now even if we were to grant that for Jones to forego the benefit offered by Smith in such a case would be to suffer intolerable harm, it clearly would not make sense to say that the harm was caused by Smith, and so such a view could not provide any grounds for punishing Smith. The most that could be at issue would be whether the contract should be enforced. As we shall see, there are indeed some contracts that should not be enforced.

The view that Jones does not act freely in accepting Smith's offer of a lifepreserver is typically based on the assumption that if there is no reasonable alternative the action is not free. On this basis some authors come to the (to say the least) paradoxical conclusion that it is possible for an offer to enlarge a person's freedom, and yet at the same time to be coercive! It enhances his freedom because it adds to his available options, but it is coercive because he has no reasonable alternative! The idea that an action that is coercive must limit a person's freedom is a mere "dogma," one author maintains.[20]

This writer, Joel Feinberg, professor of philosophy at the University of Arizona, considers the case of a business executive who is desperately unhappy in his job in New York, has no welfare payments available to him, and is offered a job in Houston which is distasteful and unrewarding, but better than the New York job. Feinberg concedes that the offer of the job in Houston enhances the executive's freedom, but holds nonetheless that he is coerced into taking it, because the New York job is "an intolerable evil."[21] Feinberg goes even further and maintains that "there is no difference in the degree of coercion" experienced in such a case, and in the case of a gunman who threatens violence.[22]

If a writer is prepared to accept such a patent self-contradiction rather than accept the obvious conclusion, because he does not like the obvious conclusion, it is difficult to see how any line of argument at all that he did not like could succeed in convincing him. There could scarcely be any clearer evidence of the rationality of the free market, than such extraordinary feats of irrationality and self-contradiction which its opponents find necessary to oppose it.

As we have seen, it does not follow from the fact that there is no reasonable alternative to an action, that the action is not free. As Aristotle remarks, even where there is no reasonable alternative, the benefit can be chosen because it is "worthy of choice."

The opposite of freedom is necessity, and an action or event is necessary when it cannot be otherwise. To return to Smith and Jones, is it possible for Jones, in danger of drowning, to reject Smith's offer of a lifepreserver? Clearly there are circumstances where he could—for example if he had thrown himself into the river in an attempt to commit suicide. But supposing that is not the case, and he is extremely desirous of being rescued, does he retain the power to reject the rescue attempt? It would seem that the answer to this must be that he does indeed retain the power, even though he has no intention of using it. The fact that one has no intention of using a power does not mean that one lacks that power. In accepting Smith's offer Jones is acting autonomously, he is still the master of his own actions—unless perhaps he were so overcome by hysteria as totally to lose control of himself, which would be a different case.

EVEN IN DISTRESS THERE IS BENEFIT

We have been making an argument that the person who engages in a market transaction in distress is still acting freely and is responsible for his decision. However, even if we were to grant, for the sake of argument, that the person in distress is not acting freely, that would not solve the problem, because we would still not have any explanation for his action, unless we recognize that he is benefiting. If we say that the worker mentioned earlier is harmed by being offered only $1 an hour, it is impossible to explain his action in accepting the offer. It is no explanation to say that he cannot help it, that he is forced to accept it. For in what sense is he forced to accept it? The only sense in which he is forced to accept it is that he has a desperate need for it. But that presupposes that it constitutes a net benefit for him. The victim of a holdup does not *need* to give his money to the robber.[23] The fact that the worker may also need more than he receives does not mean that what he receives is not a benefit.

BLACKMAIL?

The question has been asked whether there is any significant difference between certain economic transactions like this and blackmail. What is the difference between offering not to publish compromising photographs of a man with his mistress if he will pay $500, and offering someone who is gravely ill a dose of lifesaving medicine for an "exorbitant" price? After all, it has been argued, there is not necessarily anything wrong about publishing compromising photographs of a person—newspapers do it constantly. Under certain circumstances there could even be an obligation on the part of the blackmailer to carry out the activity which he threatens, as when he threatens to reveal that the victim has committed a crime. And there is not necessarily anything wrong about selling photographs for money. It seems to be merely the conjunction of these two permissible activities which is felt to be wrong. And some writers have indeed maintained that blackmail would not be punishable in a properly free society, since it does not involve violence or the threat of violence.[24]

But this is a mistake. To blackmail a person is to threaten to cause him harm. Harm is not restricted to violence or the threat of it, but includes injury to a person's reputation by defamation, libel and slander.[25] Although public persons may be deemed to have voluntarily opened themselves up to public debate, and so to negative comment, newspapers have no moral right deliberately to publish compromising photographs of private persons in order to cause them harm, and in doing so may render themselves liable to legal action. The fact that the blackmailer may have an obligation to society to reveal that his victim has committed a crime does not detract from the fact that his intention in revealing the crime under these circumstances is not to serve the cause of justice, but to cause personal harm to his victim. To be accused of a crime is harmful, even to be accused truthfully, just as to be put in jail is harmful, even when one deserves it: the whole point of jail is that it is harmful. Whether the harm is justified is another question, as we shall see in Chapters 6 and 7. That depends on the reasons for it. Imagine a case where Smith has robbed Jones and so deserves jail, but he is never accused of that crime; but he is accused and found guilty, wrongfully and corruptly, of robbing Brown and so goes to jail. Is the sentence justified? That sentence is not justified, but another one, perhaps very similar, for robbing Jones would be justified. His actual sentence is unjust, because the reasons on which it was based were insufficient. Similarly, the revelation of a crime is unjust when it proceeds from malice; and the threat to reveal it is unjust when it proceeds out of a desire, not for justice, but for personal profit.

The fact that an official has an obligation to, say, give someone a permit who has satisfied the legal conditions for one, does not alter the fact that he causes harm if he demands money for it. In each case the victim is placed by the extortioner in a situation where he must choose between paying or suffering harm, as he is in a holdup.[26] This is not the case in a market exchange. We will examine in more detail in Chapter 5, as mentioned above, the question of the difference between causing harm and withholding a benefit.

KNOWING WHAT IS GOOD

We have argued that exchanges take place only because both parties expect to benefit. But at the same time, we conceded that it is possible for anyone to make a mistake about what is really for his own good. In any given case government may know better, and so, the argument runs, it may be justified in placing restrictions on the market in order to protect people against short-term pressures contrary to their true long-term interests.

The question of law, however, as we have pointed out, is always a question of *punishment*. While it is true that we can all make mistakes, it does not follow that it is justifiable to punish one person for another's mistake. It does not follow, because an employee happens to be misguided in assessing the benefits that will accrue to him from a job, that the employer deserves to be punished. If I apply for a job paying $2 an hour when I actually need $4 to survive, the employer who provides the job has done nothing to deserve a penalty.

It is iniquitous to punish one person because of another's mistake. It is still more iniquitous to impose the punishment when the mistake is not even claimed to be certain, but merely possible. Yet this is the case with government regulation of the market.

But, it might be rejoined, if the employee is mistaken, and is doing something which is really harming himself, then the employer is at least partly the cause of that harm, and may justifiably be punished.

There are two responses to be made to this. One is that the employer is not the cause of the putative harm, but the circumstances of the market or the employee himself. We shall return to this point shortly. The other is contained in the common law concept of the benefit of the bargain.

THE BENEFIT OF THE BARGAIN

It is true that the expectation of a benefit is not the same thing as the benefit itself. However, the potential for a benefit is itself already a benefit. If I buy a house as an investment, expecting that its value will go up, and instead it declines, I have not obtained the benefit I expected to obtain, but nonetheless I did obtain a benefit, namely the potential for a capital gain on this house, which I could not have obtained without buying the house. I may know quite well that houses go down as well as up in value; and I may realize quite clearly that that is a distinct possibility in this particular case; and yet I may still decide to buy the house, because the benefit of having the potential for a capital gain seems to me sufficient to warrant the risk of loss.

This fact, that every purchase or sale is carried out for the purpose of obtaining at least a relative benefit, is reflected in the concept found in English and American common law of the "benefit of the bargain." According to this usage everyone who buys or sells anything, provided only that he obtains what he intended to obtain, is said to have received the "benefit of his bargain," even if at a later time in the light of subsequent events he comes to the conclusion that it was a mistake to engage in the transaction. A person who has received what he wanted to receive is not entitled to make any legal complaint, since he has obtained "the benefit of his bargain," and for the same reason a person who discovers that a contract from which he benefited was fraudulent, but does not act promptly to renounce it, is taken to have confirmed it, and the contract becomes valid.[27] Similarly, in a legal action for redress of a breach of contract, the amount of the award is often measured by the "benefit of the bargain," by which is meant, not the eventual profit which the party hoped to achieve as a further consequence of the transaction, but simply the good or service which he would have received had the promise been performed.[28] The amount of the award "is based not on the injured party's hopes at the time he made the contract, but on the actual value that the contract would have had to him had it been performed. The expectation of the foolishly optimistic landowner who contracted to have an oil well dug on his property is not the gusher that he hoped for but the dry well that actually would have resulted."[29] In other words, by the mere fact that an exchange takes place, it is presumed in the common law that each party benefits.

Each Individual the Best Judge

Overall the person who is in the most advantageous position to decide what is best for a particular individual is that individual himself. For what is best for an individual depends, not just on one or two isolated factors, but on all of the factors that bear on that individual's life, and no one is in as good a position to know what all those factors are, and to weigh them one against another, as the individual himself.

I may be convinced that it would be best for you to give up smoking, on the general grounds that it is likely to be injurious to your health. But perhaps from your viewpoint this is not the only factor to consider, or even the main one. Perhaps you are suffering from money worries and find that smoking alleviates some of your anxiety; or perhaps you are at a crucial stage of your career, where you must concentrate on other things, and to make a herculean effort to give smoking up just now would be an immense distraction from your main concerns. Perhaps you are suffering from deep depression, and the prolongation of your life is not something you particularly want at this point. Perhaps you are engaged in a creative enterprise, such as writing a book, and you find that, however deplorable the smoking habit may be, it nonetheless calms you and helps your inspiration. For these and a thousand other similar reasons the general and abstract proposition that it is healthier not to smoke must yield to the concrete needs of the individual. There is a very great difference between an action's being good in the abstract, that is, all things else being equal, and its being good in the concrete, taking into account the details of the situation, where all things else may be anything but equal.

Now the members of a government, being human, have as much difficulty as anyone else in discovering what is truly good for themselves, and they make mistakes about that as frequently as the rest of us. Even supposing that they are not swayed by any considerations of self-interest (which is supposing a great deal), it is excessively optimistic to think that they can be trusted to have a wisdom and insight into what is good for others that they do not have for themselves. While it is true, then, that the exchanges an individual makes may not always turn out in the end to have been for his benefit, there is no reason to expect that anyone else would do a better job making the decisions for him; on the contrary, it is more than likely that they would do a worse one, since they cannot know all the details of that person's situation.

Weakness of Will

But, it might be objected, sometimes a person's will might be weak, and he might opt for an immediate benefit which will be to his long-term detriment. Some people smoke even though they would like to quit; some take cocaine even though they know that in the long run it is likely to cause them harm.

This is true: there is such a thing as weakness of will. But a weak will is still a will, and the individual is responsible for it. The person who lights a cigarette even though he would like to quit is making a decision to prefer the certain immediate gain from the sensation of satisfaction it gives him to the merely possible long-term benefits of better health. He may not sit back and calculate calmly and rationally the various benefits of the two courses of action, weighing one against the other in a detached or theoretical fashion, but he does decide that the one benefit is to be preferred to the other.

In most cases where exploitation is alleged, however, there is no question of weakness of will. When a man applies for a job which pays only a low wage, because he has not been able to find anything better, that is not a case of weakness of will, but of a thoroughly rational and justified calculation that taking everything into consideration he will be better off with the job than without it.

The Benefit of Responsibility

Can we presume to benefit an adult human being by taking away from him his responsibility for himself? No doubt there are certain particular benefits which can be given in this way. If we put a drunkard in prison until he no longer craves alcohol, we have benefited him to that extent. But we have also harmed him, because there is nothing an adult human being has which is more precious than his autonomy, his ability to govern himself and be responsible for his own decisions. The question is, can we be entitled to harm him in this way when he is causing no harm to others? We shall take this question up more fully in Chapter 7.

The Long-Term View and Collective Bargaining

While the fact that everyone can make a mistake about what is beneficial has some relevance to the discussion of paternalistic laws, such as those forbidding suicide, or requiring car drivers to wear safety belts, it has no significance for the concept of exploitation. It is not the case that the worker who accepts a low wage because of his weak bargaining power, and who will be better off if the state imposes a higher wage, mistook a harm for a benefit. As we have seen, a low wage is not a harm, but a lesser benefit.

Despite this, the possibility of making a mistake about what is for one's genuine good is often used as an argument for collective-bargaining laws. Those who support these laws often grant that it may not be for the short-term benefit of persons in distress to forbid exchanges which take advantage of their weakness, but maintain that such a prohibition is for their long-term benefit. An employee applying for a job in a factory is in a weak bargaining position, left to himself, and may well not be able to secure the salary or protection that he needs; but if these things are required by law, or by a legally enforceable trade union contract, he will obtain them; and an employer who does not provide them will be breaking the law and will be punished.

Such a system creates an appearance of bestowing benefits, but the harm that it causes is often overlooked. Any employer has only a certain amount of money to pay out. If he is required by law to pay out more than the work done economically justifies, that reduces his ability to employ others. The employee who already has a job, then, and who is able to keep it, benefits from such a law, but those who are prevented from finding jobs which they would otherwise have had, and those who lose their jobs because their firm can no longer afford them, do not benefit.

One of the most obvious facts of economic life in the United States in the last twenty years has been the relative decline of American manufacturing. Many consumer goods that Americans buy are no longer made in America, but in Japan and other countries of East Asia. In the process hundreds of thousands of jobs have been eliminated in America and created in East Asia. What is the reason for this? A good deal has been written about Japanese management methods, as if that were the decisive factor, and about the lower cost of capital in Japan. But most people in business know that the principal reason why this takes place is the cost of labor, understood in the broad sense to include not only the dollar amount of wages but in combination with that, the terms of employment. According to Peter Drucker, all the available evidence indicates that the main cause of the high cost of labor and so of the "productivity gap" experienced by American industry is the work rules and job restrictions imposed by trade unions.[30]

Most markets are not stable, but change constantly, from day to day. To respond to these changing conditions any business must be flexible, able to move workers about from sectors where they are needed less to sectors where they are needed more. Union contracts, however, typically impose rigid job classifications which make it impossible for employers to transfer workers as they are needed. Japanese unions, which are typically company unions, and which apparently understand that workers prosper only when their employer prospers, generally have only a small number of job classifications: in the automobile industry regularly only about five. In the United States, however, company unions (unions dominated by the company) are forbidden by law, and union contracts typically impose many more job classifications: in the automobile industry, about sixty. This factor alone, the cost of unionization, is sufficient to explain the decline of American manufacturing, and the massive export of manufacturing jobs overseas. To this must be added, however, the cost of the benefits which employers in the United States are compelled by law to provide for their employees, such as unemployment compensation and worker's compensation, and also the costs imposed by other labor laws, such as those that affect hiring, firing, or plant closings. While trade unions have benefited those workers who are fortunate enough still to have jobs, nevertheless for American workers as a whole, and for American society as a whole, they have been far from beneficial.[31]

There can be no moral objection, in this author's view, to voluntary trade unions. What is morally objectionable about trade unions in their present form is the unique monopoly privileges which are given them by the existing law, which enable them to engage in coercion. Trade unions in the United States are given these unique monopoly privileges by the following provisions of the law:

— There can be only one union for each bargaining unit, which rules out simultaneous competition between unions.

— An employer cannot refuse to bargain with the union.

— The agreements which are reached between the union leadership and the employer are legally binding not merely on all members of the union, but on all employees of the bargaining unit: that is, an employee is deprived of the freedom to bargain directly with his employer regarding his own wages and working conditions and is forced to accept whatever a majority of the voting members of the union decide, and this may be a very small proportion of those in the bargaining unit or even in the union.

— Workers are prevented from suing a union for damages on the grounds that it has caused harm to them by the contract it has negotiated, and employers are prevented from suing a union for damages resulting from a strike so long as the strike is legal.

This monopoly power is usually defended by the argument that employers and employees should be at least roughly equal, or at least not "grossly" unequal, in bargaining power. Yet this is not a rational position, because of the fundamental differences between their situations. What we call a job exists only because the employer creates it. He creates the job because there is some goal which he wishes to achieve, but which he cannot achieve without help. Anyone who asks another for help surely has the right to specify what kind of help he wants, and on what conditions. The job has no objective or independent existence in its own right; it exists solely in virtue of the employer's desires and needs. Even though the employee must consent to the job and to the payment he receives for it, otherwise he will not apply for it, still the job is not created by the employee, and does not exist in order to satisfy his needs. Furthermore, an employer must typically wait a considerable time before he receives his profit: he must not only think up the goods he wishes to produce, estimate what they will cost and what they can be sold for, design them in detail, arrange financing, and take on himself the responsibility of constructing the factory, buying the raw materials and producing the goods; he must also wait, perhaps for months or even years, after the goods have been produced, until he receives his money. And after all that effort, the product may be a flop.

In the meantime the employee expects to receive his wages each month or each week. Where is this money to come from? It can only come from the capital invested by the employer. If market conditions change, and they can change with astonishing rapidity, he may lose his entire investment, and even contract very considerable personal debt, if not be forced into bankruptcy. No doubt the employee is also at risk, to the extent of not receiving his wages, but he has made no investment in the undertaking, beyond the work he has contracted to perform, and will incur no debts from the fact that it fails; his risk is not of the same order as the risk which the employer takes on.

The employee is therefore by no means on an equal footing with the employer, and to give him an equal bargaining position by law is to rob the employer of his own creation, comparable to robbing an author of his right to the book he has written, or to counterfeiting an artist's painting. Inequality of bargaining positions, then, should not be viewed as something unjustified.

As we saw earlier, every law restricting trade, no matter how well-intentioned it may be, raises prices, and reduces the level of employment. If market conditions deteriorate, these laws can easily lead to massive unemployment, as has recently occurred in some European countries. Typically this unemployment, which is the product of a legal system of protection, is then blamed on the market, and further restrictive laws are considered necessary to deal with it.

CAUSING HARM AND FAILING TO PREVENT IT

It is sometimes clear beyond a reasonable doubt that a person has suffered harm in the wake of some business transaction. A person buys cocaine and becomes addicted to it, or buys a machine and is injured by it, or takes a job in a mine and is stricken by lung disease. This raises the question of causation: are we not justified in holding that the seller of the cocaine bears some serious degree of responsibility for the buyer's fate, or that the manufacturer of the machine is responsible for the damage it has done, or the owner of the mine for the miner's disease?

This is the question of liability, and a full discussion of it requires a discussion of the idea of causation, which will be examined in Chapter 5. To anticipate briefly what will be said there, there is a difference between a *necessary* condition of the harm, and a *sufficient* condition of it. For an action to be a cause, it must fulfill both conditions. It follows that there is an important difference between causing harm and failing to prevent harm, for in the case of failing to prevent harm only the first condition is met.

For similar reasons, even if we were to concede that (*per impossible*) in some situations a party to an exchange, as the result of misconstruing the benefits accruing to him from the transaction, might not obtain any benefit at all but only harm (if for example the concept of the benefit of the bargain did not apply), it would still not be true that the other party was the cause of the harm, and so there could be no justification for punishing him. For in the absence of force and fraud the action of one party is never sufficient to cause harm to the other. If harm is done, it is done either by the circumstances of the market, or by the party to himself.

If I buy a condominium unit as an investment and its value falls instead of rising, I do indeed suffer a loss, but the cause of the loss may be merely the circumstances of the market, if, namely, there had been good reasons to justify a prudent person in making the decision to buy at that time. On the other hand, if it was a reckless decision made in the face of an obviously deteriorating market, we might perhaps say that I had caused myself the harm. What is crystal clear is that it is not the person who sold me the unit who caused me the harm, for it was my decision to buy it and I could have decided otherwise.

Similarly, if I apply for a job paying $2 an hour when I actually need $4 to survive, I might, by an extension of the term, be said to have harmed myself, but I have no grounds to call for punishment of the person who offered me the job, for it was my decision to apply for it.

IMPLIED WARRANTIES

Within this framework the question arises of implied warranties. The Uniform Commercial Code recognizes several warranties as binding on sellers even though no explicit mention is made of them in connection with a particular sale.[32] One such warranty is that of merchantability, as it is called, which requires that the goods be fit for the ordinary purposes for which such goods are used. The problems this can give rise to are illustrated by a recent treatise:

> On the one hand, American Tobacco will argue that its Lucky Strikes are merchantable since they are fit for the ordinary purposes for which such goods are used, namely, smoking. They will admit that their cigarettes would not be merchantable if they contained some foreign object such as a toenail or a mouse's ear, but they will maintain that the goods are merchantable as long as they are essentially identical to other goods that pass in the trade under the label "cigarettes." The plaintiff will argue, on the other hand, that the proper measure of merchantability is whether the cigarette causes cancer, and he will maintain that if the cigarette causes cancer, *ipso facto* it is not suitable for the ordinary purposes for which it is sold, and it is not merchantable. Thus arises the question: to be merchantable must cigarettes be non-cancer-causing, or is it sufficient that they be like all other cigarettes despite the fact that they might contribute to lung cancer in some users?[33]

If merchantability is interpreted as an element of the contract which the buyer is entitled to take for granted because of the customary way such business is done, then a supporter of free markets will have no objection to it. A buyer has a right to obtain what he is paying for, and what the seller is commonly understood to be selling him, unless the buyer waives this right by buying the item "as is." Since not every aspect of an item can be inspected by the buyer before purchase, it must be assumed in every sale that the seller guarantees that the goods being sold are of the minimum quality of which they would customarily be expected to be. If the goods are not of this quality, then even though the seller made no deliberate attempt to deceive, and indeed made no statement at all, and even though he had no knowledge that the goods sold were of inferior quality, then the exchange is not a valid contract, and the buyer has a right to a refund. The behavior of the merchant can legitimately be interpreted in the light of what is customary in the trade. For example, if a person orders a machine from a manufacturer, there is an implied understanding that the machine will be new, and not secondhand or rebuilt, and that sound material and good workmanship are to be furnished. The same kind of warranty applies to the sale of food: a person who is in the business of selling food is assumed to be selling something which is at least minimally fit for human consumption.

The implied warranty of merchantability is intended to protect the buyer against defects in the product. This raises the question: What is a defect? Commonly, a distinction is made between defects of manufacture and defects of design. A defect of manufacture is present when the item does not conform to its customary description. If I buy a bar of chocolate and the package proves to be filled with sawdust instead, I have not bought what is commonly understood to be a bar of chocolate. Or I buy a car, but it turns out to lack a motor. A defect of design, by contrast, is where the customer, for whatever reason, is unhappy with the customary description of the product, for example because it is dangerous. I succeeded in buying the bar of chocolate, but chocolate can make people fat. Or I buy a Jumping Jalopy, but Jumping Jalopies turn out to be excessively lethal to their occupants in crashes.

From the viewpoint advocated in this book, it is only defects of manufacture which can give grounds for legal complaint (and then only when the warranty is not disclaimed, i.e., when the product is not sold "as is.") The reason is that the design of the product is precisely what identifies the product. It was my decision to buy a Jumping Jalopy. I cannot blame the seller or the manufacturer for providing me with one. If the question of safety was important to me, then I should have investigated Jumping Jalopies from that aspect before I committed myself to the decision to buy one.

Another implied warranty recognized by the Code is that of fitness for a particular purpose. Where the seller knows that the buyer wants the goods for a particular purpose, and that the buyer is relying on the seller's skill and judgement to provide him with the goods he needs, then there is an implicit warranty that the goods are fit for that purpose. The justification for these obligations on the part of the seller is that they represent the customary understanding of the contract, or an understanding which is justified by the circumstances, even though they have not been put explicitly into words on this occasion. They can be obviated by the seller's stating explicity that he is selling the goods "as is," with no such warranty; or even by the way he customarily does business.

On the other hand, if these implied warranties are interpreted as providing special protection for buyers beyond what they agree to in making the purchase, so that the seller is liable for harm caused by a typical instance of the product, then from the viewpoint of a free market they are misguided, like all other measures of special protection.

The case of *Green v. The American Tobacco Co.*, which hinged on just this question, was ultimately decided by the Fifth Circuit Court of Appeals in 1970 as follows:

> We are not dealing with an obvious, harmful, foreign body in a product. . . . Instead, we have a product (cigarettes) that is in no way defective. They are exactly like all others of the particular brand and virtually the same as all other brands on the market.

The treatise we mentioned above comments:

To those who would reject the Fifth Circuit's conclusion out of hand, let us suggest the case of whiskey or butter. One might want to argue that butter is unmerchantable because it contains cholesterol, and cholesterol causes heart disease. Is whiskey or are automobiles not merchantable because they may cause injury or even death when they are used improperly and contribute to injury or death even when they are used properly?

Inspection has a special relevance here. According to the Code, if the seller invites the buyer to inspect the goods before purchase but he unreasonably refuses to do so, the implied warranties are no longer valid. And if he does inspect the goods as fully as he desires, then there is no implied warranty with regard to those defects which an inspection ought in the circumstances to have revealed to him.

Another warranty which is implied in every sale is the warranty of title: it is assumed in every sale that the seller has good title to what he is selling.[34] This is unexceptionable, and even necessary, from the standpoint of a free market.

Understood in the proper sense, these provisions seem fully justifiable, as rendering explicit what is customarily understood in a contract. We must ask, then, whether they modify what we said above about the seller not being the cause of harm to the buyer. Properly interpreted, the implied warranties are simply expressions or necessary consequences of the idea that the buyer has a right to obtain what he is paying for, given that some aspects of purchases and sales are not always stated explicitly, but are commonly understood in the light of the customary way of doing business. This is thoroughly consistent with the basic principle that every adult is responsible for his own knowledge or lack of knowledge, so long as the other has not deliberately deceived him.

THE RESTRICTIONS ON THE SALE OF MEDICINES

A case of special interest in this regard is presented by the current laws in the United States regulating the sale of medicinal drugs. We pass over the fact that many drugs cannot be bought freely, but may be sold only to those who have a physician's prescription: a measure which creates a legal monopoly or cartel, the disadvantages of which are almost never investigated; and we also pass over the fact that by contrast with the law at the beginning of this century, narcotics cannot now be sold legally at all, though both of these call for comment. For the moment however, the fact we wish to draw attention to is that no drug can be sold in the United States unless it has been demonstrated to the satisfaction of the Food and

Drug Administration that it is both safe and effective. Thus it is impossible for a drug firm to sell any drug "as is," with an explicit declaration that
it is giving no warranty, or even with a warning that the drug produces
certain unpleasant or dangerous side effects, or that it has not been clearly
demonstrated to be effective against some particular disease.

The human as well as the economic costs of this law have been
publicized for many years now. They have become especially clear in
recent times in connection with the plight of those stricken by AIDS. In
order to demonstrate to the satisfaction of the FDA that a drug is both safe
and effective, tests are required which can take up to ten years and cost
several millions of dollars. The result is that it is very difficult for small
firms to enter the market, and in many cases it is counterproductive to
market drugs which can be of use to only a small number of people, such
as those with a rare disease. Thus, many drugs which might save lives do
not get developed at all. Since the cost of producing drugs can be smaller
in other countries which do not have such restrictions, research for the
development of new drugs has declined in the United States, and increased overseas, creating the celebrated "drug lag": some medicines,
needed as a matter of life and death by some people, can only be obtained
outside the United States. Furthermore, the decision as to whether a
particular drug can legally be marketed or not comes easily to depend on
political considerations having to do with the friendly or hostile personal
relationships existing between officials in the FDA and employees of the
drug companies, as a recent case has shown.[35]

It will be clear that the law goes far beyond the idea of the implied
warranty as to fitness of purpose, which, as we observed, when properly
interpreted is simply an expression of the idea that a person has a right to
obtain what he is paying for. The principal reason given for this law is that
it is necessary to protect the public against exploitation. That is, it presupposes that even if a drug company issued an explicit statement that it is
giving no warranty for the drug, and even if it issued warnings about the
drug's safety or effectiveness, a drug company which sold such a drug to
an individual, in consequence of which he suffered harm, would itself be
the cause of that harm. It does not seem an exaggeration to say that this
conception is fundamentally confused, for it mistakes a mere precondition for a cause. Worse, it makes nonsense of the idea of personal responsibility, which is the foundation of all morality; for the concept of personal
responsibility is that sane, conscious adult human beings are uniquely the
causes of their own actions, for good or ill, and can be praised or penalized for them. Without this idea the notions of praise and blame
become merely absurd. According to the view implicit in the law we have
been considering, the individual is not responsible for his action in taking
the drug, even though warned by the drug company, but the drug

company is responsible for its action in selling the drug. But if the individual in such cases is not responsible for his action, it is very hard to see how there can be any grounds for holding the drug company responsible for its actions. We will see more of this question in a subsequent chapter. (In recent months the FDA has been prepared to loosen somewhat the restrictions it places on the sale of certain AIDS drugs which have not met its tests for safety and effectiveness, in the wake of vocal protests from the AIDS community. This concession of the irrationality and injustice of the law is of course a welcome move in the right direction, but it has occurred only for one small set of drugs, and only as the result of intense political pressure by an organized interest group.)

If an individual suffers harm, then, from something that he buys, it does not necessarily follow that some other *person* has caused him harm. In the case of someone who is harmed by a drug, it may simply be that we must say that the drug has harmed him; as well as, under certain circumstances, that he has harmed himself.

ALL EXCHANGES ARE GRATUITOUS

Since exchanges take place only because both parties expect to benefit, it follows that all economic transactions are gratuitous. Just as no one has an obligation to become an employer, or to manufacture any particular goods for the market, so no one has an obligation as a matter of justice to offer any particular wages or working conditions or benefits, or to charge any particular price for the goods he sells. No one has an obligation to buy anything, and no one has an obligation to sell anything. Anyone who puts anything up for sale is doing a favor to others, in the sense of providing a benefit for them which they have no right to expect, and anyone who buys is doing a favor to the seller, which he has no right to expect. To view something which is a favor as if it were a right, is surely very far from being a sound moral attitude.

The notion that economic equality is a desirable and necessary goal overlooks this fact, of the gratuitousness of economic activity, and consequently the fact that the various groups of people involved in the market are not all in a morally equal position in regard to every aspect of a transaction. The recipient of a favor is not in a morally equal position with the bestower of the favor. As we have seen, the recipient of a job is not in a morally equal position with the creator of the job. The consumer of a product is not in a morally equal position with the producer of it. To employ the coercive powers of government in order to ensure that people who are fundamentally and necessarily in unequal positions will be treated as if they were in equal positions can only be a futile as well as an unethical endeavor.

THE ENFORCEMENT OF CONTRACTS

Our argument has been that in the absence of force and fraud, both parties to an exchange engage in it because they expect to benefit, and each therefore necessarily acts in such a way that the other considers it a benefit. Our conclusion is that it cannot be right to punish either, no matter what the terms of their agreement. It is a very different matter, however, *not to enforce* a contract. There are some contracts which it is permissible not to enforce.

1) One case is where neither party will be harmed if the agreement is not enforced.

A contract is a mutually conditioned promise. Smith promises to give Jones a certain sum of money on condition that Jones promises to do a certain amount of work for Smith. Jones in turn promises to do this work for Smith on condition that Smith pays him a certain amount of money. The binding force of the contract comes from the fact that it leads each party justifiably to expect a certain performance from the other and to rely upon that expectation in such a way that if the other fails to perform, then the first party is harmed. This is reflected in the legal concept of detrimental reliance. If I contract with you to put a new kitchen in my home for $10,000, and you put the new kitchen in, but I then fail to pay you, I am causing you harm, because you have done the work but have not received the recompense the prospect of which alone led you to do the work. The binding force of contracts is derived from the Principle of No Harm, which states, roughly speaking, that persons should not be harmed unless they have caused harm (discussed more fully in Chapters 7, 8 and 9). If circumstances should be such that one person is *not* harmed by the other's failure to perform, then the reason for the legal obligation in that direction ceases.

Suppose we sign a contract that you will put a new kitchen in for me next year; but in the meantime you move to another part of the country, and I sell my house. Neither of us is harmed by the failure to keep to the contract, and it lapses.

Suppose Jones is about to drown, and Smith, standing by, offers to rescue him on condition that he agrees to work for Smith at a low wage for ten years. It is clear that at least after a certain length of time Smith will not be harmed if Jones refuses to work for him any longer. Just what that length of time might be would depend on the circumstances, for example on the hardship Smith had to suffer in rescuing Jones. If Smith had to suffer very considerable hardship, perhaps imperilling his own life, the situation would be different from that where he suffered no inconvenience at all, but merely threw Jones a lifebelt. In this case, presumably Smith would suffer no harm if Jones ceased to work for him after a relatively short period.

2) A second case is where it has become impossible for one party to fulfill the contract. This is the principle behind bankruptcy laws. If a person enters into a contract in good faith, and through circumstances beyond his control becomes unable to fulfill his obligation, for example to pay a debt, bankruptcy law typically provides for his assets to be divided up among his creditors, and his indebtedness is thereupon considered at an end. This can be justified on the grounds that obligation presupposes possibility. For an obligation to be binding, it must be possible to carry it out.

Sometimes it is not perhaps strictly impossible for one party to fulfill the contract, but would involve exceeding hardship; for example, if the debt could be paid off only by working for a very long time, perhaps a lifetime. Bankruptcy law typically considers this equivalent, and that is perhaps not unreasonable.

3) The Uniform Commercial Code declares that a court may refuse to enforce a contract which it deems "unconscionable." The Code does not define unconscionability, however, leaving that to judges, and in practice courts have given widely different tests for it. A classic case is *Williams v. the Walker-Thomas Furniture Co.* Mrs. Williams was a welfare mother with seven children and a monthly income of $218; she had bought $1800 of merchandise from Walker-Thomas over a period of several years. For each purchase she signed a complex installment contract which applied her monthly payments pro rata to all the items she had purchased, so that if she fell delinquent on the payments on one item, all the items on which she still owed money could be repossessed. Her last purchase was a stereo set for $514.95. After making numerous payments she defaulted, and the store filed suit to repossess all the items on which she still owed money. Two courts granted the suit, but a court of appeals reversed those decisions and refused to enforce the contract. The judge gave as his reasons a lack of meaningful choice on Mrs. Williams's part, and contract terms which were unreasonably favorable to the other party. He emphasized Mrs. Williams's lack of education, and the use of fine print by the Walker-Thomas company. Other court decisions have based findings of unconscionability on consumer ignorance, ignorance of the English language, the poverty of the buyer, or simply what the court regarded as an excessively high price.[36]

The unconscionable contract shares with bankruptcy a focus on inability, but the inability is of a different kind. In bankruptcy the debt is cancelled because of inability to pay, or hardship tantamount to inability. In cases of unconscionability the contract is cancelled by the court because the consumer is deemed unable to enter validly into the contract. The court's decision regarding Mrs. Williams was based not so much on the hardship she would suffer from the repossession, as on her alleged inability to enter into the contract itself, because of her lack of meaningful choice, her lack of education, and because the repossession clause was in fine print.

This implies that certain categories of sane adults should not be considered responsible for their own actions, while leaving it to each judge individually to determine what those categories of persons should be. The chief criterion seems to be simply that the judge finds it, as one expressed it, "shocking" that such an agreement should be made.[37]

This, however, is surely both condescending and arbitrary. It is condescending because it assumes that only those contracts should be binding, and only those standards should be valid, which an educated, middle-class judge could imagine himself observing. The inevitable consequence of such a policy is that businesses will reduce their services among the population which is not held to its agreements. And the assumption that if certain classes of people behave foolishly, they should not be held liable for their actions is, of course, an effective way of increasing the number and the foolishness of foolish actions. Furthermore such a policy is arbitrary because in many situations there is no way in which a seller can know in advance what some judge is not likely to find shocking. The mere fact that a judge may consider a price shocking does not mean that the buyer did not consider it a benefit at the time he agreed to pay it. Just as the mere fact that a person does not know the English language is no reason to reduce him to the moral status of a child.

To summarize, the Principle of Mutual Benefit points out that in the absence of force, fraud, and mistake, people buy and sell only because they expect to benefit from the transaction. It makes no sense, then, to believe that either party to a transaction may cause harm to the other. Although many people believe that there are exceptions to this principle, such as when one party is under severe economic pressure, or when the terms of trade are too one-sided, our analysis shows that the principle holds equally well in such cases. "Exploitation" as it is widely understood is an utter misrepresentation of the true situation. It is not only a fatal mistake in economics, but also a gross error in ethics, to pass laws which penalize either party to an exchange because of terms they have mutually agreed on.

3

Is the Market Imperfect?

In January, 1991, the nonprofit Venice Hospital in Florida was fined $2.3 million. Its crime was that it encouraged patients to buy from its medical equipment supply business.[1]

Eight Ivy League universities and the Massachusetts Institute of Technology were charged by the Justice Department in May, 1991, with the felony of agreeing on the amounts of financial aid they would provide to prospective students.[2] The universities, however, refused to admit any wrongdoing.

In the same month the B. Manischewitz Company was fined $1 million for agreeing with two other firms, in the course of a customary restaurant meal, on the price they would charge for Passover matzo.[3]

In August, 1991, two antique dealers were fined $100,000 and $50,000 for agreeing not to bid against one another at an auction.[4]

These are only a few of the many penalties, some much heavier, inflicted on individuals and institutions during 1991 on the grounds that they *restrained trade*. They used neither force nor fraud, all the activities concerned were voluntary; yet they were convicted of causing harm.

The laws under which these penalties are imposed reflect the assumption, common in the United States at least since the case of Standard Oil that led to the Sherman Anti-Trust Act of 1890, that the market system, desirable though it might be as the basis of the economy, functions imperfectly in some situations and must then be regulated by government. Left to itself the market can produce an imbalance of power, not only through monopoly but also through its opposite, excessive competition; and an imbalance of power is automatically harmful, it is believed. Tied in with this, in the minds of many, is the question of the environment: a completely free market, they assume, would result in the abandonment of environmental protection and conservation.

But is the assumption correct, that the market sometimes functions imperfectly? Is it possible to cause harm through peaceful competition? Does a monopolist cause harm? Does a free market in practice increase inequality? Will market freedom result in devastation of the environment?

COMPETITION

Businesspeople routinely speak of being "hurt by the competition," as if their competitors were a cause of harm to them: every business desires so far as possible to insulate itself against competition and secure a monopoly of its market. Most if not all nations assume that competitors can cause harm to a business and have laws designed to protect certain producers and sellers against excessive competition. Perhaps the best-known example of this in the United States in recent history is the agreement with Japan to restrict the number of Japanese cars imported into the United States, in order to protect American automobile makers and their workers (discussed in the Introduction).

The general fear and dislike of strong competition is reflected in the picturesque terminology frequently employed by journalists who describe commercial situations in terms taken from physical warfare, of "battles," "raiding," and "cutthroat" competition. Indeed, the whole notion of competition appears to some people to be regrettable: it implies opposition and conflict, and surely the world would be a better place if competition could be replaced universally by cooperation. In the nineteenth century the influential French writer Louis Blanc maintained that all the evils experienced in social life could be traced back to competition.

Competition, however, is simply the result of freedom of choice. If I have a choice between buying a shirt from Smith or from Brown, then automatically Smith and Brown are in competition. Their reactions to that fact may be very different, one may respond reluctantly and the other enthusiastically, but that will not alter the fact that they are in competition. The consequence is that the only way of eliminating competition is by eliminating freedom of choice. And the only effective way of eliminating freedom of choice is by law, that is, by coercion, for in a free market it will always be possible for additional producers to enter the market. But while using the power of the law to eliminate freedom of choice may be good for the existing sellers and producers, at least in the short term, it is anything but good for buyers and consumers, for it typically results in higher prices, and in all the consequences that flow from them: fewer jobs, lower quality relative to price, and less innovation. We saw in the case of the car import restrictions the notably higher prices carbuyers have had to pay. Even for the producers the results can be detrimental, as we also saw in that case in the number of jobs lost.

Even Hesiod, some 2,700 years ago, understood the difference between harmful strife and competition:

> It was never true that there was only one kind
> of Strife. There have always
> been two on earth. There is one
> you could like when you understand her.
> The other is hateful. The two Strifes
> have separate natures.
> There is one Strife who builds up evil war,
> and slaughter.
> She is harsh; no man loves her, but under compulsion
> and by will of the immortals men
> promote this rough Strife.
> But the other one . . . is far kinder.
> She pushes the shiftless man to work,
> for all his laziness.
> A man looks at his neighbour, who is rich:
> then he too
> wants work; for the rich man presses on with
> his ploughing and planting
> and the ordering of his state.
> So the neighbour envies the neighbour
> who presses on toward wealth. Such Strife
> is a good friend to mortals.[5]

Although it is extremely difficult to make an argument on economic grounds for legal protection against competition, nonetheless arguments still continue to be made on the grounds of "fairness." A distinction is often made between fair and unfair competition. Businesses typically profess to welcome fair competition, but demand protection from unfair competition. The charge of unfair competition is usually made on the grounds that the competitor sells his goods below cost. (Competitors are rarely accused of producing goods of excessively high quality, however, though logically that should constitute just as good grounds for protection.)

Quite apart from the difficulty that outsiders usually experience in establishing whether a firm's prices are genuinely below cost, however, the notion of unfair competition ignores the role of the *customer*. The crucial fact is that it is always the customer's free decision not to buy from a particular seller. All things else being equal, it will always be to the customer's advantage to buy at the lowest price he can, even if that price should be below the seller's cost. There is nothing morally wrong about his doing this, just as there would be nothing morally wrong about his accepting the merchandise or service as a free gift.

On the other hand, a customer's decision to buy from a particular seller by no means automatically follows from the mere fact that that seller has lower prices. The smaller shop can offer greater convenience and quicker service, perhaps, and this is in fact the secret of the success of many small food stores. If anyone causes harm to a seller, it could only be those persons who do not buy from him. But, as we have seen, buying is a gratuitous act, a favor. No one believes that customers have an obligation to buy from a seller. Even organized boycotts are not usually condemned as immoral or unjust. And, as we shall later see in more detail, refusing to trade with someone is by no means the same as causing harm to him. But of course the customers who do not buy from a seller cannot readily be identified. It is easier, then, to lay the blame at the feet of the competitor, who can usually be identified all too easily.

So long as competition takes place in a free market, the idea that a business can be harmed by its competitors is a figure of speech, rather than a literal reality. If it were strictly true, the competitor would be guilty of a crime, and could at the least be sued for damages, in the way that anybody can be sued who causes harm to another; but this is a possibility which even our present laws have not yet envisioned. While it is true, no doubt, that a firm can suffer in consequence of competition, it would be more accurate to say that it is suffering in virtue of its own policies, or because it cannot or does not wish to match what its competitors offer, than to blame the competitors.

The case is very different, however, when a firm uses subsidies provided by government in order to sell its goods at a price below the market, whether in its own country or another. In that case the competition no longer takes place in a free market. If the argument of this book is correct, such subsidies cannot be justified ethically. It seems clear that it can be permissible to bring political pressure to bear on such a government to change its policies, and where the market of another country is affected, that may only be possible by some measure regulating trade between the two countries. The intervention is justified because its purpose is to increase the freedom of the market. This is one of the few cases where even Adam Smith is willing to approve of government intervention in the market, on condition that it has some probability of success.[6]

MONOPOLIES

Although our analysis shows that it is a mistake to believe that buyers or sellers ought to be legally protected against competition, the analysis does not in any way depend on there being what economists call "perfect competition." This is the idea of a market in which no individual has power to influence prices, by increasing or decreasing his production or purchasing, but must passively accept whatever price happens to be prevailing. An example of this in today's market would be an American wheat farmer, since no single farmer can produce more than a tiny fraction of the world demand for wheat.[7]

Traditionally most economists have conceded that in such a perfectly competitive market there would be no need for government to intervene, since the market itself could not be "distorted" by the self-serving actions of any one producer or consumer. No one, on this theory, would have any economic power over anyone else. Regulation is needed, it is thought, because markets do not conform to the ideal of perfect competition.[8] Even that celebrated foe of free markets, John Kenneth Galbraith, concedes "It is unnecessary for government to control the exercise of private power if it does not exist in any harmful form."[9]

In the Middle Ages and the early modern period it was generally believed that in order to be successful in trade it was necessary to have a legally enforced monopoly,[10] and government policy was often directed towards fostering monopoly as a means of increasing the nation's power. It could perhaps be argued that this mentality is still evident in much European protectionism. It was Adam Smith who demonstrated that the economic power of the nation could best be increased by free trade. But in recent times the shoe has largely been on the other foot: monopoly has been viewed as something morally objectionable, and since the Sherman Anti-Trust Act of 1890, U.S. law has simply forbidden outright all collusion to set prices (making notable exception, however, for labor unions). The moral argument against monopolies and cartels is that they are prone to take unfair advantage of buyers, making use of their economic power in order to raise prices above their market level, or the "fair" price. "It was agreed by everyone" writes Galbraith, "that such power was evil and that it should be struck down or be made subject to regulation by the state wherever it was found. The regulation of monopoly represented one of the few instances where, given the competitive model, it was agreed that the state would have to exercise its authority in the economy."[11] Even those who otherwise advocate market freedom often support the law prohibiting monopolies.

Yet from the economic point of view monopolies are not something particularly to be feared. Economists point out that in a free market, so long as a monopoly does not receive support from government, it is never absolute or permanent. A firm enjoys a monopoly when it is immune from competition; but in an unregulated market no firm can be perfectly insulated from competition forever. There are substitutes for every product. At the present time, for example, many American cities have only one newspaper, and this may therefore appear to have a monopoly. But the majority of Americans now obtain their news from television, which is the real competition for the newspapers. If a genuine monopoly is achieved in an industry, and the monopolist firm raises prices above the competitive level, it creates an incentive for other firms to enter the industry in competition with it. No doubt in some industries there are natural barriers to entry, but none of these barriers are impregnable. It is often assumed that industries such as gas and electricity are natural monopolies, incapable of functioning properly in the market. Yet for many years the same assumption was made about telephone service, which is now functioning much more competitively, even if not yet entirely so.[12] Monopoly becomes absolute, and something to be feared, only when it is supported by government.

Besides pointing out that the negative aspects of monopolies are not as great as many people imagine, economists also point out that monopolies have positive features which render them of special value to society. As the distinguished economist Joseph Schumpeter has shown, monopoly power can provide much more incentive for innovation than a purely competitive market, as a result of the process which he called "creative destruction": the large short-term profits which can be obtained by the monopolist lead others to invent similar but better products in order to circumvent his monopoly. In consequence, Schumpeter argues that "perfect competition is not only impossible but inferior, and has no title to being set up as a model of ideal efficiency." He concludes that it is "a mistake to base the theory of government regulation of industry on the principle that big business should be made to work as the respective industry would work in perfect competition."[13] There is a good deal of empirical evidence in favor of Schumpeter's theory, and it is now widely supported by economists.[14]

Economists also point out that national monopolies have a special significance for international competition. In order to be competitive on the international market, it is often necessary for a firm to possess the economies of scale that can only be obtained by having so large a share of the national market that other firms cannot survive. The realization of this necessity is currently leading to pressure to weaken or dismantle anti-monopoly legislation in some industries. By the same token, international competition weakens the power of domestic monopolies.

In particular the positive role of what we may call product monopolies is often overlooked. The ability to achieve at least a temporary monopoly in individual products is essential to the market, for many products sell only because they obtain a monopoly to some extent. In cases where there are only a few competing products this is perhaps clear enough, but it may also be true even where there are many competing products. I go into a supermarket to buy some tea, and find perhaps two dozen different varieties. But there may be only one variety which meets my needs in terms of a combination of price and flavor, that is, which possesses this unique character and occupies this particular niche in the market. To that extent it has a monopoly, and the difference between this and what economists typically call a monopoly (a firm which is insulated against competition) is more a difference of degree than of kind. It is the possibility of obtaining this partial monopoly (which by the nature of the case will be only temporary) which provides the producer with the incentive to spend the time and money to get the product to the market.

A further consideration in favor of monopolies is that they alone make it possible for the potential economic value of an enterprise to be fully realized. Say that the development of the lawnmower market arrives through normal competition at the point where there are only two makers left, and where it would pay one of these to buy out the other, and it would pay the other to sell to him. Since the other firm could have the same objective, and since they know how valuable the monopoly power will be to the buyer, in order to achieve his goal the monopolist will have to offer them a high price. Now if we have a law prohibiting monopolies, such exchanges, which may be few in number but which may concern exceptionally large sums of money, cannot take place. This means that the owners of those firms are prevented from realizing the very considerable economic value of what they own. And this in turn means that there is so much wealth or capital that is not created, with consequences of the same sort as we saw above: lost jobs, higher prices, less innovation, and a lower standard of living in the society.

Does the Monopolist Cause Harm?

In order to justify legislation penalizing those who establish monopolies, it is above all necessary to demonstrate that the monopolist causes harm. This is no doubt widely believed. But is it true?

We are assuming that he has made no use of force or fraud, that any who may have sold to him to enable him to acquire his monopoly did so voluntarily. They may not have known that he was in the process of successfully acquiring a monopoly, though since that is the implicit aim of every seller in the market, the suspicion cannot usually be far from their minds, especially if they know that their commodity is in short supply.

We are also assuming that it is a monopoly in a free market, that is, that the monopoly is not specially supported by any law or legal arrangement.

Whom could the monopolist be harming? The only candidates are those who buy from him at his monopoly prices, and those who wish to buy from him but are unable to do so because his prices are too high. Again, however, we must remember that to cause harm to a person it is necessary that his condition after the event be worse than his condition before it. Is this the case when we buy from a monopolist?

Those who buy from him at his monopoly prices will only do so, as we have seen, if they expect to benefit from the purchase. Before the purchase they have their money; after the purchase they have the goods or services which, in the actual situation, they prefer to the money. In their minds, then, it cannot be the case that they are harmed. No doubt they would prefer to pay a lower price, but that is not sufficient to show that they are being harmed by paying the higher price, when the fact is that they do so because they consider the transaction beneficial.

Did Venice Hospital harm its patients by encouraging them to buy from its medical equipment supply business? No force or deception was used. If the patients bought from the equipment supply business, they did so because, taking their overall situation into account, they believed they would be better off doing that. If they bought from the equipment supply firm, perhaps they had to pay higher prices than if not. But if they did not wish to pay those prices, they could go elsewhere or not buy at all. It makes no sense to think that they were harmed.

The two antique dealers mentioned at the beginning of this chapter had engaged in what is known as a "pool": they agreed not to bid against one another at the auction, and one bought the item, then the two participated in a further auction of it. The charge against them is that they harmed the seller by artificially depressing the price he received.

But there was no necessity for either of them to attend the auction. Even if they attended, there was no necessity for either of them to bid. A person who puts an item up for auction has no *right* to receive any particular price. The argument is that auctions are conducted according to certain rules, and making an agreement beforehand not to bid goes against those rules. But this begs the question, which is whether there should be such a rule. Even the government was long uncertain whether pooling was a violation of the antitrust laws. At the beginning of this chapter we noted that the universities accused of agreeing on financial aid to prospective students refused to admit wrongdoing. Our analysis indicates that they had good reason for this refusal.

Those who wish to buy but are unable to do so because they cannot afford to pay the price, may seem at first likelier candidates for the position of having been harmed, especially if they have a desperate need for what the monopolist is selling. Since the distinctive action of the monopolist consists in the amassing of exclusive ownership together with the setting of a monopoly price, our question must be: Does he cause harm by this action to those who wish to buy but cannot afford the price?[15]

It may seem that we should make a distinction between the case where the monopolist has *created* the object over which he has a monopoly, and the case where he *acquires* a monopoly over objects which *already existed*. It is widely agreed that an inventor does not cause harm by charging a high price for his invention, nor an artist for his paintings.[16] But where the monopolist acquires a monopoly over objects which already existed, it might perhaps seem plausible to consider that the buyer's situation has been worsened. Previously he could buy the object, say a gallon of gasoline, at a price he could afford, but now that is no longer possible.

It is important to keep in mind, however, the significant difference between being robbed, and being unable to afford to buy an item. The condition of the person who has been robbed is clearly worse after than before: he possessed something, and now it has been taken away from him. But this is not true of the person who cannot afford to buy an item which he previously could afford to buy. He still possesses everything that he possessed previously. At most we could say that he has lost the ability to buy that item. But the ability to buy something is not a genuine possession. The ability to buy something is always contingent on the seller's willingness to sell, and without that willingness on the part of the seller, which cannot be taken for granted, there is no ability to buy.

Perhaps the most important thing to understand about monopolies, however, is that *government is always a monopoly*, and a much more serious and far-reaching one than any market monopoly, for it is the monopoly of coercion. Furthermore, government monopoly, unlike market monopolies, is permanent. This truth is underlined by the fact that in law governments, including state and local governments, are immune from antitrust suits. The appeal to government to prohibit monopolies is highly ironic, then: one embraces a greater monopoly as the savior from a lesser one. We shall return to this topic in Chapter 6.

Dealing with Japan

Many governments ask themselves what they can do to stem the triumphant tide of the Japanese manufacturers. A frequent response has been to accuse the Japanese of unfair trading, on the grounds that they sell their products below cost, or engage in "dumping." Most Western governments have erected trade barriers to protect their own manufacturers but recognize that this has the undesirable effect of raising prices.

There is a free-market response to the problem of the Japanese. Their superiority in the market can be attributed chiefly to two factors. One is the operation of cartels. Japanese firms club together in a variety of ways to create distribution systems, to protect their own territory and to attack foreign markets, dividing a market up between them to maximize their impact and economize on scarce resources. It is this perhaps more than any other factor which has given them their power. Although nominally Japan has antitrust laws, they are relatively weak and are only feebly enforced.[17]

What principally hinders American firms from competing against the Japanese is *American antitrust law*. Economists generally recognize that only a national monopoly may have the economic strength to compete in the international arena against the national monopolies of other countries. Similarly, it may take a cartel to compete against a cartel. If American firms had the liberty to form cartels and monopolies, as we have argued they have a right to, there is good reason to believe that the problem of trade with the Japanese would be largely solved.

From the viewpoint of morality, the one thing that must be avoided is special governmental support for cartels, since this introduces coercion and punishment where none have been deserved. It is this Japanese practice that the United States should object to, not the formation of cartels and monopolies as such; and it is this practice that the United States in its turn must avoid, if it should ever come to see that monopolies are not the evil things it has taken them to be.

The second major factor behind the Japanese superiority, from a free-market perspective, lies in the area of labor relations, specifically in the difference between labor law in Japan and the United States. U.S. law prohibits the formation of unions dominated by the employer, "company" unions. Japanese law, by contrast, allows them. The result is that in Japan employees tend to recognize that their well-being depends on the well-being of the company, while in the United States employees are encouraged to develop an unnecessarily adversarial attitude towards their employers. This difference shows itself especially in union work rules and job classifications. Japanese unions typically have few, while American unions have many. As a result Japanese employers enjoy relative flexibility in assigning workers to jobs as they are needed, while American employers are greatly restricted. This adds significantly to the cost of American products. The remedy is not to accuse the Japanese of being unfair, but to loosen up the restrictions on American employers.

POWER

In discussions of the market the concept of power sometimes figures prominently. The desirable state of affairs, it is widely believed, is that power should be dispersed equally throughout the society: any excessive accumulation of power in the hands of a few is dangerous, and those who have little or no power, such as minorities, should be "empowered." In the market power should so far as possible be equal, or at least not extremely unequal, between buyer and seller, in the interests of "economic democracy." President Franklin Roosevelt expressed this view when he stated: "The power of a few to manage the economic life of the Nation must be diffused among the many or be transferred to the public and its democratically responsible government. If prices are to be managed and administered, if the Nation's business is to be allotted by plan and not by competition, that power should not be vested in any private group. . . ."[18] John Kenneth Galbraith speaks of "the ogre of economic power," and remarks, "In the American liberal tradition, a finding that private economic power exists has been tantamount to a demand that it be suppressed."[19]

There are a number of problems with this conception, however. One is that the notion of power is essentially ambiguous, as between the power to use physical force, on the one hand, and economic power, which is the ability to make or not to make exchanges, that is, to give or not to give benefits, on the other. When the notion of power is used in contexts like the present, it typically trades on this ambiguity; but, as we have just seen, there is no useful analogy between the use of physical force and the bestowal of a benefit in an exchange. The power to use physical force is an extremely dangerous power, which must be strictly circumscribed if a peaceful and civilized social life is to prevail. In our century alone, tens of millions of people have been killed by governments wielding their monopoly of physical force. Economic power, the power to buy and sell, on the other hand, is by no means dangerous; on the contrary, it is the source of immense benefits, not only to those who possess it, but to the rest of the society. Power is to be feared only when it can do harm. Economic power by itself cannot possibly do harm, it can only do good, if the notion of doing harm is properly understood; and we shall take this topic up in Chapter 5.

Economic power is either the power to trade, to bestow benefits, or the power not to trade, to withhold benefits. The power to trade can only take effect if someone else voluntarily agrees with it. I may have $100 million in the bank, but if no one wants to sell me anything, my economic power is zero. Wealth still leaves a person entirely dependent on the willing cooperation of others. So long as force and fraud are ruled out, and political corruption, there is no way that mere wealth can do harm. No doubt wealth can provide large inducements to others to offer that cooperation, but mere inducements, however large, do not remove the individual's essential power to make his own decisions.

Of course, the power to trade is also the power to withhold trading. A firm which has set up a plant employing a hundred people has the power to close the plant down. Are they not then causing harm to their employees? A full answer to this question will be given in Chapter 5. For the present we may point out that, while it is no doubt true that the employee who loses his job suffers, this alone is not sufficient to justify us in saying that the employer causes the employee harm, for the notion of causality must also apply. The question here is analogous to whether someone who fails to give a gift can be said to cause harm. Suppose that a person has given a gift of $1,000 each year to the United Way, and in such a fashion that although he has not made any promises, the United Way has come to depend on the gift; if one year he refuses to make the donation, he does not cause the United Way harm. Similarly, if a customer who has bought supplies from a firm regularly, to such an extent that the firm depends on his custom, and he decides to transfer his business to another firm, he does not cause the first firm harm. As we pointed out in the last chapter, and will argue in more detail in Chapter 5, *failing to do good* is not the same thing as causing harm. All economic transactions are gratuitous, except to the extent that a contract has been made. Furthermore, as was also pointed out in Chapter 2, a job does not belong to the employee, but to the employer, since it is he who creates it.[20]

Economic Power and the Political Process

Sometimes writers on this subject assume that an accumulation of wealth automatically endangers fair political processes. It is a cause of concern to modern liberals that elected representatives should not receive large campaign contributions or other favors from private persons, for example, for then they will be subject to undue influence. It is sometimes even maintained that the government of the United States is controlled by an elite of the wealthy and privileged.

If this last claim were true, however, we should expect to find that the legislation that is passed would favor the wealthy. But it is difficult to see that this has been the case by and large. The progressive income tax, reaching as high as 80 percent on large incomes for many years, the antitrust legislation, the recent abolition of the low capital gains tax, and many other such laws, do not reflect a desire to favor the wealthy.

Further than this, however, such views are a manifestation of a mechanistic conception of human existence, which has abandoned belief in free will and personal responsibility and sees human behavior as the product of external forces. For those who believe in free will and personal responsibility, however, human behavior is caused, not by economic or social forces, but by the human beings themselves. If that is the case, the chief remedy for regrettable behavior will lie, not in altering external conditions, but in an improvement in the virtue and character of the individual person. Political corruption, on this view, is first and foremost a failure of moral responsibility on the part of those holding political power. The elected representative who sells his vote deserves to be punished. No doubt external forces play a role, especially in the case of the weak-willed, but it is not the decisive role. From the viewpoint argued for in this book, then, there can be no strong objection to the use of private money to finance election campaigns. Elected officials are responsible for their votes to those who elect them. If the electorate believe their officials have voted against the interests of the electorate, they can remove them though the political process. In practice it would be helpful in this if the voting records of the elected officials are well publicized.

COURTESY

Since buyer and seller are each doing the other a favor, the relationship between them is delicate. A favor is something one has no right to expect. But it is possible, and even easy, to awaken in a person—or for the circumstances to awaken in him—the expectation that he will receive a favor: for example, when he sees other people, who have no special claim to it, receiving the same favor. I see that a bank is lending money, and so I expect that they will lend some to me. I see a restaurant serving food, and so I expect they will serve some to me. If, then, the favor which was expected is denied, it can easily be felt as a personal offense. And this feeling can be strongly reinforced if the rejection is given in an unfriendly or even merely a neutral tone. When declining to do someone a favor, it is necessary usually to be especially polite and gentle, if one does not wish to cause offense. Even when *doing* someone a favor, it is necessary to be courteous; for it is an offense to one's legitimate pride to accept a favor given discourteously. Courtesy and consideration for the feelings of the other person, then, should be an integral part of every business transaction. But human beings, alas, are not perfect, and very often in the course of business patience diminishes, people become preoccupied with their own concerns, and feelings are injured. Making a living in the market can be hard; it can take a heavy toll of the spirit and lead to cynicism about human nature. The only remedy for this lies in the spiritual improvement of ourselves and of the human race, which however is scarcely something that can be accomplished by legislation, as we shall see in more detail in Chapter 6.

"MARKET FAILURE"

If a suburban homeowner creates an exceptionally beautiful garden where it can be seen by his neighbors, he improves not only the market value of his own property, but also that of theirs, at no expense to them. If a manufacturing firm can dump its waste in a public stream, it can make a larger profit than if it had to pay for waste disposal. Newspapers and television stations make their profit by reporting on the activities of third parties (that is, other than the buyer and seller of the newspaper), who may suffer severe damage in consequence, but are not recompensed by the buyer or seller. In cases like these there are benefits or costs associated with a transaction which are not reflected in the price, but are paid or reaped by someone who is neither buyer nor seller. Economists term such effects on third parties "externalities." Some go further, and refer to them and other similar cases as instances of "market failure," a term which is sometimes taken to imply a moral deficiency. But is the notion of market failure justified?

The term "market failure" seems to imply that there was something which the market ought to have done, or which it attempted to do, but did not succeed in doing. But the significant fact in such cases from the viewpoint of moral values is that one person is benefited or harmed by the activity of another. The fact that the action happens to be done in a particular case for the purpose of making a profit has no bearing on the morality of the action. If I burn old tires in my back yard and the smoke drifts into your house and makes it unlivable, then my action is causing you harm. Whether I do it merely in order to rid myself of an inconvenience, or whether I do it as a business, for the purpose of making a profit, is morally irrelevant. If I do it for the purpose of making a profit, then *I as an individual* have failed morally, but it is inaccurate and misleading to say that the *market* has failed.

Recent writers opposed to market freedom have added some additional examples of alleged market failure to this. One writer argues that markets can fail when one side has more information than the other, and gives the example of a car owner whose car needs repairs.

"Since car owners are ignorant of the cause of their car's problem, they have to depend on service station owners for an opinion before deciding which repair to buy. . . . After testing the car on their diagnostic machine, the service station owners identify the problem. But since they know that the consumers do not know what is wrong (i.e., there is asymmetrical information), the service station owners have a great incentive to lie and diagnose the problem as major when it is not."[21] The author believes that the service station owner who lies in such a case is acting with "individual rationality," and concludes that unless a profession develops a high level of ethics, regulation will be needed.

To call lying a case of market failure betrays an elementary misunderstanding of the concept of a free market. Deliberate deception, or fraud, is not part of the concept of a free market. It is certainly true that the successful operation of a market economy depends on maintaining ethical behavior, and there must be legal remedies available for people who have been defrauded. Fraud, however, is not a case of the failure of the market, but of the moral failure of individuals.

Having said this by way of a general observation, however, we can add that the individual case cited is somewhat simpler to deal with. There is no "just price" for car repairs: a mechanic is entitled to offer his services at whatever price he likes. The normal, prudent car owner, faced with the necessity of having his car repaired, obtains quotes from a number of mechanics, makes some enquiries about their reputations, and chooses what appears to him to be the best combination. If he happens to be in an area where there is only one mechanic, who quotes a very high price, he must weigh the cost against the advantage of having a mechanic there at all, and the difficulty of going somewhere else: how would he fare if no mechanic were available whatever? After all, he does not have a right to have a mechanic available everywhere.

The same writer gives as an example of market failure the case of someone who desires to purchase a used car. "The cars vary in quality from very good to very bad, but only the owners know their car's quality. Since the potential buyers know nothing, they must assume that the car they look at has the average quality of cars on the market. Hence, they are willing to pay at most the price of an average car. However, at that price only sellers with cars of quality less than the average would be willing to sell. The car buyers thus know that any car they buy must be of below-average quality, so they would be paying too much for it and would not buy. Hence, at any price either buyers or sellers would be unwilling to transact business and the market would be inactive." The market fails "in the sense that no transaction takes place despite the fact that there are traders in the market for whom such trades would be beneficial."

The fact is, however, that people pull off the tremendous feat of buying a used car rather frequently, which must surely puzzle our author. How do they do it? One possibility for a prudent buyer who does not trust his own judgement is to take the car to a mechanic of his choice to have it examined! Information, in other words, is a commodity, and has a price, and must be treated like any other commodity in the market.

A further example of alleged market failure taken from our author is that of countries such as India and Bangladesh where "the number of unskilled workers is so high that efficiency would dictate paying unskilled workers a zero or near-zero wage," a possibility which he rejects as unfair, inequitable, and coldhearted, and which he views as an argument for a minimum wage. This example is typical of objections to the idea of a free market in that it leaves out of account factors which obviously have a decisive significance. For one thing, it leaves out of account the condition of the workers before the factory in question was created. If they are willing to work for wages that are very low by our standard (presumably they will not work for zero wages), that can only be because in their view that "low" wage represents an improvement over what they had before. Second, it leaves out of account the effect of a minimum wage on employment. Any employer has only a limited amount of money to give out. If he pays some employees more, he must pay others less or let them go altogether. Thus one automatic effect of any minimum wage is to increase unemployment: the factory owner will not be able to employ as many workers as he previously did. A minimum wage will help those who can keep their jobs, then, but it will harm those who might otherwise have been employed.

The market is simply the sum total of all the individual exchanges that take place. For the market to fail would have to mean that individual exchanges fail. But this is a meaningless notion. An exchange could properly be said to fail only if it did not bring to each party what that party intended to obtain in the exchange. But this, as we have seen, is ruled out by the nature of the case: if only one party were to benefit, the exchange would not take place. In the examples we have considered, everyone who buys or sells something still receives what he intended to receive in the purchase or sale. The notion of market failure is a misnomer.

The fact that there is no such thing as market failure does not mean that the market solves all problems, however. The claim made for a free market is somewhat like the claim made for democracy, not that it will eliminate all difficulties, but that any other system will have worse ones, both from an economic and a moral viewpoint. There will always be problems in the market. One of the principal reasons for this is the impossibility of knowing the future; the impossibility, for example, of knowing when the market for a particular product will be saturated. The production process for many products takes a long time, perhaps years. The decision about the number of items to make should be based on the state of the market at the time when the product will reach it. But that cannot be known with any certainty. As a result it happens from time to time that many more houses or washing machines are built than can be sold at current prices, and the market suffers a glut. This in turn causes unemployment.

The question is, what is the best remedy for such a problem: intervention by government, which finds it just as difficult to know what the future will bring as the participants in the market do but nonetheless uses force to accomplish its ends, or the free responses of the interested parties themselves?

Some economists, recognizing the difficulty inherent in the idea of market failure, restrict the notion to those instances where the market, though it produces benefits, does not lead to the "best attainable" results.[22] But this raises the question as to the criterion for what is "best": best from what aspect, and from whose standpoint? If I offer you a low price for your house, and you sell it to another person who has offered you a higher price, this may not be the best attainable result from *my* viewpoint, but it would not entitle me to charge that the market has failed. One possibility is to describe the "best attainable results" in terms of efficiency: the most efficient allocation of resources, that is, the one with the lowest costs. However, while it is always possible for a person in business to spend more on resources than is necessary, this is a personal mistake of judgement, not a failure of the market.

Some of the most notorious cases of putative market failure appear to have been caused, not primarily by the market or its participants, but by government. The outstanding instance of this is the Great Depression. At the time it occurred it was almost universally regarded as an exceptionally pernicious example of the ordinary trade cycle, a crisis of capitalism. Now, as a result of historical research, there are grounds for believing that it was caused, or at least greatly prolonged, primarily by actions of the federal government. One of these was the action of the Federal Reserve in increasing interest rates and further restricting the money supply, precisely at the time when just the opposite action was needed. This deprived businesses of necessary capital, which led to unemployment. The other action was the passage by Congress of the Smoot-Hawley tariff bill, which imposed draconian tariffs on imports and led to similar reprisals by other countries, so that international trade came almost to a halt. But for these actions, there is reason to believe that the effects of the trade cycle would have been much less severe and would have lasted only a relatively short time, perhaps a matter of some months, instead of the ten or more years that they did.[23]

THE IRRATIONALITY OF THE MARKET

A related objection to the market is that market outcomes are often "irrational." For example, chance often plays a great role in the success or failure of business enterprises, and so in the distribution of wealth that results from them. An unexpected turn of events can enable a corporation or an individual to make "windfall" profits. The market does not simply reward people according to the amount of skill or hard work they put into it, and highly educated people such as university professors are sometimes paid less than plumbers and stonemasons. Furthermore, the abilities of individuals, and even their willingness to make an effort, are often also largely the product of chance. One person has the good fortune to be raised in a wealthy family and so receives a good education, while another comes from poor parents who perhaps have little esteem for learning and even little ability to encourage in their children the development of a good character. Even the basic natural distribution of talents is a matter of chance: nature is arbitrary. This leads some moralists, such as John Rawls, to hold that the factual distribution of talents has no moral standing, and can establish no moral claim.[24]

Market activity is generally characterized by the rationality of means to an end. Any means is rational to the extent that it secures or helps to secure the end, provided that it remains within the bounds of justice. The goal of market activity is profit, and, all things else being equal, whatever means leads to a larger profit will usually be employed. It is this feature of capitalism which has led commentators such as Werner Sombart and Max Weber to analyze it precisely as an outstanding example of a rational enterprise, and to point out the kinship between the rationality of the market or of capitalism and the rationality of science.[25] One example of this pervasive rationality of the market, and so of the middle class, which is often overlooked by moralists is its tendency to eliminate inherited class distinctions, and irrational prejudice and discrimination, since they are antipathetic to success in the market.

Despite this, it is quite true that market outcomes are often determined by chance (though the ongoing success of a business enterprise over several years cannot usually be explained simply by that means). But this does not alter the fact that in every exchange both buyer and seller benefit. The forcible prevention of exchanges (which is all that economic regulations as such can ultimately achieve) will not increase benefits overall to either one.

That a product of chance *can* be the foundation of a moral claim, however, is shown by the fact that every individual human existence itself is a product of chance, yet individual human existence is the foundation of all moral claims. In particular it is the foundation of the principle that people who do not deserve to be punished ought not to be punished. Even if the market were the very paradigm of absurdity, that would not for a moment justify punishing those who take part in it. The mere fact that a person performs an action that leads to an irrational outcome does not in the least make him deserve punishment, and so does not justify the imposition of government regulations.

INSTABILITY

Another common objection to an unfettered market is that it can be very unstable. A recurring example of this is the business cycle, the alternate succession of peaks and troughs in business activity across the entire national economy. The economy does not simply expand at a steady rate; instead it tends to leap ahead in bursts, and then go into decline, before leaping ahead again, and repeating the cycle. Even apart from these more or less regular ups and downs, unexpected events can induce wild swings in prices, which may benefit some speculators, but deprive conscientious businesspeople and workers of their livelihood and throw otherwise well-run firms out of business. The oil shortages with their attendant price increases of the 1970s, the stock market crash of 1987, the collapse of the real estate market in 1989, and the general recession of 1990 and 1991, to mention only some recent events, have meant economic ruin to many people.

Economists have proposed two chief explanations for the business cycle. One is that it is due to excessive investment, the other that it is the result of governmental policies. The theory that the business cycle is due to excessive investment can perhaps best be understood by an illustration. During the last twenty or thirty years, there have been several waves of overbuilding in Florida. Typically at some point a number of builders discover that the market conditions there are ripe for the building of condominiums, and they buy land, commission architects and engineers to develop plans, go through the lengthy and expensive process of obtaining various permits from the local authorities, and begin to build, attracting additional workers from less prosperous areas. At first sales go very well, profits are good, and other builders are attracted to do likewise. At some point, however, which it is extremely difficult if not impossible to predict in advance, since it hinges on a great number of factors, the demand for the condominiums begins to slow down, and eventually it dries up altogether. In the meantime many projects which were already underway are continued to completion, despite the slowing of the market, because once they have been started it is extremely difficult to halt them. Numerous buildings are now left empty, workers must be laid off, and unemployment becomes a serious problem; some builders go bankrupt. It may take perhaps eighteen months for the surplus units to be sold, the unemployed to find jobs, and the market to return to normal. Then, after a period of consolidation, lasting perhaps a decade, the same cycle may begin to repeat itself. In the business cycle properly so-called, such a pattern repeats itself over the entire national economy. The cause of this cycle of boom and bust is described as excessive investment, but the excessive investment is caused essentially by lack of information: the impossibility of knowing ahead of time when demand will be satisfied.

A remarkable thing about the business cycle is that it affects not merely some particular segments of the economy of a nation, but the whole national economy. The causes of it, then, must be some factor or factors which apply to the entire nation, though not necessarily to other nations. This has led to the view that it results from some policy of the national government, such as its control of the money supply.

Whether government is the chief cause of the more or less regular ups and downs of the business cycle, however, there are good reasons for believing that it is the chief cause of instability in the market overall. The principal reason has to do, as before, with the difficulty of making predictions. The market regularly takes account far in advance of the possibility of both good and bad news so far as it is in any way predictable, and when bad news breaks it often has little effect, because it has been anticipated, and the necessary adjustments have been made gradually. What is most unpredictable, and what typically throws markets into the worst confusion, is the intervention of government. A single sentence, added to a piece of legislation as an afterthought at 2 A.M., can turn a market upside down, bringing devastating losses to large numbers of people. Government is essentially arbitrary in regard to the market, because it enjoys a monopoly of coercion and is not directly affected by market outcomes.

There can be no doubt that the instability of the market presents a very serious problem. It does not follow by any means, however, that government regulation is a good way of attempting to solve it. Economists have long known—it is one of the things that can genuinely be said to constitute knowledge in the sphere of economics—that the quickest and least painful way of clearing the market and restoring it to normalcy is the simple operation of the market itself. When a shortage of gasoline leads to a higher price for it, the higher price provides an incentive to producers to produce more, thereby overcoming the shortage. When a glut leads to lower prices, the lower prices remove the incentive for production, and the lower production eliminates the glut. If governmental regulation is used to prevent a shortage from producing higher prices, as it was, for example, in the gasoline crisis of 1979, the result is merely a prolongation of the shortage. If regulation is used to prevent a glut from producing lower prices, the effect is just to prolong the glut.

The possibility should not be overlooked that free-market mechanisms can be devised to alleviate instability. Producers of products subject to market swings can cooperate, while the market is up, in establishing forms of insurance which will provide protection when the market goes down.

Quite apart from the economic aspects of stability, however, there is a moral one, the question of justice. A law imposes a penalty. If it is to be a just law, it must only penalize what deserves to be penalized. But a seller who raises his prices because of a shortage does not deserve to be penalized. He has caused no harm. As we have seen, offers to buy and offers to sell are gratuitous. Even at the higher price, he is still doing his customers a favor in selling to them, just as they do him a favor in buying from him even when he is necessitated to sell at low prices. Far from causing harm, the seller who raises his prices in a shortage is doing just what needs to be done to reduce the shortage, he is providing an incentive for producers to produce more. From the viewpoint of justice, market stability can not be a sufficient reason for imposing on a seller the penalties of the law.

ENVIRONMENTAL PROTECTION

It is widely believed that environmental protection is incompatible with market freedom, that in an unfettered market automobiles would be able to pollute the atmosphere without any control, and factories would be able to pour their garbage into the air, water, and soil without hindrance. Environmental effects usually figure prominently among alleged examples of market failure.

This is a misunderstanding of the concept of a free market. It is not part of the concept of a free market that people should be able to rob or cheat one another; similarly it is not part of the concept of a free market that people should be able to cause harm to one another's environment. The idea of a free market is that there should not be any special laws or regulations governing buying or selling, because in the absence of force and fraud, buyer and seller always benefit one another and do not harm one another. But this does not mean that the normal laws which forbid people from genuinely causing harm to one another should be abolished. Laws for the protection of the environment come under this heading.

To pollute the environment seriously in places where human beings have a right to live is to cause harm to them, and, as we shall see in more detail in Chapter 6, it is a principle of justice that those who cause harm deserve to be punished. This is true no matter what the reason for the pollution. Whether it is caused by a private party pursuing his own interests, as in the case of someone burning noxious substances in his own backyard in order to get rid of them, or whether it is caused by someone producing goods for the market, makes no difference. That some businesses pollute the environment, then, is not an objection to the free market system, any more than theft, fraud, or coercion constitute objections to it. The question of the market and the question of the environment are two distinct questions.

To see how a legal system providing for a free market would handle the problem of the environment, let us consider some particular kinds of cases. Where one individual directly pollutes the environment belonging to another individual, as in the case of the person who burns leaves or garbage in his back yard, causing smoke and soot to pollute the air of his next-door neighbor, it is clear enough that the one is being harmed by the other, and if the harm is sufficiently great or prolonged, the common law provides him with a legal remedy, the right to sue. Cases like this are easy to handle, from the point of view of public policy, because what is at stake is the property of an individual. It is a point of fundamental significance that where private property is at issue pollution is much less likely to occur, because there is an individual person who has an economic incentive to see to it that the property is preserved.

A more difficult case, and one more typical of the sort that raise serious environmental problems, is the one where, for example, a factory pours noxious effluent into a river which is not the property of any particular individual. A nuclear power plant, for instance, pours heated water into a public stream, killing large numbers of fish and perhaps quantities of plant life. Here it is not immediately clear that any individual person is being harmed directly; indeed the pollution may go unnoticed for a long period. Nonetheless, the stream is public property, and the public is harmed by its degradation.

The principal practical reason why this kind of problem arises appears to be the fact that the stream is not private property. If the stream were entirely the property of an individual or corporation, which could make a profit from it, the owner, as we just observed, would have an economic motive to see to it that the stream was not polluted, and if it were to be polluted, he would have a powerful legal remedy. We know from wide experience that this situation minimizes the incentive to pollute. Thus one important long-term solution for problems of this sort is to maximize privatization: to bring more and more property out of the public domain and into private hands.

But privatization is unlikely ever to provide the complete answer, since it is probable that there will always be significant forms of public property, the atmosphere being perhaps the most obvious one. The relationship between pollution of public property and the market needs to be clarified, then. The preservation of public property is a public good, which it is the duty of government to protect, up to a certain point.

That point is a function of the opportunity costs involved. For the protection of the environment a price must be paid. Money spent on cleaning up the environment, or on equipment to prevent pollution, is money that could have been spent for other purposes. The more money is spent on the environment, the less economic growth there will be.

This means that in every society there must be a willingness to accept a certain level of pollution. It is impossible to have an environment that is totally unpolluted, if there is to be economic growth. Environmentalists and public officials influenced by them appear sometimes not to understand this fact too clearly and speak as if no expense whatever ought to be spared for the sake of a completely clean environment.

Although initially the cost of cleaning the environment up should be borne by those who have polluted it, and the cost of preventing pollution should be paid by those who would otherwise profit from the pollution; in the end, however, the cost will be borne by the entire community. If General Motors pays $100 million for equipment to prevent pollution in its factories, this must be added on to the price of its cars and trucks, which eventually will be paid by consumers, and will result in a loss of jobs and a lower standard of living throughout the society. Since the community will have to pay the price, it seems only right that the community should determine the price to be paid, that is, to determine what level of pollution is acceptable.

Economists have made a number of suggestions about the best way to accomplish environmental protection. One is that it is better for government to tax pollution, for example at the level of harm a marginal unit of pollution causes to the public, than to legislate equipment or otherwise engage in detailed local regulation as the Environmental Protection Agency now largely does. The advantage of the tax is that it would provide an economic incentive for the desirable behavior, which appears likely to be a far more effective measure.

An alternative method recommended by economists, and recently implemented by the federal government, is tradable pollution licenses. In this system the regulatory authorities determine the total amount of emissions to be permitted in a district, and then issue permits for these emissions. The permits can be bought and sold like industrial property. Firms that do not pollute as much as their license permits can sell their surplus rights to others. The advantage of this is that it keeps the total cost of pollution control down, and provides firms with a market incentive to pollute as little as possible.[26]

Since legislation to protect the environment will always involve a penalty, it is morally important that the law penalize the correct party. The party to penalize is the party who is actually causing the harm. If, to use the earlier example, I burn some tires in my back yard, causing my neighbor's property to be covered with smoke and soot, the person who sold me the tires is innocent: *I* am the one causing the harm. Similarly in the case of automobile exhaust, it is not the producer of the car, but the driver, who causes the pollution, and it is he who should be subject to regulation, not the manufacturer. A tax on pollution would observe this distinction. (In the case of tradable pollution permits, a firm causes harm by exceeding its quota.)

Regulating the manufacturer rather than the driver has the practical drawback that it stifles innovation. If the law, rather than requiring manufacturers to incorporate one particular kind of device in their automobiles, such as a catalytic converter, simply forbids people from driving cars which pollute the atmosphere beyond a certain measurable extent, it will leave room for manufacturers to develop and offer to the public as many devices as they can invent which will effectively decrease the pollution to the level which is legally acceptable. The device which has proven in practice to be most effective in decreasing air pollution from automobiles is apparently not the catalytic converter, mandated by the U.S. government, but fuel injection, developed by the market.

Conservation

The problem of the conservation of natural resources goes beyond the problem of pollution. It would seem that mankind as a whole may possibly suffer a loss through the extermination of any living species, for example, and the preservation of wildlife requires both abstention from killing or harming them directly and the preservation of a great variety of natural habitats.

An important part of the practical answer to the problem of the conservation of natural resources also lies in the privatization of ownership. The problem here again arises largely because the natural resource in question is not owned privately, but publicly. Where a resource is owned privately, to repeat, there are particular persons who possess a personal economic incentive to preserve it. Where it is owned publicly, this is not the case. An illustration is provided by the situation of the elephant in Africa. In Kenya, where the sale of ivory has been banned for decades, elephants are nonetheless hunted illegally for their ivory. In consequence, the elephant population has dropped from 65,000 to 19,000 over the past decade, and it is estimated that it may become extinct in the next five years. It seems not to be widely known, however, that in Zimbabwe, by contrast, ivory sales are not only allowed but encouraged and are worth about $5 million a year to some two dozen tribal villages which in effect own the elephants. This has led the villagers to protect elephants from poachers, to cull elephant herds to prevent overpopulation, and in general to guard their investment in future ivory production. As a result, the elephant population has grown from 30,000 to 43,000 over the past decade.[27] The challenge for advocates of the free market is to develop analogous forms of privatization for valuable natural resources which are threatened.

Wetlands constitute a special difficulty. Wetlands are areas which are midway between dry land and ocean or stream and provide a habitat for numerous forms of wildlife. According to current law in most states, all wetlands wherever found must be preserved. This leads to some far-reaching consequences. The remains of a half-dried up pond in the middle of a building lot may effectively prevent the owner from erecting any building on his land. In one case in Pennsylvania an owner who had *created* a pond on his land was reportedly forbidden to fill it in because it was deemed wetlands. The net effect of the current law is to convert wetlands from private into public property without compensation—a procedure outlawed by the Constitution—and to inflict sometimes enormous financial losses on individuals who have done nothing to deserve such treatment.

THE DEMOCRACY OF THE MARKET

It is sometimes maintained that the market is undemocratic. We can elect our public officials, it is said, but we cannot elect our corporate leaders. It is also sometimes asserted that the democratic political process is superior to the market in satisfying human needs. In both of these respects, however, the truth is exactly the reverse. In point of fact the market is one of the most democratic devices ever invented by man.

On the one hand, it has been pointed out by Kenneth J. Arrow and others that electoral processes are inevitably imperfect. They do not faithfully express the wishes of the voting population. The "paradox of voting pointed out by Arrow is that when a poll has shown that a community prefers A to B, and B to C, it does not necessarily follow that if they have to choose only between A and C, they will choose A.[28] Arrow concludes further that there is no method of voting which will remove this paradox.[29] Again, the electoral system inescapably influences the result of a vote. For example, it makes a considerable difference whether majority rule or proportional representation is used, and if majority rule, what size of a majority, whether 51 percent or a two-thirds majority, is needed for election. There are no neutral election systems.

On the other hand, the market is extremely democratic. Every time we buy a product, we cast a vote. Every time we change our allegiance from one product to another, we cast a vote against the one and in favor of the other. Unless the makers of the product get enough votes, they go out of business. The market is far more nuanced than any political election, far more responsive to the most intimate details of people's needs. When I vote in an election I have a choice only between a very limited number of candidates, often only two. In that single choice I have to express all my hundreds or thousands of needs and desires. In the market, however, I can choose between this brand of coffee and that, this size tube of toothpaste and that, this expensive a house and that. The market makes it possible for every single item that I need to be available for separate choice, subject only to the limitations of human ingenuity and effort.

When it is claimed that the political process is superior to the market in satisfying human needs, what is meant of course is that the market only satisfies the needs of those who can pay, while the political process can be arranged to satisfy needs of those who cannot pay. But of course somebody has to pay for whatever is consumed, and the political process accomplishes nothing of a productive nature which would make it possible for anyone to pay. Government as such produces no wealth.[30] The market, on the other hand, at the same time that it satisfies people's needs, also ensures that the wherewithal required to satisfy those needs is brought into being. The market system does not merely rearrange already existing goods, but constantly creates new goods and services. The market is productive. It satisfies people's needs by producing what they need. This, government is powerless to do, at least in any effective way, as the demise of the socialist regimes of Eastern Europe has shown. We will return to the subject of productivity in the next chapter.

INEQUALITY

Opponents of free markets typically treat it as an axiom that a laissez-faire economy will result in great inequalities: if people are free to buy and sell whatever and whenever they like, some will do very much better than others, and the gap between rich and poor will become ever wider. It is assumed that a free market initially and principally benefits the wealthy, and only after some time does a small proportion of the benefits "trickle down" to the poor. By the same token, if a society experiences a gulf between rich and poor, there is a tendency to assume that economic freedom must be the cause of that. One reason for this view seems to be that when new products come out, they are frequently expensive and can be bought only by the wealthy. Similarly when new resources are discovered, it is often the wealthy who first take advantage of them, thereby gaining large profits.

There are good reasons, however, both theoretical and historical, for believing that a free market over time benefits the poor proportionately far more than the rich, and leads to a society which is economically ever more equal. The two factors which arguably have the greatest influence on the condition of the poor are prices and employment. The poor will usually be best off where prices are lowest and there are the most jobs. Now for any given quantity of resources, a free market, even though it may temporarily allow high prices in some sectors, minimizes prices in the economy taken as a whole, because it maximizes overall competition (market monopolies are ever only temporary, as we have seen, while in a free market the heaviest monopolist, government, is inactive). By the same token a free market maximizes employment because it maximizes economic activity.

If we compare the situation of the very rich and the very poor today with what it was in earlier epochs, it is clear that with a few exceptions for areas such as transport, communications, and medicine, the condition of the very rich today is relatively little improved over what it was in the time of Louis XIV or even the Caesars, for the products of the mass market have little to offer them. A washing machine is of little benefit to someone who can keep servants to do his laundry. An eighteenth-century aristocrat did not need radio or television for entertainment but could employ the best artists and musicians of the day as retainers in his own household.[31]

By contrast, the condition of the working class and the poor has been revolutionized in almost every respect, as even the slightest comparison in the standard of living will show. For they are the ones who benefit from the cheap and plentiful products of the mass market. One good measure of the condition of life is life expectancy. Average life expectancy in France as late as 1750 was about twenty-nine years.[32] Needless to say, for the poor it was considerably less. Not only is the condition of the poor much better than it was, it is also better even than that of the rich of earlier times in some respects, especially in regard to health care, communications and transport. George Washington would have been happy to have the dental services or the antibiotics available to a modern laborer.

What the *actual* effect of a free market is on the gap between rich and poor is a *factual* question, to be answered by studying the historical data. When we study the data, however, we find that, like so much else that is commonly thought about the market, the assumption that a free market fosters inequality is essentially a myth. The best-known study on this subject is probably that by the economist Simon Kuznets, who concluded from examining the data available for the United States, England, and Germany, that "the relative distribution of income, as measured by annual income incidence in rather broad classes, has been moving toward equality—with these trends particularly noticeable since the 1920s but beginning perhaps in the period before the first world war."[33]

While Kuznets's analysis has been severely attacked by opponents of the free market, there is widespread agreement among less-biased scholars that essentially it holds up: at the least, that income inequality in these three countries is basically stable, certainly that there has not been any noticeable increase in it up to the time when he wrote.[34]

It should be noted that according to Kuznets's account the crucial factor is not precisely capitalism or the free market, but economic growth, in whatever system that may take place. To the extent that economic growth has taken place in socialist countries the same phenomenon would be expected there; and there appears to be some evidence that this is indeed the case, although it is extremely difficult to make comparisons of this nature from one country to another because the data tend to be collected differently.[35] Notoriously, however, economic growth has not taken place in socialist countries to anything like the extent that it has in market-oriented countries.

By the same token, however, the market in the United States, England and Germany, as in other Western nations, has been far from simply free. Since the mid-1960s, especially, a great expansion of welfare programs and regulatory activity took place in the United States, and correspondingly there is evidence that during this time the gap between rich and poor in the United States has ceased to become narrower.

Even if it were the case that free markets resulted in ever greater inequality, however, that would be no argument against them, from the viewpoint of genuine ethical concern. The reason for this is that inequality is not necessarily harmful. We pointed out in Chapter 2 that exchanges take place only because both parties expect to benefit, and that an unequal benefit is still a benefit. Here we can point out in addition that far from being harmful, inequality is one of the usual signs that improvement is taking place. When penicillin was first discovered, it could at first be made available only to relatively few people, and so inequality was increased. Yet that inequality was the harbinger of immense benefits to the poor everywhere around the globe as infectious diseases were conquered.

If Smith's condition is improving, the mere fact that Jones's condition is improving much more rapidly causes Smith no harm. While it is true that new products are often expensive, and can be afforded only by the wealthy, this is not the whole story. The purchase of expensive new products by the wealthy makes it possible to produce them in increasing numbers, obtaining economies of scale which lower the cost of production, and eventually the price, to the level where they are affordable by the poor. The first automobiles were expensive, but the lowest-priced ones constitute an ever smaller fraction of the income of the poor, and it is now possible for the large majority of the U.S. population to buy one.

Who has benefited more from the invention of the automobile, the rich or the poor? There can be no doubt about the answer to this, and the answer is similar for telephones, gas stoves, electric irons, washing machines, refrigerators, computers, airplanes, and almost every other appliance or machine.

From the viewpoint of ethics the decisive fact is that a person who merely increases inequality does nothing by that fact to deserve punishment. The mere fact that someone else has more than I does not mean that he is causing me harm.

THE INDUSTRIAL REVOLUTION

It is often assumed, even by supporters of the idea of a free market, that although a free market may be the best solution now, there was a time during the Industrial Revolution when working conditions were so terrible that special government regulation was needed. One thinks of child labor, for example, or the very long working day, and it is assumed that the improvements we have experienced over the last hundred years would not have taken place without these regulations. Let us examine these two instances, then, of child labor and poor working conditions, from the perspective of the values and the legal system which would be associated with a free market.

There can be no doubt that by our standards today many children were subjected to extremely harsh conditions, especially in cloth manufacture, working from an early age twelve or even fourteen hours a day in low, dark rooms, often filled with a fine fluff which caused bronchial and lung troubles. However, these facts must be judged in the light of the conditions and standards which prevailed otherwise in the society. In the sixteenth century the majority of children in Europe lived in rural villages, and it was customary to employ them from a very early age, sometimes as young as three, in agricultural tasks. With the growth of the putting-out system, in which spinners and weavers produced cloth in their homes, young children were routinely employed to help, as well as in such trades as chimney-sweeping. When large factories developed, the initial move to employ children in them came from public officials, the overseers of the parish workhouses. In the south of England these workhouses contained large numbers of orphaned and vagrant children, whom the overseers did not readily know what to do with, and it apparently seemed a desirable solution to the problem to send them to the mills in the north of England, ostensibly as apprentices, to learn a trade. Once there, however, there was no one to look after their interests. Subsequently, the practice of sending their children to work in the factories was adopted by poor parents as a way of adding to the family income. During the nineteenth century, when government inspectors were appointed to see to it that abuses were eliminated, many parents went to great lengths and resorted to ingenious schemes to keep their children employed in the factories despite the law to the contrary.

From the point of view of the ethics of a free market, the first question is, who has responsibility for children? The normal answer to this must be, their parents. It is the responsibility of parents to care for their children and ensure that they receive a decent upbringing. If parents abuse their children, the children have a right to be protected by the state. It is the parents, then, rather than factory-owners, who should be the ones primarily regulated by laws designed to protect the welfare of children. Presumably the normal legal provision against child abuse should be sufficient for that purpose.

It should be borne in mind that children very often want to work in order to have their own income; and work may be one of the main ways in which children and youth, especially those in today's inner city, learn to relate constructively to the larger society.[36] Furthermore, work which is too heavy for one child may be stimulating to another. It seems a recommendation of prudence, then, to handle each case individually, rather than to make every family conform to some universal abstract law which ignores their particular situation and needs.

The working conditions of adults also need to be investigated in the light of historical conditions. It is true that, by comparison with what we now enjoy, conditions in the early factories were often wretched. But here again it is necessary to look at the whole picture, and not merely at part of it. Why did the workers apply for such jobs if they were so terrible? The answer is that for the most part they were no worse, and in some respects were much better, than the alternatives available to them. Any survey of working conditions during the Industrial Revolution must take account of the great increase in population during that period. Already during the period that preceded it considerable improvements had taken place in agriculture, and so in the food supply; and also in medicine, for example with the introduction of inoculation against smallpox. These improvements resulted in a noticeable improvement in the general level of health, which led to a decline in the death rate and an increase in life expectancy. Whereas in 1740 the population of England was six million, by 1851 it had reached eighteen million, and by 1900 it was approximately forty million, an increase of over 500 percent! This growing population could not be supported on the farms, nor could they be supported by the cottage industries prevalent before the Industrial Revolution. If it had not been for the newly created factories, it must be asked whether a large part of the new population must not have starved; even with the employment provided by the new factories, in the famines of 1795–96 and 1800–01 there were deaths from starvation.

The first workers in the new factories were mainly women and children, for the majority of working men initially refused to work there, largely as a matter of pride: until the term "factory" became established, the term "workhouse" was often used, which was already applied to the parish house for the poor, and the stigma attached to that idea hung over the factories. Even by 1816, it is estimated that men made up less than 20 percent of the employees in textile mills.[37] In judging the working conditions, we must compare them with what prevailed otherwise in the society. The factory workers were not skilled, and if the comparison is to be accurate, it must be with the conditions of the unskilled or semiskilled outside the factories. Employment for such people was typically only seasonal, casual, and part-time. The principal cottage industry consisted of the trades associated with the making of woolen cloth: carding, spinning, weaving, fulling, etc. The typical workman, or rather working family, was employed at a piece-rate by a "putter-out," who provided them with the materials which they needed and with the necessary equipment. Conditions in the cottage industries have been compared to what we associate today with a sweatshop.[38] The workers were "overworked, undernourished and at times badly treated."[39] Few earned a living full-time by their manufacturing activity in the home, most supplemented that with work on farms or roads or fishing. Within this framework conditions varied greatly from one region of England to another, and from one industry to another, some being considerably worse than others.

By comparison with this the factories offered steady occupation and regular income. The principal complaint made by the workers in the factories concerned not working conditions or wages, but their fellow-workers. William Hutton, who was an apprentice in Lombe's mill at Derby from 1730 to 1737, termed his fellow-workers "the most vulgar and rude of the human race."[40] When the brothers John and George Buchanan established the Deanston Mills in 1785, they found that "the more respectable part of the surrounding inhabitants were at first averse to seek employment in the works, as they considered it disreputable to be employed in what they called 'a public work.'"[41] A similar prejudice was encountered by David Dale at New Lanark, by Samuel Oldknow at Mellor, and by most of the early factory-owners about whom we possess information.[42] It appears that the workers in the early factories were mainly paupers or tramps.[43] Sir George Nicholls remarks that the factories employed "the worst description of the people."[44] There was a great deal of absenteeism: Lewis Paul wrote in 1742, "I have not half my people come to work today, and I have no great fascination in the prospect I have to put myself in the power of such people." This was a continuation of work habits which predated the factory system.

> In most parts of the country there were annual fairs or wakes during which little or no work was done. The journeymen of London downed tools on each of the eight hanging days at Tyburn, to say nothing of the frequent occasions when they joined in a riot or demonstration. A contest in the ring or a race-meeting often led to a cessation of labour. In 1754 the colliers of Oldham and the weavers of Manchester competed in a cock-fight that lasted three days. Coal miners left the pit to take part in a Parliamentary election, to celebrate a national victory, or, as in 1779, to seek consolation for a national defeat.[45]

Even during periods of employment most unskilled or semiskilled workers in general worked only three or four days a week. Coal miners typically worked only when they felt like it.[46] It was not from the unskilled factory workers, but from social workers, intellectuals, and already highly paid craftsmen that the demand for labor legislation developed.

The Industrial Revolution was a period of transition from a heavily regulated economy to a more lightly regulated one. Any such transition can be expected to produce economic problems, even very serious problems, as the countries of Eastern Europe are in the process of discovering; but these problems are by their nature temporary, and the market itself is the quickest and most efficient remedy for them. There is every reason to believe that the improvements in working conditions which have taken place would have taken place in any event, and even more so, simply as the natural result of the competition between employers for the limited pool of workers.

* * *

If the arguments of this chapter and the previous one are correct, then apart from the crucially important exception of the use of force and fraud, it is a mistake, and indeed a gross mistake, to think that persons who engage in market transactions may cause harm to their exchange partners or competitors.

If the thesis of these chapters is valid, the free, unregulated market is one human creation about which we can be confident that it helps and benefits people because it represents people's own judgement as to what benefits them concretely in their actual circumstances, and not the often presumptuous judgement of onlookers, ignorant of the true conditions of their lives. The evidence of this benefit is provided by history and is visible on all sides, in the myriad of goods, services, and jobs which the market creates for us when allowed to function with stringent protection from force and fraud, but without further government "protection." A government which truly wishes to benefit its people will eliminate all special aid to buyers or sellers, and all special restrictions on them, allowing them what Adam Smith called their natural liberty, a liberty which is no doubt always accompanied by risk, but which also alone can create a humane society.

4

Economic Value

Every purchase and sale hinges on the value or worth of the goods or services in question. Before we buy a loaf of bread for $1 or a house for $100,000, we want to be sure that it is worth the price, that it has the necessary value. But what sort of value is this, what exactly does it consist in? Value is not all of one kind. There are numerous different kinds of value. For example, there is aesthetic value, which is the special value we attribute to things of beauty, such as the music of Mozart or the poetry of Shelley. There is utility or use value, which is the kind of value we attach to things that we can use as means to some end we want to achieve: a screwdriver might have little use value to someone engaged in writing poetry, but quite a lot to someone building a house. There is emotional or sentimental value, which is the value we attach to particular objects associated with loved ones, or with special memories. The house that I grew up in will usually mean a lot more to me than to others for whom it is just another house; a house that I have built with my own hands will mean more to me emotionally than one I buy ready-made. There is moral value, which is the special value we see in virtue, like courage, or honesty, or generosity. There are values of personal preference, or personal taste: some people like chocolate-chip ice cream, others don't. And then there is economic value.

Economic value is simply *exchange* value. The exchange value of any item is what someone is prepared to give in exchange for it. The exchange value of a house, for example, is the highest price that some actual person is willing and ready to pay for it. That is, the economic value of the house is just whatever price the buyer and seller agree on. If someone is prepared to give me $100,000 for my house, and no one will pay more, then the value of my house is $100,000.

Suppose I have spent five years building my dream house with my own hands, lavishing my time and labor on it. Then I put it up for sale, but no one, absolutely no one, wants to buy it at any price (perhaps radioactive waste is discovered underneath it). What is its value? There is no single answer to this question: the answer will depend on the kind of value under discussion. Its emotional value to me personally will still be very high: it has cost me dearly. Its aesthetic value may also be very high: perhaps it has won an architectural award. But neither of these constitutes its economic value. If nobody wants to buy it at any price, its *economic* value is zero.

Some people find this hard to accept. After all, the house is there. Surely it must have some value. And no doubt it has other kinds of value. But its economic value is entirely dependent on its exchangeability. There is no great mystery why this should be so: it is simply what is meant by economic value.

Now a question that we wish to ask is this: Does economic value have any objective existence, or is it a purely subjective reality?

MARX

Marx maintained that exchange value is not a real value, but merely an appearance, an expression or "phenomenal form" of value. The real value of any product, according to his theory (which derives, ironically, from Adam Smith), consists in the fact that it is the result of human labor. This real or labor value is proportional to the number of hours of labor needed to produce the product. Since the two objects to be exchanged have different uses, argues Marx, the only thing they can have in common is that they represent equal amounts of labor. If two items get exchanged for one another, he maintains (say a boat for a car), then they must have the same value because they have the same price, say five thousand dollars. That is, each of them is equal to a third thing, which is neither a car nor a boat. This third thing, which is measured by their price, cannot be their use value, because the use values of a car and a boat are entirely different. But the only feature the car and the boat have in common is that they are the products of labor. The fact that the product is useful to the buyer is only a precondition of the exchange and does not make any contribution to the value of the product.

"As use-values, commodities are, above all, of different qualities, but as exchange values they are merely different quantities, and consequently do not contain an atom of use-value. If we leave out of consideration the use-value of commodities, they have only one common property left, that of being products of labor."[1]

Not the labor of the individual men who made this car and this boat, however, because "we put out of sight both the useful character of the various kinds of labor embodied in them, and the concrete forms of that labor; there is nothing left but what is common to them all; all are reduced to one and the same sort of labor, human labor in the abstract."

Marx concedes that so far as use-value is concerned, it is true that each side gains. But he refuses to allow that this has any significance, since he believes that use-value value has nothing to do with exchange-value. The value of a product which is decisive for the analysis of the market in his theory is its labor value; it is this which is reflected in its exchange value, he maintains, and in regard to the exchange value it is not true that each side gains, since the exchange value by definition is the same for each side.

For Marx, then, the economic value of a product is an objective feature of the product, as objective as the labor which went into creating it. Economic value has nothing to do with the usefulness of the item to the buyer, nothing to do with his desire for it, or with the desire of the seller to sell, which are all accidental, relative, and subjective. It is inherent in the item.

THE JUST PRICE

The widespread notion of a just price or a fair price is somewhat similar to these ideas. This is the view that a seller is not morally entitled to charge whatever price he likes, and a buyer is likewise not entitled to offer whatever price he likes, but that there is a price, or at least a narrow range of prices, which is right and just, and a price demanded over this will be exploitatively high, or exorbitant, while an offer below it will be exploitatively low. Goods have a certain value independently of any particular sale, and the price must reflect that value. If a shortage arises, especially in some item which is much needed, and sellers raise their prices as a result, this typically calls forth from the public not merely disappointment, but anger and moral condemnation, as taking unfair advantage of buyers, and there may be an outcry for legislation to prevent it. When a hurricane devastated Charleston, South Carolina, in 1989, and the prices of building materials were raised drastically, the city fathers hurried to pass laws prohibiting the increases in order to prevent dealers from making a quick profit by exploiting the public, they said.

The notion of a just price was developed at some length by theologians during the Middle Ages. For Thomas Aquinas it followed from the Aristotelian understanding of justice as equality: a just exchange will be one in which the benefits to buyer and seller are equal, and this will happen only when the price paid equals the value of the item. "If the price exceeds the quantity of the value of the thing, or on the contrary the thing exceeds the price, the equality of justice is destroyed."[2] Evidently the "quantity of value" of a thing is a reality as independent of the agreement between buyer and seller for Aquinas as it is for Marx.

How the just price can be discovered has been the subject of dispute. Some writers, such as the medieval theologian Duns Scotus, argued that it should cover the costs of production together with a modest profit, a view which is still utilized with regulated industries such as gas and electricity.[3] Later scholastic writers pointed out, however, that that would mean that it would be unjust for anyone ever to suffer a loss, and instead argued that the just price should be determined by the prevailing market price, the "common estimate" of value. They recognized that this common estimate could vary at different places and times, and so concluded that there was no single just price.[4]

The Just Wage

One form of the just price is the just wage. Several popes have taught a doctrine of "the living wage," that "wages ought not to be insufficient to support a frugal and well-behaved wage earner," as Pope Leo XIII puts it. He continues, "If through necessity or fear of a worse evil the workman accepts harder conditions because an employer or contractor will afford him no better, he is made the victim of force and injustice."[5] According to Pope Pius XI employers have an obligation to pay a wage sufficient to support not only the worker himself but also his family, and social justice demands that such a wage should be guaranteed by law. Pius allows that the financial condition of the business and the owner needs to be taken into account in determining wages. It is unjust, he concedes, to demand wages so high that an employer cannot pay them without ruin. But if the business makes a smaller profit because of bad management, want of enterprise, or out-of-date methods, that is not a just reason for reducing wages. As an additional factor he adds that wages should be regulated with a view to the economic welfare of the people as a whole.[6]

Pope John Paul II has condemned what he calls "economism," by which he apparently means the practice of looking at human labor through the eyes of the economist. Economism is materialistic, he asserts, and does not give man the dignity which is his due as a human person. It denigrates man by treating human labor as a commodity, as a form of merchandise which can be bought and sold, and thereby it reduces human beings to the status of mere instruments of production, mere tools in the hands of the capitalist, when they should rather be considered as the creators of work.[7] Views such as these are not restricted to Catholics, but are common in our society.

Another form of the doctrine of the just price is the notion of comparable worth, which has been much discussed recently. This idea is that two very different kinds of work, say that of a truck driver and that of a secretary, can both be analyzed into their component skills, such as (say) optical perception skills, hand movement skills, organizational skills, which can then be compared with one another in order to establish their value relative to one another. Although secretaries are typically paid less than truck drivers, this comparison might show that the skills involved were of equal worth, and so the secretary then would be entitled to the same wage as the truck driver.

THE NATURE OF ECONOMIC VALUE

All of these ideas have in common the view that economic value has some kind of objective or independent existence, apart from the agreement between buyer and seller. To say that a thing has *sub*jective existence in this sense is to say that a statement affirming it will be true if and only if some people believe that it is true; and to say that a thing has *ob*jective existence is to say that a statement affirming it will be true even if no one believes that it is true. That chocolate ice cream tastes good is a subjective truth because if no one thought that it tasted good, then it would not be true that it tastes good. The existence of the table I am writing on is objective, because even if no one knows or believes that it is here, nonetheless it is here.

In discussions about values it seems to be frequently assumed that all values must have the same kind of reality. Members of traditional societies often seem to assume that all values have objective reality, while many philosophers, such as the logical positivists earlier in this century and those sympathetic to their views, tend to assume that all values are subjective. It seems truer to our normal view of things, however, to say that different kinds of value have different kinds of reality. Values of personal preference, such as the good taste of chocolate ice cream, seem to be definitely subjective. On the other hand at least some moral values arguably represent something objectively true about human nature – for example, the Principle of No Harm, which we shall investigate in later chapters, namely, the principle that with certain specified exceptions it is wrong to cause harm to innocent people. Even if all the surviving members of the human race believed that there was nothing wrong about murdering innocent people, it would still be wrong.

What are we to say, then, about the reality of economic value, that is, exchange value? The fact that an object incorporates a certain amount of human labor represents only one kind of value among others. No doubt it is an important kind of value, but it is by no means the only real value in any object, and it is by no means what is decisive for the exchange. Even if we were to agree with Marx that the two objects to be exchanged each represent a certain quantity of labor—which despite his attempts to clarify it remains a thoroughly unclear concept—it is not true that that is all they have in common. What they also have in common is *a certain level of demand relative to the supply*, and it is this which is reflected in the exchange value. Exchange value is a genuine value, and not merely an appearance of value, for it represents what the two individuals desire; and it consists in whatever they agree on. But since it consists entirely in their agreement, it is purely subjective, and there is no method by which it could be ascertained objectively, apart from their agreement.

The common notion, which Marx shares, that any two items which are exchanged for one another must be of equal value is already an oversimplification, because it overlooks the reason why the exchange takes place. If a man sells a boat, he does so because he values the money more than the boat. And the buyer only buys the boat because he values the boat more than the money. Properly speaking, the boat does not have a single value: it has different values to the two men. What we call the exchange value of the boat is just the amount of money which the buyer is willing to offer and which the seller is willing to accept, given the other terms and conditions of the exchange.

Since the notion of "market value" is often used to compute benefit and loss, it should be noted that market value is not so much an actual value, as a presumptive one. The market value of an item is the highest price which the seller can reasonably expect to obtain for it at a certain time and place, based on what has been paid in the recent past for this or similar items. The market value of a house is what a seller can hope to obtain if he can afford to wait a certain length of time, say three months, in the light of the prices that have been paid for other similar houses in his neighborhood during, say, the last three months. The actual exchange value of any item, by contrast, is what someone is actually ready and willing to pay for it.

The notion of a just price is related to the idea of market value. Although the notion of a just or fair price has been defended with a good deal of theory, in practice what counts as a just price is to a large extent simply the customary price, the price that people expect to pay or to receive in the future because it is what has been paid in the past. This is shown by the fact that prices which were previously considered unjust in this view have often subsequently come to be accepted as just once they became established as customary. Even where the just price is calculated by adding a profit onto costs, the estimate of what constitutes a fair profit is typically heavily influenced by custom. It is perhaps understandable that people should become upset when they have been expecting to pay a certain amount for something they need, and then find that the seller is asking twice as much. But the mere fact that something has been customary does not necessarily entail that there is a right to it, otherwise all breaking with custom would be unjust.

The *true* just price, by contrast, is whatever an actual buyer and seller bind themselves to by contract. As Hobbes writes: "The value of all things contracted for is measured by the appetite of the contractors, and therefore the just value is that which they be contented to give."[8] A buyer who understands the concept of a free market, then, will recognize that a seller has the right in justice to ask whatever price he wishes for his goods. And a seller will recognize that a buyer likewise is entitled to offer whatever price he wishes.

The effect of the doctrine of a just price is to prolong shortages. As mentioned above, the city fathers of Charleston passed legislation in the wake of the 1989 hurricane to freeze prices in order to prevent "exploitation." Other towns afflicted by the hurricane which did not freeze prices recovered from the devastation quickly, for although the price of building materials went up sharply, that provided the incentive for manufacturers and dealers to supply the additional materials that were needed for reconstruction, and prices then came down again. Twelve months after the hurricane, however, the portions of Charleston hit by the hurricane still lay largely in ruins.[9]

Belief in the just price was arguably one of the principal causes of the famines that periodically swept Europe in centuries past, because it removed the market incentive to import additional grain as needed in times of drought. The empty stores of the former Soviet Union, and the famines recently afflicting some nations in Africa, can be clearly traced to the same cause.

Some of the late-scholastic theologians acknowledged this effect, and sought to make adjustments to the concept of a just price by factoring in allowances for shortages.[10] But to extend the just price in this way was essentially to abandon it.

Similar considerations apply to the living wage. The doctrine of the living wage implies that the economic value of an employee's labor is created by the employee's need. But in point of fact it is created by the demand for the labor, relative to the supply. If there is no demand for a particular kind of labor, then that labor has no economic value. If a workingman needs food desperately, and in order to earn it he spends long hours making spindles for spinning wheels which no one has any desire to buy, he is doing nothing to earn an income. To say that nonetheless he ought to be paid a living wage is to misunderstand the concept of a wage and to confuse it with a charitable donation. A wage is money given to a person because he has produced by his labor something that his employer wants. A wage has to be earned, and it is earned by the benefits it produces for the person who pays it. No doubt people in general, and not merely employers, have a moral obligation to help the needy to the extent that they can without injury to themselves, but this is not the result of the labor of the needy, and has no particular connection with it. The moral value of a person as a human being is one thing, and his economic value as a productive laborer is something entirely different.

The view that labor ought not to be treated as a commodity, that is, ought not to be bought and sold, because that would reduce human beings to the status of mere instruments, is a misunderstanding of the employment relationship. Employment is a voluntary agreement between two persons, one of whom offers his labor in exchange for money and the other of whom offers his money in exchange for labor. Each individual must give his consent to this agreement. In a free market no employee is dragooned into a job by force, each one has a job only because he has applied for it. The employer in advertising the job specifies what the terms and conditions of the job are. The employee applies for the job because he believes that he will be better off with it than without it, taking account of all the terms and conditions of employment. If he does not believe that, he does not apply for the job. This does not transform him into a "mere instrument" of the employer. A person is treated as a mere instrument when he is compelled by another's force to do what he does not desire to do. But to buy his labor from him when he wishes to sell it is to do him a great favor, and to place a wealth of benefits within his reach.

Treating labor as a commodity is one of the very best things that has ever happened to labor. If labor could not be bought and sold, each individual would have to fend for himself, there could be no division of labor, each person would have to provide himself with all the necessaries of existence. It is the ability to buy and sell labor more than any other single factor which has transformed human existence from the wretched poverty, disease, and early death characteristic of primitive societies to the relative comfort, health, and longevity which make the Western world, despite its many limitations, the envy of the rest of mankind. We know what it is like when labor cannot be bought and sold. It is called unemployment, and is looked upon by most ordinary people as an unmitigated disaster.

Some have suggested that employment for wages should be replaced by partnership, or some other form of employee participation in the ownership of the business. But this is naive. To participate in the ownership of a business is to share in the responsibility for it and in the risk attached to it. Many employees, perhaps most, want neither. To share in the risk of a business means that you do not have a definite income each week or month—income can fluctuate wildly depending on the ups and downs of the market, and to many working people that is unacceptable.

Just as the doctrine of the just price restricts the supply of goods, so the doctrine of the just wage restricts the supply of employment. Any employer has only a certain amount of money to pay in wages, and if he is compelled by law to pay more to some than the productivity of their labor warrants in the market, his ability to employ others is reduced.

Similar considerations apply to the notion of "comparable worth." Just as the economic worth of any form of employment is created by the demand for it, not by the need of the employee, so also it is not created by the employee's skills. A person may have highly developed skills at producing smoke signals, but if smoke signalling has been replaced by telephones and there is no demand for it, the economic value of those skills is zero. The economic worth of a secretary hinges on the general level of demand for secretarial services, relative to the supply, just as the economic worth of a truck driver hinges on the level of demand for his services, relative to the supply. No doubt the person's skills play a role in this, but they are only a part of what is relevant. The wage at which it makes sense for an employer to hire a person is determined by the employee's marginal productivity, that is, it will only make sense to hire this person at this salary if as a result the firm makes more profit than it would without him. Add to this that every job, as we saw earlier, is created not by the employee, but by the employer, who therefore has every right to determine what it shall consist in, and what shall be paid for it.

Similar considerations apply also to such notions as "exorbitant" or "windfall" profits. There is no objective measure by which a profit can be judged excessive. Such judgements express only what people are accustomed to and are typically merely the voice of envy. The only truly exorbitant profit is one acquired by fraud or force.

COERCION AND THE MEASUREMENT OF PRODUCTIVITY

The economic or exchange value of an item is given only by a *voluntary* exchange, not by one that is the result of force or fraud. If a customer buys a bag of sawdust for $30 because the seller assured him it was wheat, the $30 does not represent the genuine exchange value of sawdust. If I should succeed in persuading an acquaintance of mine to buy my house from me by the expedient of threatening to blow his car up, I may obtain money in place of the house, but the money is not a true measure of the economic value of the house. If a thug threatens to burn Smith's restaurant down unless Smith buys "protection" from him, this "protection" has no economic value, even though Smith pays a large sum for it. The concept of economic value has meaning only within the framework of a voluntary market system. Economic value represents the relationship between a voluntary supply and a voluntary demand.

Similarly, the concept of economic productivity has meaning only within the framework of a voluntary market, since a productive activity is one which results in the creation of economic value. An action is economically productive only to the extent that it produces something which other individuals desire. Neither the sale of the sawdust nor the protection afforded by the thug are economically productive.

It follows from this that various goods and services to which economic value and productivity are frequently attributed do not properly possess it. If government pays workers to produce some item which is not in demand in the market, and even more so if it then compels people by law to buy the product, no genuine economic value is created, and economic calculations based on any other assumption can only be misleading.

Throughout the United States, as in most other countries, a certain number of years of education are mandated by government. At the same time, most schools are owned by government and are paid for by taxation. Public education is not a voluntary exchange. It cannot be assumed, then, that the salaries paid to public school teachers out of taxes represent genuine economic value, or that the education the students receive has it either. Yet both educators and economists routinely make that assumption. Of course it seems reasonable to suppose that some of the education that government now provides would be provided privately if government did not, but it is only that portion of government expenditure which would otherwise be spent privately which represents genuine economic value.

Salaries paid within the context of a union contract are not simply the product of a voluntary exchange, but are imposed by the monopoly privileges of union legislation. Does the work for which these salaries are paid possess economic value? Possibly, if the firm makes a profit, but possibly not even then, if the profit comes from other areas of the firm's activities. Salaries which result from union contracts cannot be assumed to represent genuine economic value. Similar considerations apply to all employment which takes place as the result of legislation. In order to know what the true economic value of mandated employment is, we would need to calculate what the level of employment would be if the market were free.

In calculating the national income, economists customarily include all government expenditures except transfer payments, such as welfare or social security payments. It is recognized that transfer payments do not add to the nation's wealth, but it is assumed that all other governmental expenditures do, irrespective of their nature. If the U.S. government spends $40 million on a supercollider, or on the salaries of IRS agents, the assumption is made that this adds that amount to the nation's wealth. Yet economists recognize that such expenditures are anomalous, because there is no way to estimate their market value. What is the market value of a supercollider, or of the IRS? Instead of simply excluding government expenditures from the national income, however, the compromise solution is typically adopted of assuming that government output possesses economic value, and calculating it at *cost*, which would immediately be recognized as absurd if it were done with private business. It means that if government were to get as much work done by employing one person in place of two, its contribution to the national welfare would diminish, whereas if it spends more money on higher salaries, irrespective of the employees' actual accomplishments, its contribution to the national welfare increases.[11] Common sense would suggest that exactly the reverse is the case. The distortions introduced into the market by economic legislation make rational economic calculation extremely difficult if not impossible, and the conclusions of economists based on such assumptions should be regarded with the greatest distrust.[12]

Government always acts by coercion, as we shall see in more detail in Chapter 6. Every time government steps beyond its task of providing protection from crime and uses the coercive power of the law to influence economic activity as such, the result is similar to that produced by the thug, or by my threat to blow up my acquaintance's car. What may appear on the surface to be genuine economic activity is actually not so, and to count it as if it were is to be snared by an illusion. This is true of all the chief macroeconomic variables: prices, employment, and output. A price resulting from coercion is not a true price, even though money be handed over; employment resulting from coercion is not true employment, even though some kind of work may be done; and products resulting from coercion do not constitute genuine output. All these measurements are systematically distorted and rendered unreliable by government intervention in the market.

In intervening in the market, however, government relies and must rely on just these measurements. When the Federal Reserve makes a decision to increase interest rates, or not to reduce them, because of the danger of inflation, it looks to a particular measurement of inflation, such as the Consumer Price Index. But this Index lumps together not only voluntary but coerced prices. Every figure government consults as the basis for its economic policies has been falsified by its own previous interventions. In attempting to direct the economy according to some policy, any policy whatever, then, government is essentially flying blind, yet it compels the entire nation to fly with it.

Economists who favor macroeconomics sometimes reply that for many purposes rough estimates can still be useful, and no doubt that is true. Yet at the present time government expenditures make up some 40 percent of the figure referred to as the Gross National Product, and an analysis of the economy restricted to free prices and production might present a very different picture from the usual one.

5

Causing Harm

A black professor who argued that he was denied tenure by a college for racial reasons was recently awarded $1 million in damages. The Supreme Court of California ruled that Claremont Graduate School, one of the nation's leading colleges, was guilty of racial discrimination against Reginald Clark, prohibited by the Civil Rights Act of 1964.[1]

A U.S. district court has awarded $2.41 million to a woman who said a real estate management firm refused to rent an apartment to her because she has children. Carrie Titmuss, a secretary, won the award against William J. Davis Inc. in virtue of federal housing discrimination laws passed in 1989.[2]

A woman who argued that a firm refused to promote her to a management position because she is a woman won an award from a Los Angeles court of $20.3 million. The verdict was returned against Texaco Inc. in favor of Janella Sue Martin on the grounds of sexual discrimination. The award consisted of $5.34 million in compensatory damages and $15 million in punitive damages.[3]

In each of these cases a firm is penalized savagely because it does not wish to do business with a person. The laws against discrimination assume that it is possible to cause a person harm by inaction, that is, by refusing to trade with him or her. Yet this assumption, like the notion of exploitation, is a myth. It rests on a fundamental misconception of what is involved in causing harm.

JOHN STUART MILL

It is to the lasting credit of John Stuart Mill that he formulated the basic ethical principle of the liberal society: people should be free to do as they please, so long as they cause no harm to others.[4] But when do we cause harm to others? Mill believed that it is possible to cause harm to a person not only by performing an action which inflicts harm on him directly, but also by *not* performing an action that one ought to have performed to help him.

Of course everyone has long known that this is true in some circumstances. If the captain of a ship neglects to take the necessary measures to keep his ship from running aground, then by not performing certain actions he has caused harm to his employers, crew and passengers. He has an obligation to care for his ship because he has deliberately taken that obligation on himself by contract and is being paid to fulfill it. He has led others to rely on his performance of certain actions, and so he harms them by failing to perform those actions.

Mill's view, however, goes far beyond that. It says that even where a person has *not* deliberately placed himself under any obligation to perform some action, it is still possible for him to cause harm by failing to do it. "There are also many positive acts for the benefit of others, which he may rightfully be compelled to perform; such as . . . saving a fellow-creature's life, or interposing to protect the defenseless against ill-usage, things which whenever it is obviously a man's duty to do, he may rightfully be made responsible to society for not doing. A person may cause evil to others not only by his actions but by his inaction, and in either case he is justly accountable to them for the injury."[5]

This view runs counter to the common law tradition of the English-speaking peoples. However, since Mill wrote, the idea has become widely accepted in the United States also, and in recent years many laws have been passed that effectively put it into practice. For example, this applies to almost all of the laws which are based on the idea of fairness, or, as it is called, social justice. If it be asked what is wrong with refusing to employ minorities or women or the elderly, i.e., practicing job discrimination, many people will reply that it is unfair, for it causes harm to those discriminated against. If it be asked what harm is done to them, a likely reply will be that it deprives them of an opportunity they ought to have. The employer has not shot or robbed or defrauded the individual; he has simply not given him or her a job. In Mill's words, he has caused evil not by his actions, but by inaction.

Similarly, if someone should inquire what is wrong with making jobs available at a low wage, say $2 an hour, he will be told that this is taking unfair advantage of the worker. If he asks why it is unfair, a typical answer will be that an individual cannot live and support a family on such a wage. It is not that the employer has harmed the worker directly, by theft or deception, but that he is not giving him what (according to the commentator) he needs. He is causing harm by what he is failing to do, namely, pay a wage of a particular amount.

Or again, if a seller is charging a much higher price for an article than people are accustomed to, or if the price is much higher than the item seems to be worth, the seller is frequently felt to be taking unfair advantage of the buyer ("ripping him off," in the popular phrase), especially if the buyer is ignorant of the market price or needs the product urgently. The seller is not inflicting any direct injury on the person or property of the buyer, he is simply not helping him as much as it is felt he ought to help him, and this is taken as being equivalent to harming him directly.

Since some very significant laws and court decisions now rest on this view, it is a matter of importance to know whether it is sound or not. Is it the case, as Mill says, that we can cause harm to others by inaction, by failing to help them when we ought?

TWO CONDITIONS

As we saw in Chapter 2, for one person to cause harm to another, two essential requirements must be fulfilled. The first is that the condition of the person who is believed to be harmed must be worse after than it was before. There must have been a deterioration in his situation. For that is what we mean by harm.

The second requirement is that causation must have taken place. The deterioration in the condition of the other person must be the result of the action or inaction of the first person if he is to be held responsible for it and punished because of it. We must now examine both of these conditions from a slightly different perspective than in Chapter 2. There we were concerned with the question whether it is possible to harm a person by making an exchange with him. Here our question is whether it is possible to harm him by inaction, by refusing to help him or trade with him.

DETERIORATION AND THE BASELINE

To harm a person is to make his condition worse. If Brown shoots Smith, it is clear that he has harmed him because it is clear that Smith's condition is worse after being shot than it was beforehand. "Worse" implies a comparison, and the comparison in the first place is a temporal one, between the condition of the person after the harmful event has taken place and his condition immediately before it took place. The "baseline" or benchmark for the comparison is the moment just before the harmful action began.

The description of the person's condition immediately before the harmful action took place must be complete. Sometimes the person's condition is not static, but is in the process of changing, either for better or worse, and this process of change is interrupted by the harmful action of the other person. In that case the description of the harmed person's condition must include the likelihood of the change continuing, so far as that can be estimated. Suppose for example that White injures Black while Black is on his way to be interviewed for a job, with the consequence that Black is prevented from obtaining the job. The description of Black's condition just before he was injured includes a certain probability that he would have obtained the job; and so an account of the harm White has done to Black cannot be confined to the physical damage that he did to him but must also include the harm he did by depriving him of that probability that he would have obtained the job, if it is at all significant.

It is sometimes maintained that the baseline for comparison ought to be not the actual situation of the person in distress at the time the action of the other person started, but the hypothetical situation that the person in distress would be in but for the action or inaction of the other.[6] If Brown encounters difficulties while swimming and Green throws him a rope, it may be said that Green is benefiting Brown because if Green had not thrown him a rope he would have drowned. But although this may be a convenient manner of speaking, philosophically it is a mistake to formulate it in this way. We can never be certain what *would* have happened. At most we can say what would have been more or less *likely* to happen, and that may be very far from what would actually have happened. The result of such a formulation is to make all benefits and all harms merely conjectural. Smith declares that he is going to commit suicide. Suppose that I would like to have the experience of killing someone, and I shoot Smith. Could I argue that I didn't harm him, because if I hadn't killed him he would have died anyway? Assuredly not.

Where it is necessary, that is, where there is good reason to believe that some significant change would have taken place in the person's condition, everything that may be gained by formulating it in terms of what would have happened hypothetically can be gained equally well by a full description of the person's actual condition at the time of the event in question. The idea that Brown would have drowned can be formulated equally well as the idea that he was in danger of drowning. This danger constitutes an integral part of his situation at the time Green threw him the rope, and in assessing the danger we take account of the degree of likelihood involved. It is not necessary to go beyond the actual condition provided it is fully described.

Since it is sometimes questioned whether an action has harmed or benefited a person, we may note that the same baseline applies in the case of a benefit as in that of a harm. We must compare the person's condition after the action has taken place with what it was immediately before the action in question commenced. It is clear that if you give a gift of $1,000 to Robinson you have benefited him, because after you give him the money he has $1,000 more than he had beforehand. And again, the description of the person's condition before the action commenced must be complete and must include the likelihood of any change that was in process continuing, so far as that can be estimated.

We mentioned above the case where Green, standing idly by a stream, notices that Brown, who is swimming, appears to be in serious difficulties and likely to drown. He throws Brown a rope, and with that Brown succeeds in making his way ashore. We assumed, as most people probably would, that Green has benefited Brown, because before Green threw him the rope he was in danger of drowning, while afterwards he was not. But such a case is more controversial than a reader unacquainted with modern liberal thought might suspect. The modern liberal tends to deny that Green has benefited Brown, because he believes that there should be a law requiring the Greens of this world to save the Browns.

Feinberg

Joel Feinberg, whose views we encountered in Chaper 2, gives in another of his writings a representative argument for the modern liberal position on the question we are concerned with here. According to Feinberg there is a difference between "active aid" and "gratuitous benefit." A gratuitous benefit to a person in distress, he asserts, consists in restoring him not to the situation he was in just before the rescue commenced, but to the situation he was in *before the onset of the peril*. According to Feinberg, the correct baseline for gauging benefits and harms is the person's normal condition. To benefit a person it is not sufficient to rescue him from distress: it is necessary to improve his condition above what it normally would be. It will be worthwhile to spend a little time analyzing Feinberg's position, for no other modern liberal writer has developed the implications of the modern liberal position on the question of benefits and harms as thoroughly as he has.

Feinberg concedes that to save a drowning man is to benefit him in a generic sense, "for it is to affect his interest in a favorable as opposed to an adverse or neutral way. It is to prevent his interest-curve from taking a sharp decline from the baseline of its normal condition. . . . [But] it does not follow from the fact that the rescuer affects the endangered party's interests favorably that he 'benefits' him in the sense of elevating his interest-curve to a point on the graph *above* the baseline of his condition before he fell into the water. It is only the latter sense of 'benefiting' that would support further descriptions of the rescue as benevolent generosity, 'active service,' 'positive good,' and so on. . . . It is a benefit only in the generic sense of affecting the [person's] interest favorably, specifically by preventing a drastic decline in his fortunes from a normal baseline." Feinberg goes on to explain his notion of a "normal baseline" as: "the point on the interest-graph where a person's interest-line usually is, or at any rate where it was during the period before the present episode began." He summarizes: "To escape with one's life is not to become better off than one was before one's life was imperiled."

But what is the difference between "affecting a person's interests favorably" or giving him "active aid," and benefiting him? Why is it that only improving his situation above what it *normally* is can count as a benefit? Feinberg's answer to this is a moral one. A gratuitous benefit, he explains, is something which the recipient has no moral claim to. If I donate $1,000 to the Red Cross, this would be a gratuitous benefit to them, because, although I might be considered to have an obligation to give something to some charity or other, I have no special moral obligation to give anything to the Red Cross. But in the case of Green's throwing the rope to Brown, there *is* a special moral obligation to rescue. Brown has a *right* to be saved. And if Green does not save Brown when he could, in Feinberg's view he ought to be punished. For Feinberg, like the generality of modern liberals, assumes that all definite moral obligations can and should be enforced by law, under threat of punishment.

Now many if not most people would agree that Green has a moral obligation to help Brown if he can do so without excessive difficulty. This is not in dispute. The question in dispute is whether Green deserves to be punished if he does not help Brown.

The ethical tradition of the Western world, which has found expression in the Judaeo-Christian religious tradition, has typically been that there are fundamentally different kinds of moral claims: there are claims in justice, which can legitimately be enforced by law, and there are claims in charity or benevolence, which may be genuine claims, and even very strong ones indeed, but which cannot be legitimately so enforced.

Obligations in Charity

This is brought out clearly in the well-known Gospel parable of the Good Samaritan. Although the priest and Levite walk past the wounded man, doing nothing to help him though they easily could, and although it is perfectly clear that Jesus disapproves strongly of their callousness, there is no suggestion in the Gospel that they should be punished by the civil law. Similarly, the Gospel says nothing to indicate that the wounded man had a right to be helped. On the contrary, it states that the Good Samaritan showed mercy on him.[7] The view of the Gospel is clearly that the priest and Levite had an obligation to help, but it was not an obligation to be enforced by human law: it was an obligation in charity.

In Feinberg's view, which is a faithful representative of modern liberal opinion, there cannot be obligations in charity. If there is an obligation, it can and should be enforced by law, and is therefore an obligation in justice. Why does Feinberg believe this? Or, to put it in terms of causing versus allowing harm, why does he believe that the law can justly prohibit not only causing harm but also allowing it? He appears to give two answers to this question. One is that this is simply his intuition.[8] This does not allow much comment, beyond that it is not mine. His second answer is that both have the same purpose, namely preventing harms, and therefore there must be a *presumption* that both are equally legitimate.[9]

This is an astonishing argument for a moralist to make. The mere fact that two activities have the same purpose does not establish the slightest presumption that they are equally moral. The activity of a bank robber and that of a legitimate businessman have the same purpose, namely the enrichment of the individual. Does that establish a presumption that robbing banks is legitimate? Even if we confine the question to laws, Feinberg's argument undermines his own basic position as a liberal; for he rejects paternalistic laws, which aim to prevent people from harming themselves, while he supports laws which prohibit people from harming others; yet both have the same purpose, the protection of individuals from harm.

Feinberg speculates that perhaps those who support the position I am defending here are misled by the fact that persons in desperate straits characteristically implore others for their help rather than claim or demand it, and after they have been rescued, they tend to express their gratitude and even offer rewards. This can be explained, he asserts, by the fact that a person is in no mood to be morally high and mighty and make righteous demands when he is drowning.

But this is surely mistaken. Where there is a genuine right to receive help, it seems to this writer that people are typically by no means loath to demand it, precisely when they are in great difficulties. If the captain of a ship should abandon his responsibilities in the event that his ship were sinking, or if a paid lifeguard at a swimming pool looked on nonchalantly at a swimmer in trouble, it does not take any great imagination to believe that assistance would be demanded in no uncertain terms.

In the course of working his way through the problem, Feinberg seems to come to see some difficulties in making the comparison with anything other than the actual state of affairs. He concedes, as we have seen, that to rescue someone is to "affect his interests in a favorable . . . way," and he concedes further that under certain circumstances we can use as the baseline not normality but the moment the assistance began. But for this to be the appropriate baseline, he asserts, there must be no duty of assistance. If there is a duty of assistance we must use the other baseline, normality. If there is a duty to assist, then failure to assist would be to cause harm.

This reverts back to the mistaken assumption we saw above, that all duties are of the same kind, and there is no difference between obligations in justice and those in charity. The captain of a ship who fails to fulfill the duties he has contracted to do causes harm, just precisely because he had previously committed himself, and so they are duties in justice. The baseline for harm is constituted by normality, *because he contracted to preserve normality*. The priest and the Levite, who in the Gospel story walked on past the wounded man, failed in their duty towards him, but since that was not a duty in justice, which they had previously contracted to do, but in charity, they did not cause him harm. The baseline for harm is not the normal condition, health, of the man who is now wounded, but the condition he is in *when he is found by the priest and Levite*, namely, wounded.

In short, Feinberg's argument assumes what it has to prove. What it has to prove is that even in the absence of a contractual obligation to rescue, failure to rescue can cause harm. It has to prove that there cannot be obligations in charity. But in maintaining that we are entitled to use as the baseline the moment when the assistance began only when there is no duty of any kind to help, and that if there is any duty whatsoever to help, then we must use normality as the baseline, he assumes just this very point.

The absurd result would follow from Feinberg's argument that when we give a person what he needs, that is not a genuine benefit but something to which he has a right, whereas if we give him what he does not need, that is a benefit; and the more he needs it, the less of a benefit it will be to him, while the less he needs it, the more of a benefit it will be to him! This is confusing a benefit with a luxury.

Discrimination

Our discussion of the duty to rescue has been for the purpose of clarifying the first requirement for one person to cause harm to another, namely, that his situation must be worse after the action than it was before: there must have been a deterioration in his condition. Let us now apply this to some controversial economic cases.

A bank manager refuses a loan to an applicant solely on the grounds that she is a woman. Has he harmed her? Many people will reply, Of course, he has discriminated against her, depriving her of an opportunity she otherwise would have had.

But the first task is to identify the harm. If Brown shoots Smith, it is clear that Smith has been harmed. What is the equivalent here of Smith's wound, where is the deterioration in the applicant's position? If she has suffered harm, her condition afterwards must be worse than it was beforehand. Is that the case here? Let us say she wanted to start a business. Before she applied for the loan, she had, say, $10,000 capital, but she needed $20,000 to start the business. After she has been refused, her situation is still exactly the same. She does not have any more, but she also does not have any less. She has not lost anything. She is disappointed, because she had hoped to obtain the loan. She had hoped to be in a better position, and she is not. But *not being better off is altogether different from being worse off*. If the bank manager had stolen her watch, she would be worse off. But being turned down for a loan is not the same thing as being robbed. She is being denied a favor which is being done to other people. But to refuse to do someone a favor is not the same as doing that person harm.

To point this out is not to defend irrational discrimination, anymore than it is to defend the callousness of someone who could easily rescue a drowning person but refuses to do so. On the contrary, if the applicant for a loan is clearly qualified for it by all normal business criteria, and the banker's only reason for refusing to lend money to the person is an irrational prejudice, then he is harming his own business, because he is putting the satisfaction of his own emotions ahead of considerations of profit. And for this reason the general tendency of the market is to discourage irrational prejudice. But to argue as we have that discrimination does not properly speaking cause harm is implicitly to argue that we should rely on *voluntary* means, such as education and religion, not on the punitive hand of the law, to overcome it.

Our conclusion, then, is that a refusal to trade with a person does not cause that person harm because there is no identifiable harm; there has been no deterioration in that person's situation of which the refusal could be the cause.

THE CONCEPT OF A CAUSE

The second requirement for one person to cause harm to another, as we saw, is that *causation* must have taken place. If in some situation there has been a deterioration in the condition of the other person, it must be the *result* of the action or inaction of the first person. Our next question must be, then: Is it possible for a deterioration in a person's condition to be the result of someone else's inaction?

In order to answer this question we need to analyze the general idea of a cause. When do we cause anything? A cause is something which produces an effect, which brings it about. There are two criteria which jointly can prove very helpful in enabling us to identify a cause, namely, that it is the *necessary and sufficient condition of the effect*.

I am writing this at night, in a room with an electric light. What is the cause of the light in this room? Sometimes in answer to this question the reply is given: the switch, since the switch turns the light on and off. But of course switches by themselves don't produce light, so we will have to add something to this answer. What about the electric current running through the wires? This obviously plays a vital role, but again by itself electric current flowing through a wire doesn't automatically produce light. Then there is the light bulb. And again obviously the light bulb is quite crucial in producing the light, but equally clearly by itself it's not enough. It has to have electricity flowing through it. Suppose we say, then: the cause of the light which is now in my room is the electric current flowing through the light bulb. This seems a satisfactory answer. Whenever we have an electric current flowing through a light bulb, we get electric light.

As we just remarked, the cause of an effect can often be identified by the fact that it is both the necessary and the sufficient condition for the production of the effect. A necessary condition means that, if that particular condition is not realized, then the effect does not take place: it is necessary to have A before B will come about. If A is not present, then B will not be present. This light bulb is clearly a necessary condition for the presence of this light in this room. (If there were no light bulb here, the light which is currently here would not be here. If another bulb were here, say a fluorescent instead of an incandescent one, we would have light, but different light from what we are getting now.)[10]

A sufficient condition means that if that condition is realized, then that is enough to make sure that the effect takes place. If A, then necessarily B. If we have this light bulb, and it has this electric current flowing through it, is that enough to give us this light? Yes, nothing else is needed. It is central to our normal idea of a cause that the effect follow from it not by chance, but of necessity, and this is clearly true in this case: given that there is electricity flowing through the light bulb, the result, light, follows automatically.[11]

Let us now apply these ideas to some human actions. Brown pulls out a gun and shoots Smith. If our analysis is correct, Brown's shooting should be the necessary and sufficient condition of Smith's wound. Is it the necessary condition for it? That is, would Smith have sustained this wound if Brown had not shot him? No. Then Brown's shooting was indeed the necessary condition for the wound. Is it also the sufficient condition for it? Given that Brown fires this loaded gun at Smith (and Smith is not effectively shielded), will it follow of necessity that Smith is wounded? Indeed it will.

Let us consider again now the case of someone who could help a person in need but does not. Let us suppose that Jones is tying Smith to the railway tracks, and Brown, standing on a bridge nearby, sees what is happening, but since, say, he finds Smith's taste in neckties uncouth he decides not to intervene. If Brown could rescue Smith without undue danger to himself, most of us would probably feel that he has a very strong duty to do so, and that his refusal to help him is extremely reprehensible. But that is not precisely our question for the moment; our question is: Did Brown *cause* Smith's death?

We can answer this question by looking for the joint hallmarks of necessity and sufficiency. First, is Brown's failure to act a necessary condition of Smith's death? Would it be true to say that Smith would not have died this death if Brown had tried to rescue him? We can see it is possible that a train might come along just while Brown was in the midst of untying Smith and kill both of them. The mere fact that Brown tries to rescue Smith does not guarantee he will succeed. Rescue attempts sometimes fail. So we cannot say, in this case: No A, therefore no B. Brown's inaction is not a necessary condition of Smith's death.

Is it perhaps, however, a sufficient condition of it? Would it be enough, in order for Smith to die this particular death, that Brown fail to try to rescue him? If Brown fails to act, will it necessarily and inevitably follow that Smith dies in this particular way? The answer to this question is clearly, no. On the one hand, other factors must be present besides Brown's inaction, for Smith to die in this fashion; notably, Jones must have tied him to the tracks. And on the other hand, it is possible that Jones might have an attack of remorse at the last moment and untie Smith; so it is not inevitable that Smith will die, merely because Brown fails to try to rescue him. It is very clear, then, that Brown's inaction is not a sufficient condition of Smith's death.

The necessary and sufficient condition of Smith's death, given that there is a train coming, is Jones's action in tying Smith to the tracks. It is Jones, and not Brown, who is the cause of Smith's death. Jones's action was a necessary condition, because if he had not tied Smith to the tracks, Smith would not have died in that fashion. And it was sufficient, because given that there was a train coming, nothing else was needed to ensure Smith's death. To be more accurate on this last point, the sufficient condition of Smith's death is the joint fact of a) the train coming, and b)

Jones's action. If the driver of the train through no fault of his own failed to see Smith lying on the tracks, Jones alone can be blamed for his death. On the other hand, if the train driver saw Smith there, but recognized him as his next-door neighbor who plays drums at 2 A.M., and resolved to keep going, then he would bear joint responsibility with Jones.

Is Brown perhaps, however, an accessory to the killing? An accessory is someone who assists in the action. If Brown had gone to the store and bought the rope for Jones, he would be an accessory. If Brown had helped Jones escape from the scene afterwards, he would be an accessory. But Brown did not assist in the action; he simply did nothing.

We see, then, that inaction merely by itself cannot cause harm, because it cannot cause anything. Mere inaction cannot be a necessary condition of any positive or actual effect. For inaction by itself to be a necessary condition of some effect, it would have to be the case that in the absence of inaction, that is, given any action whatsoever, the effect in question would fail to take place, which is clearly not true. And mere inaction cannot be a sufficient condition of any effect, because that would mean that solely by the fact that no action is taken, some effect necessarily and inevitably follows, which makes no sense.

To say that a cause is the necessary and sufficient condition of the effect is not to provide an exclusive definition of a cause, but simply to spell out some crucial features of the idea that a cause is that which *produces* the effect, and so which must be considered to have the *power* to produce it.

Strictly speaking, when it is a question of living human beings there is no such thing as inaction: Brown is not doing nothing; he is standing on the bridge, watching. A person who is conscious is always doing something (and possibly even a person who is asleep can be said in some sense to be doing something, at least provided that he is sleeping deliberately). We speak of Brown's "inaction" only in the sense that standing on the bridge watching does not constitute helping Smith to escape. This is an important point, however, because by the same token it does not constitute helping Jones to tie him down, which would be necessary if Brown were to be the cause, or a partial cause, of Smith's death. So far as causal activity goes, standing on a bridge is just standing on a bridge.[12]

The result of this analysis is to show that there is a fundamental difference between causing harm, and failing to prevent harm. Failure to prevent a person's death is by no means the same thing as killing him. This was recognized in the notorious case of Kitty Genovese, who was stabbed to death in New York in the sight of over thirty people who could have tried to save her.[13] Although feeling ran very strong against their cowardice and inhumanity, no one suggested that they should be tried for murder.

Feinberg Again

Just as the chief objections to our conception of the baseline for harm were raised by Joel Feinberg, so it is he who has made the most detailed attempt to criticize the conception of causality that we have presented here. He makes two main arguments against it. One is that inaction *can* be the necessary and sufficient condition of harm. The other is that, even if it could not be, there is no moral difference between causing harm and allowing it. Let us look at these arguments.

Feinberg takes the by now familiar case of a nonswimmer, B, who falls off a bridge into a river. A, who is looking on, could throw him a rope, but dislikes B, and so contents himself with observing the scene. Is B's death the effect of A's inaction?

Feinberg concedes disarmingly at the outset that it "sounds much more natural to the ear" to say that inaction has "consequences" than to say that it has effects. The word "consequence," indeed, suggests from its etymology that, as distinct from an effect, it is merely something that happens afterwards, without necessarily being caused by the action in question. But since he then goes on to call it a result, this initial concession is nullified.

Feinberg analyzes the situation in this way. "At a given moment, just after B falls into the river, it is true that if A throws him the life preserver he will not drown then and there, and that if A omits to throw him the life preserver he will drown then and there. It is entirely up to A; he is in control of B's destiny . . . A's intervention was necessary to B's survival and, in the given circumstances, it would have been sufficient to tip the balance from death to life." A's omission to act, then, was a necessary condition of his drowning. And, "conjoined with the other circumstances," it was sufficient for B's drowning, because "it completed the sufficiency of a set of conditions which without it (given its necessity) would have been insufficient to produce that result."

Is A's inaction a necessary condition of B's death? If A had acted, would B certainly have been saved? It does not take any great powers of imagination to realize that there are other possibilities. Is it not possible that A might have tried to save B and failed? Perhaps he threw the rope to him, but it got carried away in the current, or B was unable to grasp it. Suppose B had a heart attack on realizing his plight, or the cold water put him into a state of shock? Suppose B had been suffering from depression and on finding that he was in danger of death gave up the struggle and decided to end it all? A thousand different factors could prevent A's rescue attempt from being successful. It is hardly plausible, then, to say that A's inaction was a necessary condition of B's death.

Was A's failure to act a *sufficient* condition of B's death? Or, if it was not sufficient by itself, was it one of the factors that together were sufficient to produce the result, like the electricity running through the light bulb that we discussed earlier?

Obviously it was not sufficient by itself: despite A's inactivity, B would not have died in this way unless he had fallen into the river. Feinberg recognizes this, but argues that A's failure to act was one of the factors that combined to bring about B's death. A's inaction, he maintains, *completed the sufficiency* of the other circumstances, in the sense that the other circumstances would not have been sufficient to cause B's death if A had acted.

This is a surprising argument, because it confuses a cause with a *conditio sine qua non*. There is a difference between necessary conditions. Some necessary conditions are productive of the effect, such as the electricity in the light bulb, some are not productive of the effect, but merely remove impediments to the production of the effect. Such a condition was sometimes referred to by medieval writers as a *removens prohibens*, a factor which merely eliminates an obstacle. If I enclose my light bulb in a box, that will effectively prevent it from casting any light in my room. Is the *absence of the box*, then, a *cause* of the light? No. The light is produced by the bulb with the electricity, it is not produced by the absence of the box. The absence of the box is a *conditio sine qua non* for the bulb to illuminate the room. If the absence of the box were a cause of the light, then the light would have an infinite number of causes, for there are an infinite number of possible impediments which happen not to be present around the light bulb in my room at the present time: cardboard boxes, tin boxes, round boxes, square boxes, boxes of every conceivable shape and size; layers of dark paint on the light bulb; aluminum foil, etc., etc. All of these absences would have to be included in any account of the cause of the light.

This objection has been urged against Feinberg by Professor Eric Mack.[14] Feinberg's response falls back on the notion of *explanation*. Very often, he says, in explaining some event, we do not attempt to list all the factors that strictly speaking ought to be mentioned for a full explanation, but we single out one or two factors which we find especially enlightening in the circumstances. We explain a drowning by pointing out that the person didn't know how to swim, or we explain a famine by citing the lack of rain for the crops. The "failure of an event to occur when it could reasonably have been expected explains why an unexpected and unusual outcome resulted."[15]

The problem with this response is that the concept of an explanation is by no means identical with the concept of a cause. Many things count as explanations which cannot be considered causes. We typically explain a person's actions, for example, by pointing to his motives or reasons, but these are not in any strict sense the same as causes. Motives would be causes only if people were machines, acting automatically as the result of whatever mechanical forces impinged on them. What counts as an explanation for us is relative to what puzzles us, but this is not true for a cause. I go into a cave, and finding electric light there, to my surprise, I ask what the explanation is for this. Many appropriate answers might be given, for example that the owner was afraid visitors would otherwise come to harm, or that some geologists are conducting a study there, but the *cause* of the light remains always the electricity flowing through the bulb. In the case of B's death by drowning, then, as the result of falling accidentally into the river, while it may be true that someone who knew A was standing nearby and was puzzled by B's death would find the explanation enlightening that A refused to try to rescue him, that does not in any way serve to make A's inaction the cause of B's death.

It is important to realize that, as we remarked earlier, the notion of a cause cannot be defined as a necessary and sufficient condition. These are simply criteria which it is often convenient to use to identify the cause. But if we take the idea of a necessary and sufficient condition in the strict sense, omitting the idea of production, it is often possible to find further effects of the effect; that is, events after the effect, which correspond to these criteria. Consider in our present case a certificate of death by drowning. If such a certificate is always issued whenever a person drowns, it fulfills the formal requirements for being a necessary condition of B's death: no certificate, no death. And since such a certificate would not be issued unless B drowned, then it is clear that B has drowned, and so it fulfills the formal requirements for being a sufficient condition. But no one will maintain that the certificate was the cause of the death, because *a cause is that which produces* the effect.

What produces B's death by drowning is the presence of water in his lungs, which prevents him breathing. If A pushes B into the water, and he drowns, then A (together with the river) is the cause of B's death, because A's action has forced him into a situation where, if he takes so much water into his lungs that he cannot breathe, this happens of necessity.

No Significant Difference?

Even when they grant that a person who merely refrains from helping another in distress is not the cause of that person's death, however, modern liberals typically see no morally significant difference between the two. Allowing a person to die when we could easily prevent it is just as bad, in their eyes, as killing him outright. One writer gives the case where Smith is having a heart attack and reaches for his medicine. What difference does it make, he asks, if Jones, who is sitting by his bedside, pushes the bottle out of his reach, or the bottle is just out of his reach and Jones could easily give it to him but does not?[16] "When we focus our attention," writes Feinberg, "on a certain class of examples, where the harm done or not prevented is extreme, and the effort required to prevent it is utterly trivial, and other morally relevant factors are identical, it is impossible to avoid the conclusion that there is no morally significant difference between them, or at least no moral difference sufficient to bear any legal weight."

If we try to apply this view in other areas of life, however, where logically it should apply with equal force, for example where it is a case of causing good rather than harm, it obviously does not work. Some of Mozart's music was composed with very little effort, for example while he was carrying on a conversation on a quite different subject. The prince archbishop of Salzburg, Count Sigismund Schrattenbach, could with very little effort have prevented Mozart from composing anything. Does anyone think that there is no significant difference between the two, between being the author of some of the most glorious music ever created and merely having refrained from preventing it? Would it be just as good to forget Mozart and hold festivals in honor of the Count?

When we read an Agatha Christie novel, are we held spellbound by the search for the person who could easily have prevented the crime, but deliberately did not?

The honor for any great achievement, and the blame for any evil, rest uniquely with the individual who produces it. Others who could have prevented it but did not may also justly receive respect or disgust, but there is no substitute for causality. What counts in any crime is above all who did it. All the evil intentions in the world, if they are never put into practice, that is, into an effective causal chain, will not serve to make a man guilty of a crime. Even the evil outcome is not essential, since an attempted murder, while not indeed a murder, is certainly and justly a crime; but even if the intentions are never so good, and the doer has nothing in mind but to benefit the victim by sending him into a blissful eternity, though against his will, it is a crime which cries to heaven for vengeance, because he has *caused* his death.

Do Moral Duties Derive from Social Rules?

The confusion over causality which now dominates so much social thinking and so much of our current law, such as liability law, derives ultimately from an unquestioned and unexamined philosophical assumption of the moral superiority of the collective over the individual. This comes to the surface with great clarity in Feinberg. Moral duties, he asserts, derive their force from social rules—rather than from individual conscience, it must be presumed. Social rules are imposed on the individual by the collective power of the society and allocate *shares* of social responsibility among individuals, he tells us. This applies not only to positive duties, such as the duty to rescue, but also to negative duties, such as the duty not to cause harm. In some matters (he does not indicate how to draw the line) what constitutes a fair share of social responsibility for one individual can only be determined in the light of the responsibilities assigned to others. An individual can only know what side of the road he ought to drive on by determining what side the other drivers have agreed to. Feinberg agrees that for the most part negative duties have precedence over positive ones, but he accounts for this by holding that with positive duties there is often a practical problem of coordination. If a fire breaks out in someone's home, I have a duty to call the fire department, but I have no duty to fight the fire myself because society has devised a system in which I fulfill my duty in this regard by paying taxes to support the professional fire fighters. It would be inefficient for society to assign everyone the duty of fighting all fires. But where sudden and unexpected emergencies arise, for which society has not made special provision, then, when the individual can provide help without great inconvenience, a sound system of social coordination assigns him that responsibility.

Now it might be mentioned in passing that the side of the road I ought to drive on is determined by the owner of the road. Anyone who owns a road has the right to decide the direction of traffic on it. It just so happens that most roads in our society are owned by government, but there is nothing strictly necessary about that; in the history of the United States some important roads have been privately owned, such as the early turnpikes.

To return to our immediate subject, however, in this modern liberal view human rights are not inherent in the individual but are assigned by society. This means that the individual has no right to be unharmed unless the society gives him that right. That is, the individual has no rights against society. And since society is represented in the concrete by (no doubt in the modern liberal view a democratically elected) government, the individual can have no rights against such a government. A theory like this not only supports a very complete socialism, but also a tyranny of the majority. It essentially abolishes the idea of human rights altogether. For the concept of human rights, if it means anything at all, means that there is a basic sphere of human life where society and government, even a democratically elected government, have no right to intrude. Furthermore, such a position runs counter to the entire drift of

Feinberg's argument in the rest of his work, which supports the traditional liberal idea that there are inherent moral limits on the power of the state over the individual. It must be wondered whether he can really mean what he says here.

Responsibility

A not uncommon response to the kind of causal analysis we have presented here is to say that although strictly speaking Brown may not have caused Smith's death, just as the onlookers did not cause Kitty Genovese's death, nonetheless such persons bear *responsibility* for such deaths, because they had an obligation to help those in peril, and they could have helped them yet did not.

As we have seen, it may very well be true that Brown has an obligation, and even a very grave obligation, to help Smith. Of course, that will depend on the circumstances: if there were a serious danger that Brown would be harmed, or if he would have to make an exceptional effort to reach Smith, such as swimming across a river, we would usually feel that he does not have a strict obligation to help Smith. Or if someone else would be harmed, the same would be true: if Brown were an ambulance driver, say, and observed the crime while driving a heart-attack victim to an emergency room, we would usually feel that he had no obligation to stop and help Smith.

But let us allow that in the case under discussion none of these things is true, and Brown does have an obligation to try to help Smith, a very serious obligation, in fact. Is he then responsible for Smith's death? The effective question this raises is the one we discussed previously, whether Brown should be punished for not helping Smith. That is, what sort of an obligation does Brown have? Are all obligations of the sort that a person who does not fulfill them can legitimately be punished? Or are there some obligations which are very real and serious obligations, but of such a nature that a person ought not to be punished for failing to carry them out? We saw that according to the sense of ethics which has characterized the Judaeo-Christian tradition, it is possible to have genuine obligations which are of such a nature that they cannot be enforced by law, namely obligations in charity or benevolence.[17]

To ask whether Brown is responsible for Smith's death, then, is to ask a question which is ambiguous. It may mean: Did Brown have an obligation to try to help Smith, and could he have made such an attempt? To this the answer may well be, yes. But the question can also mean: Did Brown have an obligation to try to help Smith of such a kind that he can be punished for not doing so? And to this the answer is, no.

Boycotts and Strikes

That a refusal to trade with a person is not a case of causing him harm is already familiar to everyone through the idea of a boycott. A boycott is an organized refusal to buy from a seller; and provided that it is entirely voluntary, and only legitimate persuasion and not any threat of force is used to persuade others to join, it is not prohibited by law, no matter how irrational the reason for the boycott might be.[18]

A strike is essentially similar: an organized refusal by employees to continue working. Although strikes in the United States and other Western countries do not take place at the present time in a free market, but within the framework of special legislation which gives monopoly powers to trade unions, still, even if this legislation were rescinded, it would always be possible for employees to withhold their labor. Provided that in so doing they do not contravene any agreement to which they have committed themselves (in practice this will usually mean that some advance notice must be given), and again that only persuasion and not force is used to convince other workers to join in, there can be no objection that they are causing harm, any more than if they were to give up their jobs with that firm and move to another. (By the same token, the employer will not be causing the strikers harm if he refuses to continue to employ them.)

When customers or workers refuse to trade with sellers or employers, then, it is commonly felt that from the viewpoint of the law this is perfectly justifiable, no matter how absurd their reasons may be. Why should it be any different when employers or sellers refuse to trade?

Perhaps it might be argued that both strikes and boycotts do indeed cause harm, but that the reason why they are not prohibited by law is that the harm is justifiable. It seems difficult, however, to make much of this, for if it were true, then only certain boycotts and strikes would be permitted by the law, namely, where the harm is not excessive, or the reasons could be demonstrated to be rational. But the law does not inquire whether a boycott or a strike causes excessive harm. Indeed it is impossible to sue a union for any harm caused to an employer or to other employees by a strike.

Similarly, the law does not inquire whether the reasons for a boycott or strike are rational. We can confirm this by asking what legal penalties would be invoked if the reasons for the strike were based on racial or sexual discrimination. Suppose that a group of black consumers decided to refuse to buy from a shopowner solely on the grounds that he was white, or conversely, that a group of white consumers decided to refuse to buy solely on the grounds that the seller was black: no doubt such behavior would be regrettable, but should it be punishable by law? Current U.S. law certainly does not punish it.[19] The same applies to a strike carried out solely for racist or sexist reasons. Suppose, for example, that a black firm is bought out by a Japanese or a white owner, and the employees strike to protest that, or conversely, that a white firm is bought out by a black or Japanese owner; then provided that there is no infraction of an agreement, the strike will not be illegal.

It seems, then, that in the one case the principle is recognized that refusal to trade cannot be considered to cause harm, but in the other case the same principle is denied—scarcely an example of triumphant consistency.

LIABILITY

Sometimes there is no dispute that a person has suffered harm in the wake of a market transaction, and the only question is: Who, if anyone, should be held responsible for it? Should a gunsmith be held responsible for a crime committed with a gun that he sold? Should a pharmaceutical company be liable if a customer falls ill from taking one of its drugs? Should a firm which makes floor polish be held responsible for the harm that comes to a baby that drinks it? Should an employer be liable for injuries which an employee suffers while on the job? If a bank robber slips on the floor of the bank and breaks a leg while trying to escape with the goods, should the bank be compelled to pay him damages? This is the problem of liability.

The common law tradition was to handle most of these questions under the general umbrella of the law of contract. It was recognized that people are capable of foreseeing the possibility of danger attaching to commercial transactions, and if they wish to insist on certain safety precautions, they can make them part of the contract. While it was acknowledged that not every aspect of a contract could be spelled out in writing, and some matters had to be understood on the basis of custom, the fact remained that it was the contract that counted. The law of torts, or accidental injuries, was reserved largely for accidents unrelated to commercial transactions. One result of this approach was that all complaints by a buyer had to be addressed exclusively to the seller, as the one with whom he had the contract. There was no possibility of suing the manufacturer, since no contract had been entered into with him. Needless to say, it was also impossible for the bank robber to sue the bank.

All this is true no longer. In the course of the twentieth century the courts and government have taken it on themselves to nullify the supremacy of contract and have extended the law of torts to commerce. At the same time the concept of legal liability has been socialized, that is, liability no longer depends on causation, but can be distributed among all those in any way related to the event. In practice this usually means that those who have the most insurance coverage must pay, whether they had any role in causing the harm or not. This is known as the "deep pockets" theory of liability. Where causation is still used as a criterion of liability, it is often understood in a much broader sense than previously. In addition, laws have been passed restricting or forbidding the sale of certain goods, such as fireworks or narcotics, because they are dangerous.

According to English and American common law, a worker injured in the course of carrying out his work had to be able to demonstrate that his employer was the cause of the harm, in order to obtain any remedy at law. With the introduction of Workman's Compensation legislation, however, this requirement has been abandoned. An employer is now automatically liable for *all* injuries which an employee receives in connection with his work. In most countries employers are required to pay for insurance to cover these costs.

In most areas of the United States a person who has sustained damage from a product which he purchased can now make a claim not only against the seller but also against the manufacturer, on three different grounds: breach of warranty, negligence, and strict liability. We have already commented on the concept of implied warranty in Chapter 2. We saw there that the implied warranty of merchantability can be understood, in a sense acceptable to a free market, as expressing conditions of the sale that are customary in the trade or with that particular firm. According to the view argued for in this book, however, that would only hold against the seller, not the manufacturer. Negligence presupposes that the negligent person has a special duty to care, a duty which he fails to fulfill, not through deliberate ill will, but through carelessness. In recent years courts have found this duty almost anywhere where there was some kind of previous relationship between the plaintiff and the defendant.

In at least forty states at the present time, however, the law provides that a manufacturer may be held liable for harm sustained as a result of the *misuse* of a product; that is, for the use of a product even where it was not at all defective, if the (mis)use was "reasonably foreseeable" (or "not unforeseeable") and not uncommon. In the case of an infant drinking furniture polish, the manufacturer may now be held responsible for the harm the infant suffers, on the grounds that such things are not uncommon, and so the manufacturer could have foreseen that it *might* happen, and should have taken steps to prevent it. Similarly there is a tendency for the courts to hold automobile manufacturers strictly liable if their vehicles are more than usually dangerous to their occupants in the event of an accident, since car accidents are common and foreseeable.[20]

A particularly striking example of the socialization of responsibility is the concept of "market-share liability," where even foreseeability was abandoned as a criterion.

In 1971 researchers discovered a weak but definite statistical link between DES (a synthetic form of estrogen) and clear-cell adenocarcinoma, a form of cancer, in daughters of women who had taken the drug during pregnancy. The *DES daughters*, as they came to be known, sued five of the companies that had manufactured DES decades earlier. But no plaintiff could identify which firm had manufactured the medicine her mother had used. Unable to disentangle the causality knot, the California Supreme Court cut it clean through. It simply parceled out liability in proportion to the share of the DES market each manufacturer had held back in the 1950s.[21]

The result of this socialization of liability has been an explosion of liability awards. This is the principal reason for the sharp rise in the cost of health insurance in the United States, which is currently the subject of much discussion. It has also had the consequence that many valuable products and services are no longer made available in the market because the cost of providing them has become too high. This is especially true in the field of medical products.

Between 1965 and 1985 the number of U.S. vaccine manufacturers shrank by more than half; by 1986 the nation depended on a single supplier for vaccines against polio, rubella, measles, mumps, and rabies. In the 1960s there were eight U.S. manufacturers of whooping cough vaccine; by 1986 there were only two. . . . "Who in his right mind," the president of a major pharmaceutical company asked in 1986, "would work on a product today that would be used by pregnant women?"[22]

We shall argue in the later chapters of this book that it is a basic principle of justice that a person can be liable only for harm that he himself has caused.

The key to the question of liability is the fact that a cause is never merely a necessary condition, but always also a sufficient condition, for the production of the effect. The mere fact that if some action had not taken place, the effect in question would not have occurred, is by no means enough to establish causality. As we have seen, causality means that, given that this action took place, the effect followed of necessity. No number of merely necessary conditions can amount by themselves to a sufficient condition. For, to repeat, to cause something is not merely to make it possible, or to pave the way for it, or to remove impediments that would have prevented it, or even to create a predisposition for it, but to produce it, to bring it about.

Sometimes confusion may be occasioned by the fact that there are different kinds of necessary conditions. There are those that are productive of the effect, for example, and those that are not, as mentioned above.

Furthermore, a sufficient condition may be made up of a number of elements, each one of which is necessary to the sufficiency of the condition. The sufficient cause of a *contract* is the pair of mutually conditioned promises which constitute the agreement. Each element of these promises which the parties understand to be essential to the agreement is essential to the agreement, so that if one of them is not fulfilled, the contract has been broken. If it is agreed, for example, that a particular date is of the essence of the contract so that if goods are not delivered by that date then the contract has been broken, then this is not merely a necessary condition of the contract, but a condition which is necessary to make up the sufficient condition of the contract, which is the agreement.

By contrast, it may be a necessary condition of the contract that the buyer have received an inheritance: if he had not, he would have had no money to make the purchase. That he should have the money for the purchase is a *conditio sine qua non*. But it is not an integral part of the agreement. Similarly, if the buyer has previously been in a coma, it is a precondition of the contract that he have come out of the coma, since otherwise he would have been incapable of making an agreement. His coming out of the coma is a *conditio removens prohibens*, but it does not constitute an integral part of the agreement. The bundle of conditions which are necessary to make a sufficient condition is not identical with the necessary conditions of the contract.

FRAUD

Our argument has been that in the absence of force and fraud, exchanges take place only because both buyer and seller expect to benefit. In the absence of force and fraud, then, each party acts without impediment, is responsible for his own actions, and must be presumed to accept whatever risk is involved in them. Although harm may happen to one of the parties *in the wake of* an exchange, and so of the seller's action, in the absence of force or fraud it makes no sense to believe that it was caused by the seller. *Post hoc* does not imply *propter hoc*.

If fraud is present, however, the situation is very different. If the exchange takes place because the seller has deliberately deceived the buyer, or vice versa, the fraudulent party has broken the contract and is the cause of whatever harm comes to the other from the exchange. (The same will be true if force should be used, but this is not a question in cases of liability.)

Although there is no dispute that the fraudulent party has caused the other harm by reason of his fraudulent claim, it may be helpful to indicate in some detail why this is so. For the sake of clarity we will draw a distinction between the contract or agreement to exchange, and the exchange itself. Let us suppose that a manufacturer has claimed that his floor polish is safe for babies to drink. The buyer accepts this claim, and for that reason buys the floor polish. The exchange has taken place. But it then turns out that the claim was fraudulent: the buyer's baby drinks it and is harmed. The contract has been broken, and the manufacturer is liable for damages to the buyer. The exchange was harmful to the buyer. The question of causality, then, is the question, what was the necessary and sufficient condition (or conditions) for the harmful exchange?

Clearly the fraudulent claim is a necessary condition of the harmful exchange, because we are assuming that the exchange would not have taken place without it. (If it should be clear that the exchange would have taken place anyway, the fraudulent claim is irrelevant.)

Further, the fraudulent claim is an integral part of the sufficient condition of the exchange, and the part which causes the harm. We observed earlier that a contract is a pair of mutually conditioned promises which derive their joint binding force from the fact that each party is led by the other to rely on his fulfilling his promise and is therefore harmed if he does not fulfill it. Smith agrees to put a new roof on Jones's house if Jones will pay him $5,000. Jones agrees to pay Smith $5,000 if he puts a new roof on Jones's house. If Smith puts the new roof on, relying on Jones's promise, but Jones then fails to pay, Smith has been harmed because he has lost his labor. If Jones pays the $5,000, but Smith then decamps, Jones has been harmed because he has lost his money. The claims or promises that each party makes, and that the other party relies on, then, are not an extrinsic factor added on to the contract, but constitute its essence. The exchange takes place only because of them, that is, because of the contract. The total sufficient condition of the exchange is the joint agreement or contract between the two parties. The agreement of the defrauded party, however, is given only because of the fraudulent claim of the other. The fraudulent claim, then, is the cause of the harm.

Whether one party to an exchange should be held responsible for harm which comes to the other will depend, then, on whether there has been a fraudulent claim. If the manufacturer of the floor polish claimed that his product was safe for babies to drink when it was not, he has made a fraudulent claim. If the pharmaceutical company claimed that its medicine was safe when it was not, it has made a fraudulent claim. If the employer claimed that his workplace was safe when it was not, he has made a fraudulent claim. But *if there has been no fraudulent claim, there cannot be liability*.

In interpreting claims made, the implied warranty must be taken into account, in the sense indicated in Chapter 2. If a particular trade is customarily carried on in a certain way, or if a particular company customarily trades in a certain way, this may often reasonably be assumed as part of the terms of the contract, without needing to be spelled out explicitly. However, there is no foundation for imputing a general implied warranty of safety.

Is there a duty to prevent foreseeable harm in the absence of a fraudulent claim? As we have seen earlier, there may very well be such a duty, depending on the circumstances, but if so it is a duty in charity or benevolence, not in justice, and cannot legitimately be enforced by law. Failing to prevent harm is by no means the same as causing harm, and those who fail to prevent harm do not deserve to be punished, or be required to make reparations.

The question of negligence arises when one has a duty to perform but performs it carelessly, causing harm but not intentionally. This can be a factor in exchanges only within the framework of the contract. If one party to the contract is negligent in fulfilling its promises, to that extent it has caused harm and can be held liable.

So-called "strict liability" is liability even though there has been no fraud or negligence. An example of this would be where a party has taken every precaution to avoid causing harm, but harm nonetheless results. While this can happen outside of contractual relationships, it is scarcely possible for one party to an exchange to cause harm in this fashion to the other party within the framework of the exchange. To make a purchase is to make a decision to obtain the item because one believes one will be better off with it, in the light of one's knowledge of the item and the seller's representations. In making such a decision one implicitly takes on oneself whatever risks may be attached to the item.

Why is it that there can be no liability in the absence of force and fraud? The reason is that there is no action of the other party which functions as a sufficient condition of the harm. Granted, harm has taken place. But in making the decision to buy the product, the buyer has implicitly accepted whatever risk attached to it. If he did not accept the risk, he would not buy the product. If he wanted to buy the product without the risk, he would have inserted a clause into the agreement of sale to that effect, and it would then have been up to the seller whether he wanted to accept that clause or not. The seller has done nothing that the buyer did not want him to do. The seller's action in transferring ownership of the product to the buyer was not sufficient to cause the harm, because it would have been ineffective without the buyer's agreement. By contrast, where the seller has made fraudulent representations, these are sufficient to cause the harm, because they are what moved the buyer to agree. In this case the buyer did not intend to buy what he actually received, say the poisonous floor polish. He took possession of it rather than of a safe one for no other reason than that the manufacturer assured him it was not poisonous.

If a person consents to a market exchange, he takes on himself the responsibility for any harm which may follow from his possession of the object, just as he does if he accidentally finds some natural object and appropriates it and suffers harm as a result. If he finds a piece of uranium and puts it in his pocket and suffers a serious burn or cancer, no one else has caused him harm, because it was his decision to take whatever risk was involved in putting it in his pocket. Similarly, if he obtains it in a market exchange, no one has used force or fraud on him, it was his decision to gain possession of the object.

In order to see how the concept of causality which we have outlined applies in cases where harm occurs in the wake of a purchase, let's analyze some typical instances.

If Green sells a gun to White, and White uses it to shoot Black, is Green responsible for the injury to Black? That is, has he caused harm, or assisted in causing harm, to Black? We are assuming that Green had no intention of harming Black, or of assisting to harm him. Is Green the cause of White's action? First, is Green's sale of the gun to White a *necessary* condition of the injury done to Black? That is, if Green had refused to sell it to him, would that have effectively prevented White from injuring Black? Whether it would have prevented him from injuring Black in this specific way will depend on how easy it would have been to obtain another gun. But a refusal by Green to sell the gun to White obviously would not prevent White from injuring Black in many other ways. If White is determined to injure Black, there is no end to the number of weapons he could use for that purpose. It seems clear, then, that Green's sale of the gun to White is not a necessary condition of his injuring Black, although it may be a necessary condition of his injuring him in this specific way.

But as we have just pointed out, for causation to take place it is not sufficient to have a necessary condition, or any number of necessary conditions. No matter how many necessary conditions are present for the effect to take place, they can never be sufficient to constitute a cause of the effect. In order to be a genuine cause, *at least one of the necessary conditions must also be sufficient to produce the effect.*

Is Green's sale of the gun to White, then, a sufficient condition of the injury done to Black? That is, given that Green sells the gun to White, will it follow of necessity that White will shoot Black? Certainly not. White could change his mind and decide not to shoot Black. We see, then, that the sale of the gun to White cannot be considered the cause of the injury to Black. The true cause of the injury to Black is White himself.

(The situation will be very different, of course, if White informs Green that he plans to use the gun to shoot Black. In that case Green becomes an accessory to the crime.)

This analysis of causation enables us to shed additional light on certain particularly controversial kinds of market transaction already discussed in Chapters 2 and 3. Our argument in those chapters was that an exchange does not take place unless both parties to it expect to benefit. Even though the individual concerned believes that he benefits, however, there are cases where the typical verdict of observers is that he is mistaken and does not, in point of fact, truly derive a benefit, but suffers harm. It commonly follows, then, that they assume that the other party to the exchange is the cause of that harm. An example is the sale of narcotics: it is widely taken for granted that anyone who sells narcotics to a person, at least for recreational purposes, is doing that person harm, and this assumption is reflected in laws which impose heavy penalties on drug dealers. But is this a valid analysis of the situation?

There is no question but that a person who takes narcotics merely for recreation may be sacrificing a great deal for the sake of a momentary pleasure. In the vast majority of cases it will seem to be clear to observers that the individual is harming himself – although that is not a judgement to make automatically, and a certain sense of modesty is appropriate in passing such a verdict: in order to be certain of it in any particular case we would have to know all the circumstances of the person's life and understand fully the motivation that leads him to it. We should be able to recognize the possibility that for some people in some circumstances, which we are not always well equipped to judge, such as perhaps when they are suffering from chronic stress, the benefits of taking narcotics even recreationally may outweigh the harm. Let us assume, however, for the sake of argument, that that is not the case. Our question here is: Is the person who sells narcotics causing harm? In particular, if the buyer incurs an addiction, is the seller the cause of that?

If we analyze the relationship of buyer and seller (in the case of sane adults) from the standpoint of causality, we see that the seller cannot be the cause of the buyer's actions. It is not the seller but the buyer who *produces* the buyer's actions. Although the action of the seller may be a necessary condition of the action of the buyer, in the general sense that the purchase of drugs would not take place without some seller or other (and the ease of finding another seller must be taken into account in judging this), still, the seller's action cannot be a *sufficient condition* of the buyer's action. For the buyer's action does not follow of necessity from the seller's offer. The buyer is an autonomous person in his own right, a free agent; it is his personal decision, and no one else's, to buy these drugs.

A desire to spare the feelings of those who are experiencing hardship can sometimes make us reluctant to stress their responsibility for their own actions or condition. And in dealing with social problems this tendency is often heightened by the inclination of social scientists to explain human behavior by reference to external or social factors which are beyond the control of the individual. This can pose a very serious problem, however, since any prospect a person might have of a lasting improvement in his situation can only come from his ability to resist being merely the passive object of external forces and to take the initiative in regard to his own life, shaping his circumstances to his own needs and desires. For in general, no one else can know what he needs as well as he does, and no one else will be as concerned about his needs as he will be. In the end he must be able to stand on his own feet and guide his own steps.

To treat a sane, conscious adult as not responsible for his actions is to treat him as a child, and that, no matter how well meant, is not only demeaning to him, but deprives him of his principal source of hope. What begins by looking like an attractive solution to a problem, then, and even like a requirement of benevolence and concern, can easily result in moral and spiritual disaster.

This is true even if the person is an addict, because although it may be extremely difficult for an addict to overcome his addiction, it is not impossible, as the powerful example of many testifies. There is no doubt that narcotics are an immense problem in the United States at the present time. But the only humane answer, and also arguably the only effective answer, lies in the conviction of each individual that he has the power to overcome their attraction, and in his resolution to do so. All efforts to help him which treat him as a mere response mechanism, wholly at the mercy of influences beyond his control, are doomed to fail—as the current policy of legally prohibiting the sale of narcotics has failed.

The case of selling alcohol to a person who is already obviously drunk is different. One of the conditions for moral responsibility is that the person be conscious. A sleepwalker may do some things that conscious people do, but it is universally recognized that sleepwalkers are not responsible for their actions. Similarly a person who is drunk is not properly conscious and in possession of himself and is not responsible for his actions. To sell him more alcohol is to cause him harm, then, and genuinely to take advantage of him unjustly. On the other hand the act of becoming drunk is one that a person must take responsibility for under normal circumstances.

But, it might be objected, does not the case of selling to children tell against our definition of causality? Children are not fully responsible for their actions, and so an adult who sells or gives narcotics to a child is truly causing harm to him. Yet the providing of the narcotics does not seem to be either a necessary or a sufficient condition of that harm. Suppose the adult decided not to provide the drugs to the child. It would not necessarily follow that the child would not take the drugs. He might obtain them from someone else, for example from another child. So the sale or gift is not a necessary condition of the harm. And again, the mere fact that the sale takes place is not enough to guarantee that the child will take the drugs; he might change his mind.

There are two different points here, deriving from the two different conditions. Let us consider first the question of the necessary condition. It is true that in many cases the child might obtain narcotics from some other source, though they would not be these identical narcotics, but only others which have similar effects. This particular sale is indeed a necessary condition for this particular harm to be done. As we remarked above, this is true of sales to adults also.

The difference between the two cases lies in regard to the sufficient condition. The child does not and cannot have the same intrinsic power of resistance that the adult has, or ought to have. The child does not have the same mature responsibility for his own actions as an adult has or should have; he is at the mercy of his feelings and whims, he does not have the same power of acting on principle. He may change his mind and not take the drugs because, for example, he does not like them. But if he does take them, it will be because the other person has given them to him. Since the child does not have the same intrinsic freedom of action, there is a sense in which he has to do whatever he does. He is not the master of himself. If he takes them, then to a certain extent (which of course lessens as he grows up) he could not properly speaking help taking them. No doubt an adult addict also is not the master of himself. But if he became an addict as an adult, then he is responsible for the fact that he is an addict.[23] And as an adult he retains the ability, given him by his genetic endowment as a person, to overcome his addiction. Even though that may be extremely difficult, the example of thousands of addicts who have successfully overcome their addiction shows that it is possible.

One adult cannot be the cause of another adult's actions, except through force or deliberate deception. This does not mean that responsibility cannot be shared, however. In the case of a person who pays another to commit a crime, both the one who commits the crime and the one who pays him are fully responsible for it.

Our argument, then, is that adults are the causes of their own actions and that the mere fact that someone sold them an item with which they then cause harm to themselves or others, or from which harm results accidentally, does not mean that the seller has caused or joined in causing that harm.

6

The Individual and the Community

To many people complete market freedom means a deficient sense of community, an extreme individualism which isolates human beings from one another, reduces their concern for others, and leaves them lonely victims of alienation. The market, in this view, stands for narrow self-interest, and the dominance of "economic man," who is not swayed by any considerations of the public good but aims only at his own benefit. Defenders of the free market frequently find themselves assailed as if they had been defending mere selfishness and greed. For similar reasons the market system is sometimes described as being opposed to democracy, on the grounds that democracy means involvement in the life of the community, a sense of participation and communal responsibility.

Government, on the other hand, is typically held in high esteem by those who have this view, as the embodiment of unselfish and impartial concern for the welfare of society as a whole, and the savior from the ruthlessness of the marketplace. Although the Founding Fathers were suspicious of governmental power and were much concerned to restrain it, an attitude which characterized the majority of Americans until well into the twentieth century, the Great Depression wrought a vast change. John Kenneth Galbraith writes, with evident approval "In the United States, as in the parliamentary democracies in general, the great majority of the people have come to regard the government as essentially benevolent. To the extent that the New Deal in the United States had revolutionary significance the revolution was in attitudes of the great masses of the people toward the federal government. Within the span of a few years a comparatively detached and impersonal mechanism, hitherto identified with tariff-making, tax-collecting, prohibition, Farmers' Bulletins and the National Parks, came to be regarded as a protector and even as a friend of the people at large and their shield against adversity."[1]

Government regulation of the economy is not felt, in this view, to be in principle anything negative or regrettable. Although from time to time particular regulations might prove to be misguided, the remedy will usually lie, not in abandoning regulation, but in improving it. There is no significant moral difference between law and other means of achieving a desirable end. Regulation is simply one means among others for doing what needs to be done. Some activities belong to private individuals, namely those concerned with merely private good, and some belong to government, namely those concerned with the common good. Persuasion, bargaining, and agreement are suitable means for achieving a private good; law and regulation are the suitable means for achieving the common good. Both kinds of activity are simply means to an end, to be used as the occasion requires. If anything, law and regulation may be seen as something positive, the concrete expression of a sense of community.

In an extension of this view, the political system and the economic system are not seen as two separate systems to be kept distinct from one another. The political system of democracy should also embrace the economy, it is felt, so that we enjoy *economic democracy*, which means that all those who are affected by business and economic decisions should be guaranteed by law a voice in making them. Society, we are told, provides each individual with the indispensable material out of which he fashions whatever it is that he achieves; the community is the necessary condition for the existence and the accomplishments of the individual; the individual owes everything to the community, and therefore fundamentally there can be no such thing as truly private property. Everything belongs of right to the community.

A book which received much applause when it was published a few years ago may serve as a representative of this school of thought.[2] The authors of this volume see America as a "culture of separation," characterized by the self-centered pursuit of happiness and an excessive esteem of the virtues of private life, which is reflected in its emphasis on the market. Market activity is characterized by "intrinsic meaninglessness in any larger moral or social context," and necessarily produces "alienation." The reward of work should be the "approbation of one's fellows" rather than the accumulation of wealth. Our social world needs to be fundamentally transformed and "reconstituted" by government, reducing competition (that is, free choice), and "reducing the punishments of failure and the rewards of success" which result from the market, in order to make it more human. The ideal of freedom is "highly individualistic," for "freedom to be left alone is a freedom that implies being alone" and is not conducive to the development of a "just economy," for the economy will be just only when it has become communal and has banished poverty.[3] Public life, that is, participation in governmental activity, is inherently more meaningful and valuable than private life.

In the light of such opinions, which see government as the savior from the evils of a free market, it will not be out of place to ask some questions about the nature and function of government. What is government? And how does it compare with the market as an expression of the sense of community?

PHYSICAL FORCE

The defining characteristic of government is that it is that individual or group which exercises a *monopoly of the use of physical force in a particular territory*. What makes a government be a government, rather than merely, for example, a private club, is that it, and it alone, has the authority to fine, to imprison, and to put to death. The power of government is essentially physical. As we pointed out in an earlier chapter, it is the power of the army and the police, of the gun and the execution chamber. (The governmental power to fine is a physical power, for it includes the power to take the money by force, for example by attaching a person's salary, and if the individual refuses to pay the fine he may suffer a further physical penalty, such as imprisonment.) These powers are not simply incidental to government: they constitute its very essence. They are both necessary and sufficient to make a government. No government can exist without possessing them and exercising them effectively, and any individual or group which does possess them and exercise them effectively constitutes the government by that very fact.[4] It may not be a just government, but it is certainly the government.

The essential role of physical force in establishing a government is evident from the nature of law. A law, as we pointed out in Chapter 2, is not merely a suggestion, or a wish, or an educational device. Every law is constituted a law only by the fact that it has a physical penalty associated with it. The effect of every law is to punish. A law without a physical penalty would be a joke. I do not say a just law, but any law; for a law, like a government, may be unjust, but still a law.[5] All law is coercive, by definition. It is with good reason, then, that Locke defines government, or political power, as "the right of making laws with penalty of death, and consequently all less penalties."[6]

Now punishment is not a good. As Bentham says, "All punishment is mischief: all punishment in itself is evil."[7] It may be a necessary evil, but it is still an evil. The same holds true, then, for all law and government. They are not a good, but a necessary evil. This may not under all circumstances be a particularly pleasant or inspiring thought, but it is the reality.

It may perhaps be objected to this definition of government that private organizations can impose penalties: clubs can fine their members, firms can discharge employees, and these penalties can entail very serious consequences for those individuals. This is certainly true, but there are fundamental differences between the ability of a private organization and that of government to inflict punishment. Private organizations can impose penalties only conditionally, depending on the desire of the individual to belong to them. An employer can discharge only those who desire to work for him. A club can only fine those who wish to continue being members of it. And no private organization is empowered to imprison or execute. But the ability of government to impose penalties is not conditional on any action or desire of the individual penalized: governmental power is absolute. And as we have seen in Chapter 2, there is a fundamental difference between refusing to employ a person and causing that person harm: causing harm is by no means the same as failing to provide help.

Is the Use of Force Always Harmful?

The distinctive actions of government are always accompanied by the use or threat of physical force. But is force always and necessarily harmful? Is it not possible that under certain circumstances the exercise of force on a person may benefit him? Most societies have laws based on this premise. People are threatened with a lesser harm in order to protect them from a greater one. Restrictions are placed on the sale of alcohol, cyclists are commanded to wear helmets and car drivers seatbelts; many drugs may not be bought without a physician's prescription, suicide and the use of narcotics are forbidden. Many of the laws restricting economic activity can be understood in the same light, for example the laws which give trade unions monopoly power on the grounds that individual employees left to themselves would succumb to the superior bargaining power of the employer. While it is true that in some such cases an activity is forbidden by law because it is considered immoral or because it is felt that there is an unjustifiable cost to society, the idea of protecting the individual against himself also is widely assumed to have played a role. In the case of minors or the insane, it is generally recognized that it may sometimes be necessary to use force on them for their own good; and, it may be asked, why should it not be possible for sane adults sometimes to be in an analogous situation, where the thoughtless exercise of freedom could be harmful to them, especially where they are in a vulnerable position? In the case of convicted criminals it might seem that the use of force is not necessarily harmful, since they deserve it.[8] Similarly, the use of force to restrain someone from committing a crime which he is threatening to commit may seem not to be harmful, since it is in his own best interests as well as in the interests of the intended victim.

Nonetheless our contention is that the use or threat of force on a sane, conscious adult is always harmful to him. This does not mean that it is always wrongful. The just punishment of a criminal by legitimate authority does not wrong him, but it does harm him, otherwise there would be no point in inflicting it. For on the traditional view of punishment, the purpose of it is to balance or redress one harm with another. The fact that a person deserves to suffer harm does not make what he suffers cease to be harm. (In the next chapter we will argue that in the case of a sane adult, harm is wrongful when the person being harmed has not caused harm.)[9]

The use or threat of force is harmful because it takes away the power of choice. To those who do not possess the power of choice, or do not possess it in fully developed form—the insane, the unconscious, or minors—it will not always and necessarily be harmful.[10] But to those who do possess the power of choice—sane, conscious adults—to deprive them of this power is to deprive them of that which most distinctively makes them persons. The use of force violates a person's sovereignty over himself, his ownership of himself. The significance of self-ownership can perhaps be seen most clearly by comparison with its opposite, slavery. We consider slavery morally repugnant because it means that one person owns another. The power to dispose of his own actions is taken away from him and given to another. The use of force on a person constitutes a kind of temporary slavery. Slavery is simply the erection of the use of force into an enduring legal institution, making it permanent and as of right. (It might be added that death is caused by physical force, in one form or another, and by that alone.)

The idea that it can be permissible to cause harm to a person in order to prevent him from suffering a greater harm rests on a number of confusions. For one thing, since we cannot predict the future of individuals, we can never know for certain that any particular individual is actually going to suffer the harm that we wish to protect him from. All we can have by way of advance knowledge is a statistical likelihood. But while a statistical likelihood can be of great help in estimating commercial matters like insurance costs, it is no substitute for knowledge in cases where punishment is in question—it is not some statistical average that suffers punishment, but a particular individual. We are not entitled to punish a person merely because of some statistical likelihood that he will be harmed, any more than we could be entitled to execute him (or, if you wish, jail him for life) because of some statistical likelihood that he will commit a murder.

A law does not merely penalize those individuals who were going to be harmed, but everyone, including possibly a great number who were never going to be harmed. A law requiring cyclists to wear helmets threatens all cyclists with punishment, not only those who have accidents.[11] A law prohibiting the purchase of narcotics threatens all users, and not merely those who would otherwise become addicts. And to threaten harm is already to cause harm to a certain extent.

Yet even if we could (in an impossible hypothesis) know for certain that a particular individual was going to suffer the harm in question, that would not justify us in inflicting a previous harm on him, albeit a lesser one. For a person must deserve to suffer harm. To take it on ourselves to inflict harm on someone who does not deserve harm, no matter how well-intentioned it might be, is to arrogate to ourselves dominion over the life and person of the other, to treat him as if he were our property, and not a person in his own right. It is to play God.

Legitimacy

We pointed out above that the authorization to use physical force is the distinctive and defining power of government. It may be objected, however, that physical force is not sufficient to establish a legitimate government, but only a tyranny. It would describe, for example, the German occupation of France during the Second World War, or the Iraqi occupation of Kuwait. But a legitimate government, such as that of the United States, rests on the voluntary support of the people.

It is true that the legitimacy of a government is not necessarily settled by its ability to use force; although it often is, in the sense that a government which initially has been established by force can subsequently come to be accepted or at least no longer rejected by the people. What constitutes legitimacy for a government is a complex question, for legitimate governments can come into being in a variety of ways. Legitimacy cannot be confined to those governments which are created by popular election in what is now the customary democratic fashion, for then almost all the governments which existed before the nineteenth century would be illegitimate and their acts legally invalid. It seems safe to say that in the history of mankind, government has to a large extent been exercised by military figures who commanded the armed force of their societies. Democratically elected governments exist because of a willingness on the part of the armed forces to submit to civilian control, and in the overall light of history represent a recent and exceptional piece of good fortune. Furthermore, the democratic form of government can probably be maintained only in societies which possess a well-developed middle class, which means that it must be possible for societies which do not have such a middle class to have governments which are legitimate even though undemocratic. But even an illegitimate government can still be a genuine government. The Nazi government of France was certainly illegitimate, but it was equally certainly the government of France at that time. The Bolshevik government of what became the Soviet Union was imposed by force and may well be considered to have been illegitimate initially, but it would be difficult to maintain that by 1930 it was not the legitimate government of that country.

Representative Government

But perhaps it may be argued that in the case of a *representative* government the authority to use force is not the decisive factor making it a government: a democratically elected government has moral power which other forms of government do not have, because it can rightly claim to represent its society. There is an obligation to obey its laws which is not necessarily present in the case of other forms of government. With such a government it is the representative function rather than the coercive function which is paramount in interpreting its relationship to society.

It may well be true that a democratically elected government has a moral power and authority which other forms of government lack. But this in no way diminishes the role of force in constituting it a government. It still remains true that every law is a law only because it is backed up by the threat of physical punishment. Take the coercive power away from government and it is no longer government. The power of a government to represent its people arises only because it possesses coercive power. Given that we need government, that is, need an authority fitted out with the right to use physical force, for the purpose of protecting us from aggression, both from other individuals and from other societies, it follows necessarily that government must treat on our behalf with other governments, and with the society as a whole, thereby representing us, whether it is what we would call technically a representative government or not. And again, given that we need a government, the least dangerous way to accomplish that is to have it elected by the people and responsible to them, thereby becoming a representative government in the standard sense. It is not as if "society" needed someone to "represent" it in any event, apart from the exercise of physical force.

The view has become common that the principal task of government is to provide for those who are disadvantaged, to care for those who are unable to care for themselves, and to create an equal society. But even according to this view, which is very different from the traditional conception, it is essential that government possess the right to use physical force within its territory, for otherwise it will be impossible for it to carry out redistributive programs effectively.

LAW

Some legal scholars consider the statement controversial that every law is constituted a law only by the threat of penalty associated with it. It has been objected that there are certain kinds of law to which this does not apply, for example laws which do not directly forbid actions, but exempt certain actions from punishment, or confer powers, or delimit powers; such as the laws which declare that a will or a contract lacking certain formalities is null and void, or the laws prescribing electoral procedures.[12]

However, given that the law says: "If you do these actions you will be punished," it is merely the obverse of this that there should be laws which say: "These other, but related, actions are not to be punished." Laws which exempt certain actions from punishment are parasitic upon laws that threaten punishment, and have no meaning without them. For example, the provisions of a valid will can be enforced by the threat of punishment. A law which requires two signatures for a will to be valid says in effect that wills which lack the two signatures cannot be enforced by the threat of punishment. This kind of analysis holds good for procedural laws in general.[13] This is not to say that laws which make exemptions from punishment, confer powers, or delimit powers are not genuine laws, of course. Law might perhaps be defined as a rule for the infliction of punishment.

H. L. A. Hart, in discussing this question, objects that a person who does not follow the prescribed form in making a will or a contract does not break any law and is not threatened with any penalty.[14] But this misses the point. Wills and contracts are legally binding only because they can be enforced with penalties. It is not the person who makes the will, but those who carry it out, who are threatened with punishment.

Hart responds to objections of this kind with a more general argument that laws play a variety of roles and perform different social functions and that this fact is distorted if the chief emphasis in understanding law is placed on coercion and punishment. Laws are primarily social rules for behavior and for the most part need to be obeyed voluntarily, he maintains. The role of coerion and punishment is merely to provide "a *guarantee* that those who would voluntarily obey shall not be sacrificed to those who would not." The primary significance of law lies not in its threat of penalties, not in what happens in courts of law, let alone in prisons, but "in the diverse ways in which the law is used to control, to guide, and to plan life out of court." Hart considers that the laws which confer powers, such as the power to make a will, or a contract, or trust, belong in a special category, because they "are thought of, spoken of, and used in social life differently from rules which impose duties." The use of law to judge and penalize people is merely "ancillary," he believes.

But the only reason why anyone uses the law to guide and plan his life out of court is that if he does not, he will find himself subjected to an involuntary encounter with a judge and a prison. If Hart's thesis were correct, then when the sanctions of a particular law are no longer enforced, we should still expect the law to be obeyed. But for the most part that is not what happens. The public are typically quick to notice that a law is no longer being enforced, and what we find then is that they do not obey it.

The power to make a contract or a will is not first given to the individual by the law. These are powers or moral rights which every person has. The formalities of the law are or should be for the purpose of ensuring that these powers are recognized and protected in the society. And the fact that many people look on such power-conferring laws in a different light from those which impose duties does not of itself necessarily mean that this view is correct. On the contrary, from the point of view developed in this book, it is naive to imagine that the punitive aspect of law is not always its most distinctive feature. To the extent that law confers power, it does so only by the threat of punishment. A similar comment applies to the laws which confer legislative and judicial powers, for these are simply powers to determine what actions will be punished.

Ronald Dworkin argues that the law in its entirety consists not only of the laws proclaimed by governments, but also of certain moral principles, such as that a criminal should not profit from his crime, and these do not directly have any specific punishment attached to them. His argument is that judges sometimes appeal to such principles in making decisions.[15] But this can be explained in another way. The reason for having a legal system is to impose on the society a certain moral order, an order of justice, and so if the law in a particular case is not clear, the judge is sometimes empowered to render judgement according to his own conception of justice, or the conception which he believes is predominant in his community. The judge's decision is law, because he has the power to impose it by force; but the principles of justice are not law until they are so imposed.

GOVERNMENT ALWAYS A MONOPOLY

What distinguishes government from other human activities is not merely that it has the right to use physical force on persons, but that it has a *monopoly* on that use within its own territory. Government does not brook competition. A government which does not possess a monopoly is not a government.

This can be seen graphically by examining a society which does not possess an effective government, such as Lebanon has recently been. For some dozen years there have been numerous warring factions in that country, each possessing an army, and each occupying a particular territory, but not in such a fashion as to hold an undisputed monopoly of force within it. There has been a nominal government, but not a real one. Having a real government means that one armed force has established its sway over the others, whether by aggression or by negotiation, so that it is recognized as paramount, and can see to it that its commands are carried out. And whatever armed force does so establish its power over the others thereby automatically becomes the government of Lebanon. It seems that this may at long last have happened, and peace has apparently returned to that devastated country.

Now all monopolies have certain well-known features which have been studied intensively by economists, and it will not be irrelevant to indicate some of them here briefly. Stated in economic terms, these features can be summed up under three headings: misallocation of resources compared to a competitive market, lower output, and higher prices. These features should not be understood exclusively in economic or monetary terms, however, but have a broader significance. They are features of the overall way in which any government treats human beings.

In economic theory resources are allocated efficiently when for every good produced, the marginal cost, that is, the cost of producing one more of it in a particular time-period, is equal to the price of the item. If the cost of producing one more dress would be $30, but the best price that can be obtained is only $20, then the supply of dresses exceeds the demand. This means that too much in the way of resources is being used to make dresses. If by contrast the cost of producing one more pair of shoes would be no more than $20, then the resources used in producing the dress would be better used in producing the pair of shoes. "Better" here means that no one would be worse off, and at least one household would be better off. Conversely, if the marginal cost of producing a coat is $40, while a price of $50 can be obtained for it, then there are too few coats being produced: the demand exceeds the supply, and not enough resources are being devoted to the production of coats.

Now a producer in a perfectly competitive market will charge a price for his product which equals his marginal cost of producing it, and will adjust his production up or down till it reaches that point (the demand curve, relating price to quantity, is horizontal, since he cannot influence the market price, or market value, of his product, but only the quantity he produces). In a perfectly competitive market, then, resources are allocated efficiently. But a monopolist will charge a price for his product higher than the marginal cost of producing it (the demand curve for a monopoly is downward-sloping, since a monopolist can influence the market price, but if he raises the price, he must expect to sell less). That is, the demand exceeds the supply, not enough of the goods are being produced. Resources are being underutilized, output is lower, and prices are higher than in a competitive market.

This applies to all the goods and services that government produces, to all the resources that it uses, and to all the prices it charges; that is, the taxes and penalties it imposes, apart from those functions which only government can perform, such as the national defense and the justice system. (This exception is necessary because there is no way in which the efficiency of government in such matters can be measured.)[16]

To say this is to say that, so far as we can measure its efficiency, government is inherently inefficient in the allocation of resources.[17] But this is to make much more than a merely economic statement, important though that is. For the monopoly of government is not merely a monopoly over some material product such as shoes or dresses, but over the use of physical force on human beings for life and death. Whereas the power of an ordinary monopoly is limited to the particular products it produces, the power of government has no such limits. We have seen that monopolistic exchanges which occur in a free market are not truly harmful, but on the contrary beneficial in the way that all market exchanges are, and that free market monopolies can bring certain specific benefits of their own, such as incentives for innovation. But in the case of governmental monopoly the situation is very different.

Monopolies which occur in a free market are only temporary. For in a free market as soon as any monopolist raises his price above the market level, it will be profitable for someone else to enter into competition with him.[18] "In [Britain and Germany] during the twentieth century, as elsewhere in the past, monopolies and large firms that were assumed to be monopolistic were always being formed and always fading or vanishing."[19] Even cartels which have been set up between governments, such as OPEC, have proved to be chronically unstable. It is the search for ways to enter into competition with the monopolist and thus share his exceptional profits which leads to greater innovation.

The Allocative Inefficiency of Monopoly

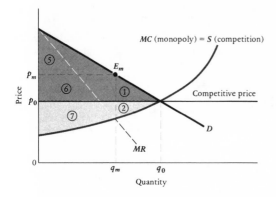

Monopoly is allocatively inefficient because it produces less than the competitive output and thus does not maximize the sum of consumers' and producers' surplus. If this market were perfectly competitive, price would be p_0, output q_0, and consumers' surplus would be the sum of areas 1, 5, and 6 (the dark shaded area). When the industry is monopolized, price rises to p_m, and consumers' surplus falls to area 5. Consumers lose area 1 because that output is not produced; they lose area 6, because the price rise has transferred it to the monopolist.

Producers' surplus in a competitive equilibrium would be the sum of areas 7 and 2 (the light shaded area). When the market is monopolized and price rises to p_m, the surplus area 2 is lost because the output is not produced. But the monopolist gains the area 6 from consumers (6 is known to be greater than 2 because p_m maximizes profits).

While area 6 is transferred from consumers' to producers' surplus by the price rise, *areas 1 and 2 are lost.* They represent the deadweight loss resulting from monopoly and account for its allocative inefficiency.

The Allocative Efficiency of Perfect Competition

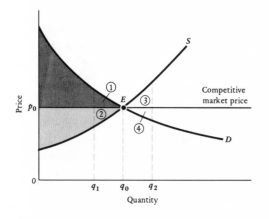

Competitive equilibrium is allocatively efficient because it maximizes the sum of consumers' plus producers' surplus. The competitive equilibrium occurs at the price-output combination, p_0q_0. At that equilibrium consumers' surplus is the dark shaded area above the price line, while producers' surplus is the light shaded area below the price line.

For any output less than q_0 the sum of the two surpluses is less than at q_0. For example, reducing output to q_1, but keeping price p_0, lowers consumers' surplus by area 1 and lowers producers' surplus by area 2.

For any output greater than q_0 the sum of the surpluses is also less than at q_0. For example, if producers are forced to produce output q_2 and sell it to consumers, who are forced to buy it at price p_0, producers' surplus is reduced by area 3 (the amount by which variable costs exceed revenue on those units), while the amount of consumers' surplus is reduced by area 4 (the amount by which expenditure exceeds consumers' satisfactions on those units).

Only the competitive output, q_0, maximizes the sum of the two surpluses.

The monopoly which government possesses in its own territory, however, is not temporary, but permanent. Not only does it remain in place for the society as a whole, but if the government so wishes, it can prevent an individual from escaping its monopoly by physically restricting or abolishing his freedom of movement.

For every good and service which a market monopoly can provide, no matter how unique, some peaceful competition is possible. Some other item can be discovered or invented which will fulfill the same function. Market monopolies are never absolute. But in the case of government no peaceful competition is possible. No other item can be found which will take the place of the right to use physical force.[20] The only competitor for a government is another government, which means war, or the partial equivalent of another government such as the mafia, which rules where it does by force and must be fought with force.[21]

THE ABUSE OF GOVERNMENTAL POWER

This is not to argue that government should be abolished. It is necessary that there should be an authority which has an exclusive monopoly on the use of physical force in society in order to protect the individual against harm caused by others in the society, and in order to protect the society against harm caused by other societies. The example of Lebanon shows what can happen in the absence of effective government. But the monopoly on the use of force which government does and must possess nonetheless makes it extraordinarily dangerous. There is no power which can be so easily abused. Government by the nature of the case possesses in the army and the police, which justify its existence as the protector from harm, almost illimitable potential for causing harm. And if we survey the history of governments even only in the twentieth century, it is not difficult to see that this is no idle observation. The governments of Germany, Japan, the Soviet Union, and China alone have been directly responsible for at least fifty million deaths. It would be difficult to find any corporation which had a similar record. Government is a Frankensteinian monster, which human beings create, but which threatens at all times to devour its creators. Government is necessary, but it is not a necessary good, it is, to repeat, a necessary evil.

This potential for causing harm is the principal reason why a democratic form of government is necessary: in order to subject government effectually so far as possible to rational control by the society. Democracy is necessary, not so that each individual can "participate" and be "involved" in society, but because democracy is the most effective means of ensuring the protection of human rights against government.

But, it might be argued, given that we have a democracy, are we not sufficiently protected from the abuse of government power that we can justly look upon it as benevolent? After all, we do have a system of checks and balances in place, and government policies that do not meet with popular approval are often speedily reversed.

There can be no doubt that a democratic or representative form of government is much less likely to be abused than other forms, but that does not mean that government is necessarily benevolent. The United States had representative government for almost a century before the Civil War, yet that government and the courts supported slavery. Even after the Civil War, blacks were subjected to constant abuse of governmental power in some portions of the country. There is good reason to believe that the Great Depression was due principally to government policies such as high interest rates and laws restricting international trade. To this day, anyone who has been in a dependent relationship with government can testify to the arbitrary way in which governmental power is likely to be used. In any issue, the chances are that an elected government will respond not to the internal requirements of the issue itself, but to what they believe will win votes, and while this is better than ignoring the desires of the people, majority rule is by no means always sensitive to questions of human rights. The government bureaucracy, for its part, responds to its own career motivations, as Public Choice theory has made clear.[22]

ECONOMIC DEMOCRACY

At the beginning of this chapter we mentioned briefly the notion of economic democracy. One advocate of this is Peter Bachrach, who has expressed the not uncommon view that the political sector should be extended to include the economy. Major economic decisions should be made by the political authority. Bachrach holds that large firms such as General Motors, which "authoritatively allocate values for the society," should be nationalized, or otherwise subject to legal control by employees, suppliers, customers, and consumers in general, as well as stockholders. The economy must be "democratized" in this sense in order to secure the survival of democracy. The reason for this is that "the majority of individuals stand to gain in self-esteem and growth toward a fuller affirmation of their personalities by participating more actively in meaningful community decisions."[23] He recognizes that only government has a monopoly on the legal use of force but does not consider that a sufficiently distinctive mark of government because he thinks of economic power as similar to the use of force. Bachrach is honest enough to admit that his system may not be workable, either politically or economically, but thinks that it "borders on dogmatism to reject this challenge out of hand."[24]

Such an approach fails to see the moral difference between voluntary agreement and the use of force. In what sense of "authority" does General Motors "authoritatively allocate values for the society?" General Motors has authority only over its employees and only on condition that they wish to remain its employees. It is an abuse of the notion of authority to apply it to the relationship of a firm with its customers or suppliers, whose only bond with it is a free decision to trade with it. Presumably Bachrach means by "authoritative" here merely that General Motors is effective in persuading Americans to accept what he thinks of as its materialistic values, that is, to buy more cars made by General Motors. But if General Motors is so effective in communicating its values to American society, how does it happen that the company is now suffering such a severe drop in its share of the market? The reason it is experiencing this decline is that increasing numbers of Americans have rejected the cars which General Motors makes because they have found that Japanese cars are better made and cost less. Americans can do this because General Motors is precisely not a government, imposing its will by force, but merely a participant in the market, subject like other participants to competition and the voluntary choices of customers.

Political systems, which are set up by the use of force, are not the moral equivalent of the market system, which develops by voluntary agreement. Bachrach's approach has lost the sense of moral outrage at the unjustifiable use of force on people who have done no harm. Although he claims to reject elitism, his theory is essentially elitist, like all forms of social engineering, in that he is willing to treat human society as a guinea pig for forcible experimentation. Even though his proposals may not be workable either economically or politically, that should not deter us from trying them, he maintains. If it fails, that is, if we discover we have used force on an entire society to no purpose, why then, we will know we were wrong! This scarcely seems a humane attitude.

THE DEHUMANIZING EFFECT OF UNNECESSARY LAWS

Since it is of the essence of law to threaten the use of force, a society which is subjected to unnecessary laws is threatened constantly with the unnecessary use of force. It was pointed out above that the use of force on a person automatically diminishes his autonomy, which is arguably the most precious possession any person has. It is by the use of his autonomy, by exercising his power to make decisions even when that means

making a mistake, that a person acquires maturity and becomes a responsible individual. A society which habitually indulges in the unnecessary
use of force on its citizens inhibits their growth towards maturity, lessens
their sense of personal responsibility, and lowers their standards for the
treatment of others, making them more ready to employ force on each
other. No doubt it is possible for the majority in a society to obey the laws,
and so to be subjected only to the threat and not to the actual use of force.
But if the threat is not fully equivalent to the use, it is equivalent in large
measure. Unnecessary laws brutalize.

Law, then, is not a neutral or indifferent instrument for the achievement of an end. It is an instrument which ought to be avoided so far as
at all possible and used only when necessary. In a civilized society there
will be a positive presumption *against* the use of legislation as a solution
for problems.

No doubt there will be disagreement as to what laws are necessary.
But someone who takes the idea of necessity seriously here will not be
disposed to confuse it with what merely "seems to be a good idea." To say
that some means is necessary to achieve some end is to say that the end
cannot be attained without the use of that means. Necessity should be
demonstrated, not merely assumed on the basis of some abstract theory.
We have argued in the previous chapters that at least the laws enacted to
protect buyers and sellers from one another, and to protect against
competition and monopoly, rest on misunderstandings and are unnecessary. But quite apart from the question as to what laws are necessary, it
would be possible to have general agreement that in itself legislation is a
burden, which in the absence of a clear and certain necessity ought not to
be imposed.

THE MARKET AND HUMAN VALUES

If government does not stand necessarily for concern for others, market
freedom does not stand for selfishness and greed. True, in a free market
there will be no legal penalty for selfishness. But to hold that people
should not be punished by the law for being selfish is not to condone
selfishness. The law does not punish those who tell lies or speak foolishly, or who fail to keep their appointments, but that does not mean it
endorses lies and foolish speech and unreliability. Freedom implies the
freedom to make mistakes, but to advocate that people should have
freedom is not to advocate that they should make mistakes.

Since market freedom is solely a question of what laws there are and
has nothing to say about people's motivations, logically speaking the
accusation can scarcely be leveled against it that it embodies greed and

selfishness. It may make more sense to direct such a charge against capitalism, where motivation plays an explicit role. In the Introduction it was pointed out that free markets are not identical with capitalism, and to defend the one is not necessarily to defend the other. Nonetheless it cannot be denied that in the modern world there is a very close link between them, and so perhaps for the sake of clarity an argument for market freedom should take account of this question. Even as an accusation against capitalism, however, the charge is misdirected.

There is such a thing as legitimate self-interest, which is not to be identified with selfishness. Selfishness is a spiritual immaturity. But legitimate self-interest is simply a concern within certain reasonable bounds to continue to exist and to carry out those activities on which one's continued existence depends or by which it may be made easier. This is not spiritual immaturity, but on the contrary something as good as existence itself and may even be considered an obligation incumbent on a rational person.

The market system does not require selfishness in order to operate. It works very much better when it is animated by a humane concern for the welfare of employees and customers, and, we might add, a similar concern on the part of employees for the welfare of employers. The market system presumes, however, that many people will be animated by self-interest, and it sees nothing wrong with that. The genius of the market system is that it channels people's natural self-interest in such a way as to make it productive for others, since, as we have seen, every exchange benefits both buyer and seller.

The economic superiority of the market system over socialism stems from the fact that it needs fewer conditions in order to operate successfully. If we compare two systems, one of which needs to have only one condition fulfilled in order to operate effectively, while the other needs two, the first will be twice as likely as the second to succeed, other things being equal. Although the market system will certainly function better if buyers and sellers are animated by generosity and concern for others, it does not *need* more than selfishness, a condition which is easy to fulfill. But this is not true of socialism. Socialism will not work unless there is a heroically high level of *unselfishness*, a condition which is extremely difficult if not impossible to fulfill in the present state of development of the human race. When people say, as some still do, despite the recent events in Eastern Europe, that in the ideal world socialism would prevail, what they have in mind is the idea of a society in which people are concerned for one another's welfare. That would indeed characterize the ideal world. But what they overlook is that to make this ideal a *precondition* for the survival of society is to destroy society.

For the rest, it is remarkable how the proponents of economic regulation are willing to overlook selfishness and greed when exercised by their own favorites. The terms demanded by trade unions, for example, must smack of these vices to an impartial observer at least as often as the terms proposed by employers, but are rarely if ever castigated. On the other hand, the market can be severe in its punishment of the "capitalist's" selfishness and greed, for these can easily lead him to overreach himself, to bite off more than he can chew, with devastating results. But even the capitalist who goes bankrupt after acting prudently and rationally, merely because of the unpredictable forces of the market, is not typically overwhelmed with sympathy from the proponents of social compassion.

COERCED VS. VOLUNTARY COMMUNITY

At the beginning of this chapter we posed the question of the relationship of the individual to the community. We noted the view, which has become widespread among the educated elite, that the idea of a free, unimpeded market stands for selfishness and a lack of a sense of community, whereas government regulation of the market is felt to be necessary in order to create community and participation. In the light of the essentially coercive and penalizing role of government on the one hand, however, and of the essentially beneficent nature of the market on the other, it becomes clear that the question about community needs to be put in different terms. The choice between an unregulated market and a regulated one is not a choice between selfishness and community, but a choice between *two kinds of community, one voluntary and one created by force*. We need only to state this second notion, however, in order to see that it has grave problems. Is it possible to create a genuine community by law, that is, by the use of physical force?

If by a community we mean a group of people who share an inner attitude of mutual concern for one another's welfare in a positive sense, it is surely clear that law by itself, no matter with what penalties it may be fitted out, is utterly incapable of creating such a reality. The army and the police can no doubt alter people's external behavior, but they cannot transform their hearts. The threat of imprisonment may compel people to live or work in the same place, but it cannot make them love one another. Concern for the welfare of others is something that must develop willingly.

But, it may be replied, the law can induce people to change their external behavior towards one another, and the value of that ought not to be underestimated. Perhaps we cannot compel people to love one another, but we can compel them not to discriminate against one another in employment. Furthermore, the law can perform an educative role, holding up a standard of behavior which can gradually, over a period of time, have an effect on people's inner attitudes.

It is of course true that a threat of imprisonment can concentrate the mind. But it is also possible that the effect of that on people's inner attitudes may be just the opposite of what is intended. It is possible, and even likely, that by compelling them to do something against their will, you will make them hate and detest it even more violently. The communist parties of Eastern Europe and China were not more beloved after forty years of power.

If you wish to compel people successfully by law to behave in a certain way, you must first convince them that it is *just*. And for that to be successful in the long run it must actually *be* just. It is our contention in these pages, however, that government restriction of economic freedom is inherently unjust.

It is remarkable that so many philosophers and teachers, intellectuals and academics, who have dedicated their lives to the proposition that reason and persuasion are superior to mere force as means of settling disagreements, in the matter of the economy have become ardent supporters of the use of force.

Even if it were possible to create a genuine community by the threat of punishment, however, it may be questionable whether that would always and under all circumstances be desirable. Even though a group of people are mutually concerned for one another's welfare, that very fact can be the cause of other problems equally if not more severe. One typical feature of closely knit communities, for example, is intolerance of diversity, dissent and innovation: there is pressure to conform to the social norm. Closely knit societies typically experience a diminution of privacy: it is felt to be acceptable to subject the life of the individual to scrutiny, even where it does not impinge particularly on the existence of others. Small towns are notorious for their narrow-mindedness, and escape to the anonymity of the city can be experienced as a liberation.

On the other hand, it is easy to underestimate the positive effects of freedom. It is not necessarily the case that a free society will be a selfish society. On the contrary, if the experience of the United States is any guide, the opposite is true. In this respect the author, as one who first came to the United States as an adult, feels entitled to speak from personal experience. Americans are justly known for their generosity, their concern for others, and their tolerance of diversity, by comparison with other peoples. Possibly this is a cultural trait which is essentially independent of their experience of economic freedom. But possibly it is in large measure the product of this freedom. This is an empirical question, to be settled by empirical means. Do other societies which have free economies exhibit similar tendencies? (A test case might perhaps be Hong Kong, since it has enjoyed a good measure of economic freedom, and the people of Hong Kong are culturally very similar to those of mainland China. Historically the focus of the Chinese people's concern has been above all their family. However, a transformation of character towards a universal generosity must conceivably take some length of time, which it seems Hong Kong is not to have if the dictatorship of the mainland is extended to it in 1997.) In the meantime we shall formulate this as a thesis, to be tested empirically: all things else being equal, a society that enjoys economic freedom is likely to be a more generous, tolerant, and caring society.

NONMARKET VALUE SYSTEMS

The economic success of capitalism has made possible the development of a large and growing segment of society which can afford to occupy itself with kinds of activity which are guided by their own internal values and standards rather than those of the market. Artists, scientists, physicians, academics, teachers, journalists, lawyers, including those who teach in law schools or are judges, and many other professions identify themselves by standards which to one extent or another explicitly reject the standards of the market. A natural consequence of this is a tendency on the part of such people to despise the market system itself and to feel that if the universe were properly organized, some other system would prevail in which the kinds of standards and values which describe good work in a profession would alone govern success or failure, independently of the market. A recent example is provided by the editor in chief of the *New England Journal of Medicine,* one of the most influential members of the medical profession, who was reported as stating that "the American health-care system, abetted by deluded White House policies, has become dangerously profit-oriented and desperately needs to reaffirm basic professional values. . . . Business and professional values do not mix comfortably in the practice of medicine," he is described as saying, and "an emerging commercial-industrial approach to health care is converting much of the health-care system into a vast and competitive marketplace."[25]

The rejection of market values as standards for the professions in and of themselves is perfectly right and necessary. Exchange values are by no means the only values. The standards of good scientific work, of good scholarship, of literary merit, of artistic achievement, of faithful reportage, of responsible medical care—all of these standards are different from the standards of the market and independent of them. So long as such activities do not form part of the market and are not market activities, there is no reason why market values should supervene on them. So long as the artist is painting only for his own gratification, he can and should judge his work according to the internal standards of art which decide what is good and what is poor artistic work. So long as the physician or the professor is not charging a fee, he can and should follow the internal standards of his profession which dictate what is good medical or academic work.

But once such activities are used for the purpose of making a living and a fee is charged for them, they are used as items in an exchange; they are introduced into the market and transformed into market activities, and it is illogical and self-contradictory to expect that market values and standards should not apply to them. So long as the physician dispenses care free of charge, he can follow exclusively the dictates of his professional conscience, but as soon as he wishes to obtain an income from his work (which he is of course fully entitled to do), he is in competition with all the other physicians who desire the same thing; and for that purpose different standards may apply.

Some forms of surgery may be attractive, not for medical reasons, but for cosmetic ones. What makes a best-selling novel is not necessarily literary merit; what makes a professor popular is not necessarily the high quality of his scholarship; what earns a physician the largest income is not necessarily that he has the most scientific approach to illness. Whether there is a demand for literary merit on the part of the buying public is a different question altogether from the question whether a particular novel or poem possesses literary merit. Coping with these two sets of standards at the same time is often a complex and difficult task, but it has to be accepted as part of life. It is often easy to feel that professional standards are superior to market standards, and while in a certain sense this is true, in another sense it is false. It is true in the sense that from the viewpoint of literary merit Tolstoy is superior to Agatha Christie. But there is a reason why Agatha Christie sells more copies than Tolstoy; namely, that she provides harassed people with relaxation, and this also is valuable and meritorious, and in a way which does not easily lend itself to a simple comparison of "better" or "worse" with Tolstoy. The desirability of maintaining high professional standards and the consequent rejection of the standards of the market so far as those professional standards go should not lead to a rejection of the market *system*.

IS SOCIETY PRIOR TO THE INDIVIDUAL?

The question whether government regulation of the market can be morally justified is sometimes discussed in terms of the question whether society is prior to the individual, or the individual to society. Aristotle maintained that society was prior to the individual, on the analogy of living organisms, where, he said, the whole is prior to the part, in the sense that the part, such as a hand or a foot, can have no independent existence as a living thing if it is once cut off from the organism.[26] To maintain that society has priority over the individual is in general to hold that the existence and needs of the individual should be subservient to the existence and needs of the society, and therefore it can be legitimate to sacrifice the individual for the sake of society. This has typically been the view of most traditional societies, and in the twentieth century, of totalitarian ones. To maintain, on the other hand, that the individual has priority over society is to assert the opposite, that society exists only to further the well-being of the individual, and that the individual has a worth in himself which cannot be subordinated to social concerns. This has typically been the stance of those societies which embody a commitment to human rights. A third position sometimes taken is that individual and society have equal priority, neither one having precedence over the other, though it is not very clear what the implications of this might be.[27]

Those who defend government interference in the economy almost invariably reject the view that the individual is prior to society. At the least individual and society are seen as having equal priority, and often it is held that the individual derives everything of significance from society. This view seems to stem largely from the fact that human beings enter the world as children of other human beings, dependent on them, and through them on the larger society, not only for their existence but also for their education. This is no doubt true, but to go on to replace the idea of society with the idea of government in this equation is to exaggerate the extent to which society and government are one. Society is not identical with government, and to be dependent on society, that is, on the help of other human beings, is not by any means the same thing as to be dependent on government. It is not government which gives birth to the child and brings it up, but its parents. In order to make a case for government interference in the market, it is not sufficient to establish a dependence on society.

Furthermore, the thesis of dependence on society fails to do justice to the creative freedom of the individual. However much it may be true that society is a necessary condition for the achievements of the individual, it is not a sufficient condition for them. No doubt Columbus could not have achieved what he did without the help of many other people, but it still remained up to him, to his imagination, his initiative, his courage, his determination, his seamanship, his leadership of men, to his own irreplaceable will and his own unique character, that he crossed the Atlantic successfully. No amount of study of society will enable us to predict the accomplishments of a Newton, an Edison, or an Einstein, not to mention the host of ordinary people who keep the world running.

A society or community is not an entity with an independent existence, it is a set of relationships between 'individual people. To say that individuals are dependent on society is just to say that they are dependent on other individuals.

To see individuals primarily as members of society does not do justice to their unique reality. Only individuals laugh, only individuals cry, only individuals love and hate, imagine and invent, think and feel, make decisions and regret them, only individuals ask questions, and only individuals have a conscience. "Society" does none of these things.

COLLECTIVE RESPONSIBILITY

Traditional societies typically see the individual chiefly as a member of a group, of a family or a tribe. One consequence of this is a doctrine of collective responsibility: the entire tribe or family is held answerable for the transgressions of the individual, and "the sins of the fathers are visited on the children." It was a revolutionary step forward when this primitive conception was abandoned, largely under the influence of the Judaeo-Christian religious tradition, and each individual came to be treated as an entity in himself, to be praised or blamed solely for what he alone had done. This is the origin of the idea of human rights. As we shall see, it is exceedingly difficult if not impossible for a communitarian philosophy to maintain the idea of human rights in a consistent manner. Human rights are essentially individual rights. The doctrine of "group rights," which gives special legal privileges to special groups,[28] however deserving they may be, and the doctrine of reverse discrimination, which makes it possible to inflict legal penalties on an individual solely because of his membership in a group, are directly hostile to the concept of human rights.

ABOLISHING CHANCE

Redistributive theories of justice often have their origin in the desire to remove the dominion of chance over people's lives. If the individual is left to himself, there is always the possibility that he may fail due to no fault of his own. Whereas if society has the enforceable obligation of taking care of its needy, then, it is believed, every individual can be guaranteed at least the minimum necessary for survival.

But this idea is an illusion. Redistributive schemes do not eliminate chance, but merely distribute it over the society, which itself always remains subject to chance. As soon as a society attempts to provide economic guarantees to any large number of citizens, the combined weight of chance in a purely negative sense begins to drag the entire society down. This is essentially the fate which socialism inflicted on the nations of Eastern Europe.

Furthermore, the chance involved is no longer just the sum of the individual instances of chance, which would be bad enough, but is systematically increased. Just as any insurance system increases the incidence of what is insured against, just as any system of insuring houses against fire, for example, will result in an increase in the number of fires, so any attempt to provide economic guarantees for a whole population increases the likelihood of economic deterioration for that society. *A society cannot guarantee itself merely by passing laws.*

We are irretrievably dependent on the voluntary benefits that others make available to us. So long as it is possible for one individual to make a life-saving discovery or invent a life-saving technique, so long will others be dependent on him for their lives. This is not a condition that can be eliminated, or that we should wish to eliminate if we could.

SOCIAL COHESION

Among the things that are usually counted as good for any society is a certain minimum of cohesion, social unity. Now it is often argued that redistributive schemes are necessary in order to preserve social unity: if serious economic inequalities are evident, the cohesion of society will be threatened. But again, this is a misjudgement; for redistributive schemes do not increase the unity of a society, but detract from it because they make the policy of the society inimical to an important and valuable section of it, the wealthy and talented. A wealthy or talented person has no economic motive to remain a member of a redistributive society; indeed he has every economic motive to leave it because he is systematically discriminated against, not merely by individuals in the market, but, what is a much more serious matter, forcibly by the law. Socialist societies have acted wisely according to their lights in prohibiting emigration, for otherwise every competent person not held by emotional ties will seek to emigrate from them, as we witnessed dramatically in the case of East Germany during the autumn of 1989 in the flood of emigration which took place as soon as it was allowed. And this phenomenon is by no means restricted to socialist countries, but is also evident in the "brain-drain" from more highly redistributive societies in the West, such as Great Britain, to ones which are less so, such as the United States.

Redistributive societies alienate not only the talented and wealthy, however, but also the disadvantaged, because they foster an unjustified resentment against other members of the society and against the society itself. Redistributive societies convey a very clear message to the less fortunate that they are entitled as a matter of justice to live off other people's labor and to receive something for nothing. Some people imagine that the outcome of this will be, if not gratitude and love towards the society, at least reconciliation and peace with it. But in point of fact the result may more typically be hatred and contempt for the society, for, human nature being what it is, it may be assumed that the benefits being received stem not from the moral sense of others but from their mere weakness and from the recipients' emerging power, a view which perhaps will encourage them to exercise more ruthlessly the power they have. Furthermore, it is the society at large which is now likely to be taken as the cause of their current as well as their past misfortune. The remedy can lie only in measures which harm the rest of society. Society is no longer a cooperative venture from which all may look to benefit, but a zero-sum enterprise in which gains for some must be obtained at the price of harm to others. It is not a great step from this to the view that anything which harms the others will be good for oneself. It scarcely needs saying that this is likely to be exceedingly destructive of the society.

If we genuinely wish to have a society which is animated by a spirit of concern for others, a society in which human beings can prosper and flourish, then we will wish above all else to have a society which is free. And for the bulk of mankind there can be no doubt that the form of freedom which they chiefly prize is economic freedom.

7

Justice and the Principle of No Harm

LAW

The idea of justice regulates the use of force, and so is intrinsically linked with the idea of law. To say that something is unjust is by that very fact in the common understanding to say that it should be forbidden by law.

Because of their relevance to the topic of this chapter, we shall repeat here some observations made in previous chapters. All laws threaten to *punish*, and to do so *physically*.[1] To make a law is to threaten to punish by the use of physical force, by means of the police, handcuffs, prison, and possibly death, those who break the law. A fine is no exception to this, for if a person refuses to pay the fine he may be taken forcibly to jail. Law can never be merely an educational tool, or a gentle suggestion. It is precisely because laws threaten punishment that justice must be enforced by law. The idea of punishment is inseparable from the idea of law and from the idea of justice.

The question as to what is just and unjust, and what laws to make and what to rescind, then, is inescapably a question about punishment. It can be formulated as the question: Who ought to be punished?

In general terms there can be only one answer to this question: those who deserve punishment. A law which punishes people who do not deserve punishment is universally felt to be unjust and intolerable. We quoted earlier the forceful statement of F. H. Bradley on this subject, but we take the liberty of repeating it here:

> Punishment is punishment only when it is deserved. We pay the penalty because we owe it, and for no other reason; and if punishment is inflicted for any other reason than because it is merited by wrong, it is a gross immorality, a crying injustice, an abominable crime, and not what it pretends to be.

Therefore the question as to what is just and unjust can be raised by asking: Who deserves punishment?

The answer to this question cannot be: Whoever breaks the law; or even: Whoever breaks the laws passed by a democratically elected government. For it is possible to have unjust laws, including those passed by a democratically elected government. There cannot therefore be any blanket rule that whoever breaks any law deserves punishment.

(To be sure, there are certain kinds of law, chiefly having to do with procedures for interactions between people, where just by the fact that there is a law, a special expectation is created that others will observe the law, and in those cases a person may cause harm to others just by the fact of breaking the law and will deserve punishment. The reason he deserves punishment, however, is that he has caused harm, rather than simply that he has broken a law. An example might be a traffic law. Traffic laws are not in general good examples of law because the justification for their existence comes not so much from the necessity of governing as from ownership of the road. Anyone who owns a road is entitled to make what rules he likes for the use of it, as we observed earlier, and in the system currently in force most roads are owned by government. But given that there is a law requiring cars to drive on the right, if a person willfully drove on the left against a stream of traffic, it might well be the case that he caused harm by that simple fact. Had there been no law, for example if the case instead were that of riding a bicycle on a path where no direction was prescribed for traffic, no harm would have been done by driving on the left. The fact that there is a law establishes a presumption in this case which others are entitled to rely on regarding the way people will behave. It would be a mistake, however, to universalize this, and conclude that the task of government is to preserve "order" in some general sense and that therefore to break any law is to cause disorder and harm. There are many laws which can be broken without causing any harm whatsoever, and there are many laws obedience to which causes harm.)

It has no significance for the justice of a law if in point of fact few get punished because few break the law. An unjust law does not become just by the fact that it is obeyed. It is the *threat* of undeserved punishment which makes the law unjust.

THE PRINCIPLE OF NO HARM

When do people deserve punishment? There seems to be widespread agreement, among those not distracted by considerations of self-interest or ideology, on a set of related principles which provide the answer to this question, focusing on the idea of harm.

1) Human beings ought not to be harmed against their will, unless they have caused harm.

2) Those who deliberately cause harm to the innocent (that is, to those who have not caused harm) deserve to be punished proportionately.

3) Those who do not cause harm deliberately do not deserve to be punished.

4) Those who cause harm inadvertently must repair the harm, and if they do not do so deserve to be punished.

To this we must add:

5) Under certain circumstances, specified by the Principle of the Double Effect, it is permissible to do an action deliberately which will have the undesired effect of causing harm to an innocent person.

The relevance of these principles to the market will be sufficiently clear. We have shown in Chapters 2 and 3 that, so long as there is no mistake, force, or fraud, buyers and sellers do not harm one another, but benefit one another, no matter what the terms of their agreement; and that competitors likewise do not cause harm to one another. It follows from the principles of No Harm that there can be no moral justification for laws which punish people for engaging in any kind of market activity unless it involves force or fraud. Further, redistributive laws, such as the imposition of taxes on some in order to pay for subsidies to others, or the "deep pockets" theory of tort liability, since they cause harm to people who have not caused harm, are similarly violations of the principles of No Harm.

In the remainder of this discussion when there is reference to causing harm, it should be understood that it is the *deliberate* causing of harm that is meant, unless something else is specified. That is, our focus is on the first three principles.

The first principle expresses what I take to be the basic principle underlying the concept of justice. It is directly necessitated by the view that all human beings possess an equal dignity as human beings. To say that human beings are essentially equal is above all to say that no one ought to inflict harm on another unless that other has himself caused harm or is threatening to cause harm.[2]

As may be imagined, the principle has a long history. It can be found at least implicitly in Cicero. Locke lays it explicitly as the foundation for his argument that government must have the consent of the people:

> "Reason . . . teaches all mankind, who will but consult it, that being all equal and independent, no one ought to harm another in his life, health, liberty, or possessions. . . . Every one . . . may not, unless it be to do justice on an offender, take away, or impair the life, or what tends to the preservation of the life, liberty, health, limb, or goods of another."[3]

The reason for the second principle is that it is necessary to sustain the first. To be unwilling to punish those who cause significant harm is not to be serious about the first principle. Of course punishment should be administered with humanity, but it must be administered. While a private individual may be willing to forego punishing someone who has harmed him, the law has no right to waive punishment. Where harm has been done the law must sternly if regretfully inflict punishment, otherwise it fails to defend those entrusted to its care. It is not sufficient to meet the demands of morality as expressed in the principles of No Harm that the treatment of the offender should be restricted to reformation or deterrence, which are essentially psychological aims rather than moral ones. Humanity towards the criminal, desirable though that is, is no substitute for justice for the victim.

The third principle is simply a necessary consequence of the first and second. Since no one ought to be harmed unless he has himself done harm, and since punishment is a form of harm, it follows necessarily that people who have done no harm should not be punished.

In the discussion that follows, when mention is made of the Principle of No Harm, without any additional qualification, it refers to all three principles or sub-principles taken together as a unity. The individual sub-principles are referred to as the First, Second, and Third Principles.

THE FIRST PRINCIPLE
HUMAN BEINGS OUGHT NOT TO BE HARMED AGAINST THEIR WILL, UNLESS THEY HAVE CAUSED HARM.

CRIME

Perhaps the best approach to the Principle of No Harm is by means of the concept of a crime. Crime is of course a legal concept, but it is also and prior to that a moral one. As a legal concept crime is whatever some society has declared to be a crime by threatening to punish, and so it admits of a great deal of variation between one society and another. Activities which incur no criminal penalties at all in one society may incur heavy penalties in another. But the legal concept of crime is dependent for its moral force and authority on the fact that it represents an attempt to put into practice in society a certain moral perception of special importance, a perception which is widespread if not universal. This perception is that there are certain actions which are morally outrageous and which cannot be tolerated. Such actions are chiefly the deliberate infliction of injury to a person's body or property, and those which cause notable harm to the society as such—for example, treason. These activities constitute what we may consider to be the core or essence of the idea of crime. Other actions which may be classified legally under the same heading derive their association with the idea of crime by extension from these core actions, for example because of a theory which declares them to be equally harmful in some respect, or because their exclusion is felt to be a necessary condition for the effective exclusion of core crime.

The core moral perception that certain actions are intolerable is in the first instance a perception on the part of the members of the society. As a consequence there is often a considerable gap between what the law condemns as a crime and what the average man or the public at large considers to be one. "To the average citizen crime means both something less and something more than the legal term implies. He tends to view traditional offenses against the state, life, property and morals as crimes, but to his mind a great many petty offenses do not merit that designation. . . ."[4] "Crime means to the ordinary man something that is sinful and immoral."[5] The concept of a crime is not simply a factual or descriptive category, but in the first place an evaluative one. The designation of an action as criminal has to be earned. And the moral sense of the public at large is likely to be all in all a better guide to the criminal status of an action in the moral sense than the fact that it is declared to be a crime by the law — a fact which is recognized legally by institutions designed to give a voice in the administration of justice to typical members of the society who are not legal experts, such as the jury or the lay judge.

A person commits a crime in the moral sense, then, when he performs an action knowingly and willingly which causes substantial harm, either to an individual or to society. The moral detestation of such activity exemplifies the First Principle, that persons who have not caused harm ought not to be harmed. The criminal law which is a product of that detestation expresses the Second Principle, that those who cause harm to the innocent deserve to be punished. Since the large majority of people accept the concept of crime, detest crime, and support legal punishment for it, in that sense and to that extent they already accept the Principle of No Harm. Causing harm to the innocent would seem in fact to be the quintessence of what we mean by the notion of "morally wrong." Anyone who wishes to cast doubt on this principle has the burden of coming up with an alternative theory as to the principle on which it is wrong to commit murder or robbery.[6]

THEORETICAL BASIS OF THE PRINCIPLE

If it is true that the Principle of No Harm is simply an unpacking or explication of what is implicit in the elementary belief that it is wrong to kill or injure an innocent person, then the task of providing a theoretical justification for it is not as urgent as it is in the case of other moral beliefs. For the validity of this insight cannot be dependent on some prior philosophical theory. That actions such as murder and robbery are criminal and deserve punishment is one of the most fundamental moral intuitions of mankind, and one which has the strongest claim to acceptance on its own terms. We do not need a theoretical construction to tell us that it is valid. Although theoretical considerations may be useful in clarifying this insight, as they can also muddy it, any moral theory we develop must assume its essential validity and be dependent on it.

Nonetheless, there are theoretical reflections which can lend support to the principle. There are, in the first place, arguments for it which might be employed, but which we shall not employ: It could be defended on the grounds of utility, as Mill does.[7] A rule utilitarianism may support the principle on the pragmatic grounds that it is needed to maximize human happiness or well-being.[8] We shall return to the question of utilitarianism more fully below, where we shall see some of the reasons which make it unfit to provide the sole foundations of morality. The principle could also be defended on the grounds of self-interest. Given that society consists of many persons who have powers roughly equal to mine, it might be to my benefit to reach and keep an agreement with them that none of us shall harm another. Both kinds of arguments, if indulged in exclusively, would have the effect of reducing the Principle of No Harm to nonmoral factors, however, which runs counter to our ordinary conception of morality.

The common conception of morality, and especially of justice, is that it is something entirely different from utility, and also from self-interest. The common conception of morality, and especially of justice, is essentially of the sort which it is customary to call Kantian. This kind of conception assumes that the moral point of view is inherently different from a nonmoral one, and especially from a self-interested one. The chief difficulty of the Kantian conception of morality is that it is thought to provide no method for settling disputes as to what ought to be done, but must rely on moral intuition, which appears to be subjective and always open to question. Whether this is really true, however, may prove to be not quite so clear as is commonly assumed. But even granted that the Kantian position suffers from this problem, the problems afflicting the alternatives to it are still greater. On the other hand the great virtue of the Kantian conception is that, in contrast to utilitarian and egoistic theories, it corresponds faithfully to what is commonly meant by morality. Here I will attempt briefly to point out some considerations which give support to the principle from a Kantian position.

We may begin with the notion of a species. In biology the notion of species refers to physical characteristics, but when we are dealing with human beings it is necessary to understand the notion of species in a deeper sense, because many of the characteristics which distinguish human beings from other species are mental and spiritual. Human beings possess the ability to make free choices (we shall assume). To that extent their actions are removed from the realm of physical necessity. But this does not mean that they are removed from every kind of necessity. There is a unique kind of necessity, neither causal nor merely logical, which arises specifically in regard to free choice, that is, in the way in which one being with free choice, a person, deals with another person. We call this moral necessity, or obligation. The primary moral necessity is not to use physical force to damage the integrity of the person.

The fact that a being has the ability to make free choices implies that it has the power of self-government, or autonomy. The integrity of the person includes his bodily integrity but is not restricted to that; it also and most especially therefore embraces his power of self-government. The most fundamental obligation is, then, not to deprive a person, by physical force, of his power of self-government, subjecting him again to the dominion of physical necessity. Coercion, the use of physical force to deprive an adult human being of the power of self-government, is intrinsically harmful and wrong, unless he has deserved it by causing harm to others.[9]

Because they possess the ability to make free choices, human beings possess the ability to understand and employ moral concepts, an ability possessed by no other species of which we have knowledge. On this basis we may derive three concepts, that of moral equality, and its counterpart pair, moral superiority and inferiority. The ability to make free choices, and so to grasp and employ moral concepts, confers a moral equality on all human beings as members of the human species. It also makes them morally superior to other species.

The basic moral concept is the one mentioned above, that of moral necessity, or obligation. The first necessity is to respect the moral equality of other persons by respecting the freedom of choice and power of self-government which they possess as members of the same species as ourselves. The impartiality and universalizability of moral judgements is derivable from the equality of human beings as members of such a species.

The line of thought we have followed here was stated in its essential points by Locke:

> Reason . . . teaches all mankind, who will but consult it, that being all *equal and independent*, no one ought to harm another in his life, liberty or possessions. For men being all the workmanship of one omnipotent and infinitely wise maker, all the servants of one sovereign master, sent into the world by his order, and about his business, they are his property, whose workmanship

they are, made to last during his, not one another's pleasure. And being furnished with like faculties, sharing all in one community of nature, there cannot be supposed any such *subordination* among us, that may authorize us to destroy one another, as if we were made for one another's uses, as the inferior ranks of creatures are for ours.[10]

But if I have the physical power to benefit myself by using physical force on another person, depriving him of his freedom and autonomy, what grounds are there for me not to do it? The answer to this lies in the fact that I am not only this particular individual, I am also a member of this species. The full reality of an individual person is not exhausted by those features of his existence which are individually and uniquely his, but also includes the features which he shares of necessity with others of his species. In causing harm to his fellow-man he is negating the value of his own nature and placing himself spiritually in a state of contradiction.

It is true that since the rise of the empirical sciences in the seventeenth century the concept of human nature or essence as a collection of necessary properties has been widely rejected by philosophers, since such necessity is neither an empirical concept nor one of logic. But the result of this has been to abolish any difference in principle between persons and other kinds of beings, and to undermine the most ordinary insights of morality. If there is no *essential* difference between human beings and cabbages, why should there be any moral difference between shooting a cabbage and shooting a human being? Philosophical attempts to find substitutes for the concept of human nature have been notoriously unsuccessful.

FREE WILL

The view has become widely accepted among theoreticians that there is no such thing as free will. The chief reason for this is the fact that we observe the undisputed reign of causality throughout the material universe. There are no exceptions that we know of to the rule that everything has a cause which predetermines the outcome of events, and it is difficult to see how human actions could be an exception. While this picture has been modified slightly by quantum physics, which has shown that on the atomic level events are only statistically predictable, it is not felt in general that the deterministic world-view needs to be fundamentally overturned because of this. Besides, free will is not an empirical phenomenon.

The assumption that human actions are essentially predetermined either by external or internal forces is especially common, perhaps, in the social sciences. Much of sociology treats of human behavior on the assumption that it is necessitated by social factors. Psychologists not infrequently assume that it is determined by psychological forces. Theoretical criminologists have almost universally abandoned the traditional view that criminals possess the power to act otherwise than they do.

On the other hand, however, it can scarcely be denied that there are powerful reasons to accept the view that sane, conscious adults have free will, reasons which are often not given their due. The first reason is our direct universal consciousness that we have the ability to choose, to do otherwise than we do.

Further, if the free will hypothesis is correct, we would expect to find that the behavior of individual persons was steadfastly unpredictable by any explanatory theory. And in point of fact this is exactly what we do find. If human behavior were predetermined, as that of inanimate matter is, it ought to be possible to discover causal laws which would enable us to predict it. It should be possible to devise theoretical explanations with the same predictive power as those of physics and chemistry. Attempts to construct such theories have been made for at least a century. But they have been a total failure. We do not possess a single theoretical explanation of human behavior which allows successful prediction of the actions of individuals. It is true that the behavior of large masses of people is often statistically predictable, but this is not on the basis of any explanatory theory. To the extent that explanations are available for human behavior, they are exclusively based on our knowledge of people's motives and purposes.

Against this the reply is made that some deterministic systems are too complex to admit of reliable prediction, such as the weather. Our understanding of human beings is still in a primitive stage, as it has been of the weather system, it is said. As our understanding progresses, prediction will become possible. Social scientists not infrequently speak as if the discovery of a reliable explanatory theory of human behavior were just around the corner.

But surely there is a significant difference between the kind of failure that we experience in predicting the behavior of complex deterministic systems like the weather and our difficulties in predicting human actions. In the case of the weather our ability to make predictions of individual events improves dramatically as our mastery increases of the various factors that make the weather up, so that astonishingly accurate predictions can now be made about certain aspects of it. Predictability with such systems improves incrementally. But this has not been the case with our attempts to predict the behavior of human beings. Despite all the theories that have been advanced, and all the mass of information that we possess about human beings, we have made no significant progress in devising explanatory theories which produce verifiable predictions.

Perhaps the strongest reason to believe in free will is not so much a theoretical reason as a practical one. Human society is impossible without the assumption of personal responsibility, and personal responsibility makes no sense without free will. The assignment of personal responsibility is indispensable to the dealings that human beings have with one another. If individuals are not considered to be responsible for their actions, all ordering and regulation of human interaction collapses. The simplest transaction, holding a conversation or buying a loaf of bread, becomes unfathomable, because there are no longer persons speaking and acting, but merely bundles of impersonal forces, which can be neither praised nor held to account.

But the assignment of personal responsibility would be merely a charade unless it is possible for persons to act differently than they do. If in point of fact the actions of individuals are predetermined, then in esteeming them or holding them to account we are merely engaged in a vast game of playacting and pretense. How could we dare inflict on a person, even one who has committed the ghastliest of crimes, the suffering of even a mild imprisonment if he had no power to do other than he did? This is sometimes defended on the grounds that the threat of punishment becomes one of the factors predetermining behavior, and that if the threat is made it must be possible to carry it out. But such an approach is profoundly cynical. It is not only consistent but a logical necessity on the part of those who do not believe in free will to wish to abolish all punishment, as some do. Yet even making every allowance for the desirability of replacing punishment in some instances with other kinds of treatment, everything we know about human nature tells us that there could be no more effective recipe for bringing the human enterprise altogether to ruin than a system in which human beings may destroy one another with impunity.

THE RATIONALITY OF INTUITIONS

We remarked above that the Kantian approach to moral questions is generally felt to suffer from the defect that it provides no methods for settling disputes as to what is right and wrong, but must rely on the intuition of the individual, which is subjective and always open to question. Yet intuitions are not wholly insulated from the sphere of reason and argument. The intuitions which an individual has, need to be consistent with one another. Yet it very often happens that they are not. It also very often happens that these inconsistencies remain hidden to the person who harbors them. In practice it is frequently easier for another person to detect inconsistencies, paradoxes and contradictions in an individual's beliefs than it is for the individual himself. Reasoned debate and mutual criticism in a spirit of inquiry between those of different points of view can go a very long way in helping us to see the adjustments that are needed in our moral beliefs for them to make sense. What is necessary above all for this to be successful is a willingness to acknowledge the difficulties of our position. The chief reason there is so much difficulty in reaching agreement on moral beliefs is arguably that we find it extremely hard to accept the possibility that we may be mistaken.

Although, as we have argued, the Principle of No Harm is widely, if not universally held, since it is generally accepted that behavior such as the murder and injury of innocent people is outrageous and should be punished, there are at least two kinds of difficulties to which the principle is exposed. On the one hand when it is formulated in a theoretical discussion, it is often felt to invite criticism on the grounds of a lack of clarity, such that it cannot be implemented realistically with consistency. What is "harm?" And who is "innocent?" Are these ideas not altogether vague and unclear? An important part of a defense of the principle will consist, then, in clarifying its terms, to show that it is sufficiently definite to be put into practice. On the other hand it is usually felt that the principle must allow of certain exceptions, and part of our aim will be to show that this is not the case.

THE NOTION OF HARM

Is the Notion of Harm Entirely Arbitrary?

In Chapter 5 we analyzed the idea of causation involved in the doing of harm. Here we shall examine other aspects of the idea of harm. It is sometimes asserted that the idea of harm is culturally conditioned, since conceptions of harm differ widely from one society to another: some customs which are valued in some societies are rejected as harmful in others. Especially in matters of sexuality, marriage, and the family, conceptions of right conduct are often greatly at variance with one another. This is also true of the idea of property. In some tribal societies the idea of strictly private property seems scarcely to have existed, and views about justice have varied accordingly. Even in Europe, conceptions of property differed widely as between the feudal period and modern times. To many people this means that all moral values are relative to cultural and historical circumstances, and are therefore purely arbitrary and conventional; and there is no such thing as an absolute value, something that would always and under all circumstances be good, or evil.

Despite these considerations, however, in point of fact thoroughgoing relativists are hard to find. Socialistic thinkers, for example, are not usually relativists—they typically hold to certain values as absolutes, for example in their conception of the exploitation of employees by employers. Even modern liberals tend to believe that such things as discrimination and slavery are absolutely wrong, and it is interesting to see how even such an explicit relativist as David Wong is prepared to strain his system to call such views not merely different, but false.[11]

As a purely factual matter it is by no means certain that different societies really do hold to fundamentally different values. When we investigate the different practices more closely, we may find that their fundamental beliefs about what is right and wrong are identical, only they are applying them in different circumstances, or against a different background understanding of the world. One society believes in caring for its elderly, another in hastening their death; but on examination we discover that in the second it is believed that they will be happier in a future life. Tribal societies often appear not to possess the idea of private property within the tribe: when a member of the tribe brings food home from the hunt, others help themselves without asking his permission; or if one needs a spear, he takes another's. But tribes are just extended families, based on blood relationship, and the concept of property within a family is different, even with ourselves, and allows a good deal of latitude. But between tribes and between families the idea of private property is held tenaciously: what belongs to one tribe does not belong to another, and any attempt to infringe on the property of a neighboring tribe will be a justification for war. The feudal concept of property was based on the assumption that the ruler, as the one with the obligation to defend the territory, owned the land, and that everyone else held their land on lease from him. While this assumption is different from ours, that does not mean that the fundamental concept of property was different. This is supported by the continuous development which has taken place in legal concepts, so that decisions made by courts in the Middle Ages can still sometimes serve as precedents today.

Even if we were to grant that views about what is right and wrong differ fundamentally from one society to another, however, the relativistic argument rests on a fallacy, and an obvious and well-known one at that. The mere fact that a belief is widely held does not mean that it is right. What people do, and what they ought to do, are not necessarily the same. The question about whether a belief or a practice is right or wrong is not a question about what people actually do, or about the beliefs or practices which they actually hold to; it is a question about what they *ought* to do, which is something altogether different. No amount of anthropological investigation can settle the question of obligation. Even if every society in the world condoned murder, murder would still be wrong. Anyone who thinks differently simply does not understand what the notion of morality means.

If morality were entirely relative, it would be impossible to criticize the morals of any society. For if morality is entirely relative to the society, then whenever people do what their society approves of, they are doing right. If a tribe of headhunters believe it is all right to kill people for food, then is it all right for them to kill people for food? That confuses conscience with rightness. If they truly believe they are doing right, then they are excused from the burdens of a bad conscience. But that does not mean that their action is right.

The lengthiest defense of moral relativism in recent years has been given by the philosopher mentioned above, David Wong. Wong argues that moral values contain both subjective, or relative, elements, and objective, or absolute, elements; that is, on the one hand everyone must reach his own moral judgements, so that no two people agree totally about moral questions, but on the other hand we typically have the feeling that there ought to be agreement, that our moral rules must somehow correspond to reality. Only relativism can do justice to the subjective side, he maintains, and yet relativism if properly understood is also capable of explaining the objective aspect. He goes about this task of explaining the objective aspect of morality in a relativistic way by developing the idea that a moral system does not need to be universally valid; it is sufficient if it is "adequate." What makes a moral system adequate? That it "meets the standards for moral systems," he replies. What standards? Wong does not tell us in any detail. He merely remarks that "standards are part of the most basic normative language," and that for a particular society there may be very many criteria that a moral system must meet—one important one being that it "provide a relatively effective resolution of . . . conflicts."

Wong argues that on this basis it is possible for a relativist to criticize a moral system as being inadequate, firstly if it rests on mistaken factual assumptions about the world, and secondly and more importantly, if it does not provide effective resolution of social conflicts.

On this theory it is the criteria for the adequacy of a moral system which then become the absolute values. If a moral system must provide an effective resolution of social conflicts, then the effective resolution of social conflicts constitutes an absolute moral value. This would fail to be true only if the criteria were completely different for every society. If there is one criterion which every society shares (as Wong seems to imply), then that will be absolute.

Absolute and Relative Values

I am by no means concerned to argue that all moral values are absolute. On the contrary, I would argue that there is only one absolute value, the one represented by the Principle of No Harm. This is a negative value, pointing to something which is always and under all circumstances evil, namely causing harm to innocent people. I would argue that while there are many genuine positive values, none of them are absolute, in the sense of being good for all people always and under all circumstances. Whether a particular thing is good for a particular person, as we have previously observed, depends on the circumstances of that particular person, and on the consequences which the thing in question will have for him, which is often extremely difficult if not impossible to predict. Apart from the Principle of No Harm, it is only by trial and error that we discover what is good and what not, and even this knowledge is subject to revision according to changing circumstances. (In addition, the implementation of any particular positive value always requires that we forgo other positive values, some of which might conceivably have been better. That is, in the case of things that are good there are always trade-offs: if I decide to play tennis at 6 P.M., I must give up the idea of having a five-course dinner at that time.)

In these pages, however, I am not concerned with value theory in general, but with one principle and one principle only, the Principle of No Harm, as it was formulated above, and my argument is that that principle is indeed absolute and allows of no exceptions.

There is some truth to the view that we have some latitude in deciding what is harmful, although the point is often exaggerated. But within certain limits we can draw the net more or less tightly. For the most part, however, this latitude is restricted to matters of custom: a different custom may be felt to be harmful merely because it is strange. If, for example, we have the custom that employees are to be paid before they do their work, as is the case in some European countries, an employer who delays payment till afterwards may be felt to be acting harmfully.

In some matters, however, it is true that the criterion, the standard, of harm is itself conventional or relative, in the sense that it can be more or less stringent. Examples of this are our standards for air and water pollution, or for safety in the workplace. A hundred years ago our ancestors seem by and large to have been content if the air was not altogether unbreathable. They had other things on their minds, presumably, and were willing to put up with a good deal of what we would consider air pollution in order to have the benefits of the cheaper and more abundant goods produced by the factories. We are, as a society, more affluent than they were, and we can afford to be more concerned about the impurities we breathe, so that our standards for clean air are more stringent than theirs. Consequently our conception of when industrial emissions are harmful is different from theirs. In an underdeveloped society, however, people are typically more concerned, as our ancestors were, to obtain the benefits of industry and often consider our standards a luxury they cannot afford. So some standards of harm are relative.

It would be a great mistake, however, to assume that therefore all standards of harm are relative. Killing a person is harming him, in any society. Maiming a person is harming him, in any society. Robbing a person is harming him, in any society. Making a contract with a person and then breaking it is harming him, in any society. Defaming a person is harming him, in any society.[12]

As G. K. Chesterton put on the lips of Father Brown, talking to the archcriminal Flambeau:

> Reason and justice grip the remotest and loneliest star. Look at those stars. Don't they look as if they were single diamonds and sapphires? Well, you can imagine any mad botany or geology you please. Think of forests of adamant with leaves of brilliants. Think the moon is a blue moon, a single elephantine sapphire. But don't fancy that all that frantic astronomy would make the smallest difference to the reason and justice of conduct. On plains of opal, under cliffs cut out of pearl, you would still find a notice-board, 'Thou shalt not steal.'[13]

Many customs have both beneficial and harmful aspects, and it can happen that one society focuses its attention on the beneficial aspects of a custom and neglects the harmful ones, while another does the opposite. It is true that some primitive societies have considered any stranger fair game for robbery or murder, but when they have been exposed to more universal moral standards, experience has shown that they typically come to agree with them. In general prolonged discussion tends to bring a larger measure of agreement as to what is genuinely harmful and what is not. With regard to doubtful cases, or cases about which different cultures differ, the question must be whether a particular state of affairs can reasonably be considered harmful, when its consequences have been examined thoroughly.

The Baseline

We have discussed the question of the baseline or benchmark for judging whether a person has been benefited or harmed in Chapters 2 and 5. The basic notion of harm is that of harm to an individual person. A person suffers harm from some event when his condition after that event is worse than it was before that event, as a result of that event. The comparison of the "before" with the "after" is an integral part of what we mean by harm. Once that is understood, many cases which are widely felt to be instances of harm prove not to be so. To return to the earlier example, if I am short of money and I ask a banker for a loan, but he refuses to give it to me, he does not harm me, because my condition after his refusal is no worse than it was before. I needed money before, and I still need it afterwards, but he has not increased my need. If I would like to stay at a hotel, but they refuse to let me in because they object to my behavior or appearance, they have not caused me harm, because they have not made my condition worse.

As we pointed out in the earlier chapters, the baseline for assessing harm is not some abstract condition of "normality," or of how things would have been otherwise, but the actual condition of the person at the time of the event in question. As we remarked there, a full description of that actual condition will include any likelihood of change for better or worse, so far as that can be estimated, in the absence of the event alleged to be harmful.

Consent

When we consent to a harmful action, the obligation on the part of the other not to perform the action ceases. *Volenti non fit injuria*. The argument was made above that harm is immoral chiefly because it violates the self-government of the individual possessing free will. The incision which the surgeon makes, cutting through skin and muscle in order to remove an inflamed appendix, certainly harms the body, but we allow him to do it to us because otherwise he cannot remove the diseased organ, and so long as he does not exceed his commission we have no grounds for complaint.[14]

It has sometimes been concluded as an objection that if this were true then duels would be permissible, since each party in a duel consents to the possibility of being killed, on condition that he has the chance to kill the other. On the other hand those opposed to duelling have usually argued that the necessary freedom of consent is not present, since duels take place typically under the threat of disgrace. The view of the present writer is that a challenge to a duel is akin to blackmail. Further discussion of this question is continued in note 15 to this chapter.

Damage

The original or root notion of harm is that of physical damage to the integrity of a living body, as in the infliction of a wound. Since a human being is more than a physical body, the logic of the idea requires that it be extended to include the other aspects of human existence, such as the mental, personal or spiritual. The use of force to restrict the movements of an adult against his will is universally recognized as harmful, because it impairs his liberty. Entering into an agreement with another person, in such a way as to cause him to take some action which depends for its success on my carrying out what I have promised and then failing to do it—that is, breach of contract—is harmful. For similar reasons, depriving a person by force of the fruits of his labor is harmful, a topic we shall explore further later in this chapter, in discussing the idea of property.

Not every kind of loss, however, constitutes damage or harm. I have a close friend, whose company I greatly enjoy, but he decides to move to some remote region of the globe: I suffer a loss, but it would not be apt to say that he has damaged or harmed me. Only those losses constitute damage or harm which impair the integrity of the person, understood in its full sense. The object which is lost must stand in such a close connection with the person that it makes sense to think of the person himself as being damaged. While it may not be possible to make this criterion more definite by means of general rules, in practice, courts of law and other judges typically have surprisingly little difficulty in agreeing on what constitutes harm in concrete instances. The best indication of this is the body of common law which has been built up in the courts of the English-speaking peoples by the decisions of countless judges and juries on just such questions and which distinguishes harm from mere loss. This common law is not based on statute, but on the sense of justice of the judges and juries, and it exhibits a considerable degree of consistency over centuries. It is noteworthy that the common law is in general not redistributivist, but affirms, for example, the binding validity of contract. The principal difficulties in deciding when one person has harmed another arise in regard to the question of causation, rather than of harm itself.

It does not seem necessary, in the light of this, to make use of the idea of a *right* in defining the meaning of harm. Some writers, such as Joel Feinberg, have felt that this is necessary in order to allow for the fact that not every deterioration in a person's condition can be considered a case of harm. Feinberg defines harm as loss or damage which infringes upon a person's rights. But if it were part of the definition of harm that some right is infringed upon, then it would be a tautology, a meaningless claim to maintain that persons have a right not to be harmed: it would be simply tantamount to saying that they have a right not to have their rights impaired. But it is not meaningless to say that people have a right not to be harmed. It is often assumed, as we shall see, particularly by utilitarians, but also by others, both conservatives and socialists, that under certain conditions it can be permissible to harm a person against his will, even one who has not caused harm, for example when the good of society appears to demand it.

If a person can be harmed only by some action which violates his rights, then we would be forced to the conclusion that the imprisonment of a criminal (or even the execution of a murderer, on the assumption that the death penalty may be deserved) does not cause him harm. To say the least, this seems a far-fetched and paradoxical view, and one to which the criminal is certainly unlikely to assent.

Perhaps it would be more faithful to our actual use of language to say that the word "harm" is used in various senses in this respect: sometimes we use it in the sense that Feinberg has in mind, as when we say a person is harmed by an action because it violates his rights; and sometimes we use it in the sense indicated just now in the case of the execution of the murderer, so that harming someone is not necessarily a violation of his rights. For our present discussion all that is necessary is that the term does not have to imply a violation of rights, and it is surely clear that this is indeed the case. Although our reason for saying that a person is harmed may be that some right of his, which we have conceded on other grounds, has been violated, those are not the only circumstances in which we consider that a person is harmed.

Interests

The notion of harm is sometimes defined in terms of interests: a thing is harmful to me if it is a setback to my interests. Thus Feinberg again: "One person harms another . . . by invading, and thereby thwarting or setting back, his interest."[16] This way of speaking is especially common in the legal profession. It has the apparent advantage of objectivizing benefit and loss, making them less dependent on our current feelings. To have an interest in something is to have a stake in it, to be at risk in it, so that I stand to gain or lose depending on the outcome of it. In this sense I can have an interest in something even if I do not know about it or desire it. For example, the question could be asked: if a person's house were burglarized while he was away, how could the burglary harm him, until he comes to know about it? The response is made that he has an interest in the preservation of his property, independently of his knowledge of it. By the same token a person can be said to have an interest in his own health or safety, which should be protected even though he himself is negligent about it, so that laws will be considered justified which restrict the sale of dangerous medicines, or which command the wearing of seatbelts or crash helmets. An object of an interest is "what is truly good for a person whether he desires it or not."

This notion has its uses, chiefly in speaking about what is usually the case, or what is the case all things else being equal; but it is filled with pitfalls. Who is to decide what is truly good for a person, whether he desires it or not? As we pointed out in a previous chapter, many things are good in the abstract, or in principle. All other things being equal, friendship is good, wealth is good, leisure is good, and much else besides. But in the concrete other things are often not equal. In the concrete what is good for a person depends on his circumstances, and that means all his circumstances. It can be extremely difficult, even for the individual himself, to know all of his circumstances, and well-nigh impossible for anyone else. Friendship is good, but should I be friends with Smith, who is secretly a member of the mafia? Wealth is good, but if sudden wealth leads me to indulge in narcotics, my last state may be worse than my first. In order to know whether something was truly good for a person we would have to be able to predict its consequences for him, which is notoriously impossible. And so we constantly make the most elementary mistakes about what is good for ourselves, let alone for others. In speaking of what is in a person's interests, then, we should bear in mind that for the most part we can only be describing what is good for him all things else being equal, so that there are severe limitations on the usefulness of this idea. The appearance of objectivity which it gives is largely illusory.

The notion of harm, by contrast, must be genuinely objective. When it's a question of punishing a person because of harm he has done, the harm must be clear and evident. Everyone has an interest in not being harmed. But if harm consists in setting back a person's interests, and if a person can have an interest in something that is good for him, whether he desires it or not, then harm comes to be in the eye of the beholder. So then even when a person is willing and anxious to work for $2 an hour, and considers that a blessing, we may pass a law punishing the employer who pays him that, because we take it on ourselves to decide that "it is not in his best interest" to work for such a small amount, and we blithely ignore the possibility that he may now lose his job because his work is not worth that much to his employer.

Another difficulty with the notion of interests is that it frequently trades on one of its primary meanings, which is to have not merely a potential for benefit or loss, but a right, a legal claim or share. To have an interest in a firm, for example, usually means that I have a legally enforceable financial share in it. To explain the notion of harm by means of the notion of interest runs the risk of begging the question, then. To make it useful, it has to be specified that the notion of interest is not being used in the sense of a right, but merely in the sense of a (potential) benefit or loss. But then the idea of interest does not seem to express anything that cannot equally well be expressed by such ideas as benefit and loss. And as we have just noted, these two ideas by themselves do not make sufficient allowance for the difference between loss in general and the special kind of damage to a person which we call harm. So the notion of an interest does not seem to be in principle any clearer than the notion of harm, which it is supposed to explain.

Offense and Hurt

Offense and *hurt* are sometimes thought to be entirely different from harm. An occurrence which is unpleasant or painful is not necessarily harmful, it has been said, because it may not have any further negative consequences for the individual's well-being. My feelings may be hurt by some remark of an acquaintance, but that does not mean he has caused me harm, on this view, since he has not brought any change about in my objective situation. Similarly offense does not of itself constitute harm: different people find very different things offensive, and there is often a large degree of subjectivity involved in such feelings. To use an example given by one writer, a man who wears in public a tie with a picture of a naked girl on it is likely to offend many people's feelings, but he is not causing them any harm, for similar reasons. If everything were to be forbidden which causes offense, it is argued, very little would be allowed. It is possible to be offended at anything whatsoever. But if hurt and offense are different from harm, then the actions which cause them obviously do not fall within the purview of the Principle of No Harm and should not be forbidden by law.

Thus Joel Feinberg maintains that the Principle of No Harm does not warrant the prohibition of even public obscenity unless it causes some more far-reaching and longer-lasting harm. Feinberg defines harm as a setback to a person's interests, and asserts that there is no interest in not being hurt as such, nor is there an interest in not being offended. Although he concedes that pain is an evil, and that to suffer pain is to be "in a harmed condition," he holds that pain is not harmful, since of itself it does not cause any further negative effects.[17] (He grants that people do have an interest in not being tortured, but only on the grounds that they have an interest in peace, and the pain of torture is sufficiently intense to violate that interest).[18] He goes on to make a distinction between ordinary or common offenses, which are of a more personal or subjective nature, and are relatively shallow, and "profound offense," which, roughly speaking, offends against one's moral sense and is of a more impersonal or objective quality. He is not, however, in general inclined to support legal prohibition of even profoundly offensive behavior if it is easy to avoid witnessing it. (Although he seems willing to make an exception for manifestations of racism.)[19]

Since pain and offense are evil, however (which Feinberg acknowledges), they are forms of harm, even if they do not have any further negative consequences for the well-being of the person. But if that is so, they fall within the scope of the Principle of No Harm. The feared conclusion does not follow from this, however, that all behavior at which some people might take offense ought to be prohibited, just as not all actions which cause harm ought to be prohibited. The reason for this is that there are different kinds of offense.

There is an important difference between grave or serious offense and light or slight offense. Only serious harm should be punished by the law, since all the punishments of the law are serious, and only grave offense should count as prohibitable harm.

There is a difference between reasonable and unreasonable offense. It can be reasonable to take offense at some actions, for example at a public display of obscenity. There are other actions at which it is unreasonable to take offense, for example at scientific research which points to a conclusion one does not like, or at obscenity confined to a private location where it can be seen only by the willing. One important consideration is whether the offensive words or actions were provoked. A person who is causing annoyance he could easily stop, should not be surprised to find himself at the receiving end of an offensive utterance. On the other hand, the provocation must be proportionate to the offense.

Especially, there is a great difference between speech or actions which deliberately cause offense or pain, and those that cause offense or pain only as an unintended consequence, and are primarily aimed at achieving some other effect. A deliberate, unprovoked personal insult, or the deliberate, unprovoked causing of any pain or offense clearly constitutes harm and is ruled out by the Principle of No Harm; and it can legitimately be prohibited by law provided it is sufficiently grave.

In the case of actions which are done for some other purpose, such as the expression of a political program, or of a scientific truth, or of artistic values, or even simply for entertainment, and where the hurt or offense follows as an unintended consequence, the Principle of Double Effect applies. Since we will have occasion to refer to this principle again later, a digression to discuss it may be in order here.

The Principle of the Double Effect

Suppose we foresee that an action we are contemplating may have a bad effect as well as a good one. Is the action invariably wrong, or are there circumstances in which it is morally permissible? Suppose, for example, that a terrorist has taken a hostage and is threatening to kill him unless his demands are met. A police sharpshooter could perhaps shoot the terrorist, but there is a risk that he might shoot the hostage by mistake. Is it morally permissible for him to try to shoot the terrorist?

The Principle of the Double Effect answers this question by providing three criteria:

1) The evil effect must not be the cause of the good effect. This rule is necessary because the end does not justify the means. We may not do harm in order that good may come of it.

     This condition would be satisfied in our example, because the evil effect, the death of the hostage, would not be the cause of the good effect, the death of the terrorist.

2) The evil effect must not be deliberately intended.

     This condition would also be satisfied, since the sharpshooter does not intend to kill the hostage, but only the terrorist. In practice it is of course important not to deceive oneself about one's real intentions.

3) The harm caused must not be greater than the harm prevented, or the good done.

     The harm caused would be the death of the hostage. The harm that might be prevented by shooting the terrorist would include the death of the hostage, and perhaps much more besides. So this condition would also be satisfied.

As we shall see in more detail below, the Principle of the Double Effect is not utilitarian, and those who subscribe to utilitarianism do not accept it.

Some examples of actions ruled out by the principle:

1) Smith steals from Jones in order to provide his mother with money for a life-saving operation. This contradicts the first and second conditions, since the theft from Jones would be the cause of the benefit to Smith's mother, and since Smith intends to steal from Jones.

2) The terrorist is in such a situation that if the bullet misses him it will certainly go into a high explosive, which would kill many people if it exploded. In that case the harm caused, namely the death of the many other people, would clearly be greater than the harm prevented, namely the death of the single hostage.

Offense Continued

Let's return now to the question we were considering previously, of an action which is performed for some good reason, such as expressing a political program, or explaining a scientific theory, or even just for enter-tainment, but which may give offense to some people. We are assuming that the offense is reasonable and grave. If we apply the Principle of the Double Effect to this, the result seems to be as follows:

1) The good effect is not obtained by means of the evil effect: the offense, if it happens, is not what *causes* the advance in scientific knowledge, or the political program, or the entertainment. If the entertainment were provided by the fact of the offense that would of course rule it out.

2) The evil effect, the offense, is not directly intended. If it were, again that would rule it out.

3) The harm caused, namely the offense, must not be greater than the harm prevented or the good done. The good done would be the advance in knowledge, or the political debate, or the entertainment. If the foreseeable offense was great, however, while the foreseeable entertainment was slight, this condition would not be satisfied. On the other hand if the entertainment value was high, while the foreseeable offense was not, the condition would be satisfied.

Between genuinely offensive behavior, on the one hand, and mere subjective dislike on the other, there is a wide range of behavior which must be examined individually to see whether and to what extent it actually causes harm. That harm must then be weighed against the good intended.

Harm Must Be Demonstrated

The charge that an action causes harm is a serious one, for it raises immediately the question whether the person performing the action should be punished. It is important, then, that harm be definite, it cannot simply be a vague idea. As we pointed out earlier, harm must be demon-strable, it cannot simply be assumed merely as the result of an abstract theory. Mere opinion, or emotion, no matter how intense or widespread, is no reliable guide to whether harm has been done, either to an individual or to society. The traditional procedure in courts of law, where evidence is weighed on both sides of the case before a verdict is reached, is a good guide to the kind of procedure that should be gone through before legislators decide that harm is being done, whether to an individual or to society. We do not convict a person of a crime until it has been proven that he is guilty. It is not unreasonable to require a similar standard for the law itself which proclaims a particular action harmful and threatens punishment for it. When a person has been murdered or robbed, the harm is plain to see. But the idea of exploitation, for example, is essentially a speculative notion. When a worker himself considers his job a benefit, it is a mere flight of fancy for someone else who is not in his position to condemn his place of work as a sweatshop. As we pointed out in previous chapters, the first thing that must be demonstrated is that the person's condition has worsened, and the second thing is that the activity in question has caused that worsening. Perhaps few of our laws would pass such a test.

UTILITY AND UTILITARIANISM

Historically the chief arguments for economic freedom have been made on the grounds of its utility, understood not so much in the strict sense of this term typically employed by philosophers – that it will bring about the greatest happiness of the greatest number – but in the somewhat broader sense of the beneficial effects which a free market brings for the society. It is on these grounds that Mill in principle supports free trade, and the same is true for the economists, as one would expect, from Adam Smith to Milton Friedman and James Buchanan. Although the approach taken in these pages is very different, nonetheless in the opinion of the present writer the validity of the argument for the utility of free markets has been established beyond any reasonable doubt by the economic prosperity they have brought to all classes of people to the extent that they have been tried.

At the same time, however, utility in a somewhat different sense is also frequently appealed to as a ground for restricting market freedom. Although there is good reason to believe that most people agree with the Principle of No Harm as a general rule, in the sense outlined above, the view is also common that it must be possible to make exceptions in cases where the benefits to society of economic regulation outweigh the harm.

Judge Robert Bork, in the hearing conducted by the U.S. Senate on his nomination to the Supreme Court, testified that he had once accepted the No Harm principle as absolute and so had held that the law requiring public accommodations not to discriminate on the grounds of race or color was wrong because it coerced innkeepers. But he had now come to the conclusion that it was a good law because the benefits of the coercion outweighed the harm done by it. Since then he has defended the same conclusion with the argument that there are no general principles to decide competing claims of association and nonassociation, because there are no general principles to decide *any* matter of legislation: "No legislation rests upon a principle that is capable of being applied generally," and so "the proper approach for the legislator is necessarily ad hoc, to ask whether the proposed law will do more good than harm."[20]

The argument of this book, of course, is that it is not only possible but necessary for legislation to rest upon a general principle, namely the Principle of No Harm. And furthermore, our argument is that coercion itself is harmful, so that to pass a law is already to cause harm just by that very fact. Whether a law will do more harm than good is a utilitarian consideration, and the question is whether that can be accepted as a moral principle. For the claim must be, not merely that the legislation is useful, but that because it is useful, it is just.

It is important to note that the problem in the case of utilitarian argumentation regarding law is that the good effects of a law are expected to result from something which is harmful, namely coercion. This is often disguised by a manner of speaking which treats law as if in itself it were a neutral action, neither beneficial nor harmful except for its effects. But this is not the case. Since law is coercive, and coercion is harmful, to enact a law is to expect that something which in itself is harmful will produce benefits.

A recent author defending utilitarianism, tells a story about an expedition exploring a cave near the ocean. While they are in the inner recesses of the cave the tide rises, threatening to imprison and drown them. Realizing this, they make their way back to the mouth of the cave. However, the first one to try to get through the exit is an extremely fat man, who gets stuck in the exit, preventing anyone else from getting out. Another member of the party, who has a stick of dynamite, proposes to explode the fat man. This course of action would be just, says our author, because the benefits, namely the salvation of the remainder of the group, say twenty people, outweigh the harm done to the one individual. Here the beneficial effect, the salvation of the twenty, is brought about by the destruction of the fat man, which is deliberately intended as the means to that end.

Now there is a serious question whether the conception of causality employed here is really accurate. The assumption is made that it is possible for harm to cause good. But is this really true? If we apply the account of causality given earlier in Chapter 5, it is surely not. For we saw there that to cause something is to bring it about, to produce it; and the marks which distinguish a cause are that it is the necessary and sufficient condition of the effect. But is the destruction of the fat man *necessary* in order to save the others? That will surely depend on their ingenuity and imagination in devising other solutions. Perhaps the walls of the cave were thin elsewhere, and an explosion there would be just as effective; perhaps a really good shove would have succeeded in dislodging the fat man; perhaps the tide really was not going to rise to a dangerous level after all, and so on. It will be very difficult if not impossible *to know* that no other solution was possible, for even if those present did not succeed in finding one, that does not mean that no other solution was possible. Sometimes in discussing such examples the reply is given that the discussion was being held on the assumption that there was no other solution. But this assumption is never justified in real life.

Will the destruction of the fat man be *sufficient* to save the others? Here the answer is even clearer. We can well imagine that the fat man might be exploded, yet the others might not be saved after all, for a hundred different reasons. Perhaps the explosion brought the roof of the cave down on them, perhaps the tide had risen too quickly outside, perhaps the boat they thought was waiting for them had sunk, and so on. Here again the assumption can never be justified in real life at the time the harmful action is performed that the good effect will actually take place.

If this analysis of causality is correct, then we can be left with a situation where the destruction of the human being is deliberately intended, and is brought about successfully, yet nothing follows from it. It has been futile. And this will apply to all cases where a law is defended on utilitarian grounds that it causes more good than harm, for laws always cause harm deliberately, as we saw in Chapter 6.

Even apart from this analysis of causality, however, any line of argument which understands the morality of our actions as something which depends entirely on their consequences suffers from the flaw that it is often impossible for us to know in advance many if not most of the consequences of our actions. When it is only a question of deciding what to do in a positive sense, aside from the causing of harm to others, it makes sense to take the likely consequences of an action into account as best we can, because we are then balancing one uncertainty against another. But this cannot suffice when it is a question of causing harm as the means for producing good, because the harm is certain, while the benefit is not. A strict utilitarian must be prepared to condemn an innocent person to slavery or death if circumstances arise in which the utilitarian expects that that would provide a greater benefit to others. But this is repugnant to the moral sense because there is no proportion between the certainty of the injury and the uncertainty of the benefit. Even if he does not accept our analysis of causality, the utilitarian can never be certain that the good effects which he desires or anticipates will actually occur.

Even if we employed a broader notion of causality, it would still pose grave problems for utilitarianism. In human life cause and effect in the broader sense often reinforce one another, so that it becomes impossible to tell the one from the other. The law prohibiting discrimination in public accommodations may serve as an example. Following the Civil

Rights Act of 1964, for several years there were black riots in over a hundred cities, resulting in many deaths, thousands of injured, and the destruction of millions of dollars' worth of property. These riots are usually attributed to the anger of rising expectations in the black community. Was the Civil Rights Act a cause of the riots? In asking what were the benefits and what was the harm which resulted from that law, should we take the riots into account or not? Suppose that instead of passing laws forbidding discrimination in employment and housing, the political parties had made a concerted effort with religious bodies and other private organizations such as schools and colleges to persuade whites to give up voluntarily the practice of discrimination, could that have achieved essentially the same effect without instigating riots? These are difficult questions to answer. How different people answer them will largely depend on their preconceptions. Those who support the law will assume that the voluntary effort would have been ineffective and will maintain that the riots should not be taken as caused by the law. (Some apparently even consider that the riots were justified, as an expression of justified anger: a frivolously irresponsible opinion, considering the harm done to innocent people.) Others, however, may point to many remarkable achievements that have been accomplished on a voluntary basis and may believe that the riots should indeed be considered an effect of the law.

Further, positions of the consequentialist[21] or utilitarian sort assume that it is possible to weigh deliberate injury against positive benefits in a single scale. But the two are unsymmetrical and incommensurable. Deliberate injury done to another against his will has a different moral status and belongs in a different moral category from the conferring of positive benefits. Suppose, to use a grotesque example, that Smith is extremely rich, and enjoys hacking people's arms off. He hacks Jones's arm off, against Jones's will, but gives him ten million dollars in payment. Even if he could know for certain in advance that once the injury has healed, Jones will be happier as a result than he would have been otherwise (which of course Smith never could know, since Jones is always free to change his mind), the injury he has done to Jones is not the sort of thing that could be compensated for by giving him any positive benefit. (Much less could it be compensated for by giving *someone else* a positive benefit.) Deliberate injuries can be weighed against other deliberate injuries, and positive benefits can be weighed against other positive benefits, but a deliberate injury cannot be weighed against a positive benefit.[22] The fact that courts of law make monetary awards to those who have suffered injury is merely a makeshift, employed because no more appropriate form of compensation is possible.

Our author justifies the deliberate killing of the fat man on the grounds that twenty human lives outweigh one. But this is not a true case of weighing one human life against twenty, because the death of the fat man would be brought about deliberately, while those of the others would not be. A true case of weighing one life against twenty would be if I were the captain of a ship faced with the choice of rescuing either a boat containing one person, or another boat containing twenty people, in a situation where it was not possible to save both. Or if I were the pilot of an airplane which was out of control and heading for a crash into a group of twenty people, and the only way their deaths could be avoided were if I were to remain with the plane instead of bailing out, suffering death myself. In such cases a genuine comparison is possible and it would indeed be true that twenty lives are more valuable than one. For here I am not deliberately intending to kill or injure anybody, I am simply trying to minimize harm which will already inevitably occur.

In order to be certain that the benefits will outweigh the harm, we would have to know everything that would happen if the other choice were made. Suppose, for example, that if the fat man had lived, he would have become a great poet, scientist or statesman; that he would have invented a vaccine which would have saved the lives of millions of people; or, without going so far, that he would have become the father of a number of children, who with their children and their children's children would otherwise never have lived. In the minds of many people that might very well change the balance. Yet there is no way of knowing what he would have accomplished if he had lived. We can never know, we can only *hope*, that the benefits will outweigh the harm, which is a very different thing indeed.

It will be clear that utilitarian arguments when used to defend the causing of harm suffer from defects which in the opinion of the present writer are nothing less than fatal. Utilitarianism cannot provide either support for the Principle of No Harm or an acceptable alternative to it. The fundamental objection to utilitarianism was formulated by Kant: persons are ends in themselves, and it can never be permissible to reduce one person to the status of a mere means to the welfare of another. To cause harm to an innocent person in order to bring about some good effect for others is to make that person merely a means to the ends of others. Other writers have pointed out that utilitarian argumentation eliminates the separate significance of the individual person, for it sums the happiness or well-being of individuals. Whether the aim of the utilitarian is to maximize total happiness or average happiness, the separate value of the individual is lost, it is only the total agglomeration which counts, and vast happiness accruing to one or a few individuals can outweigh in principle moderate injury to thousands.[23] This surely misses what we mean by morality. All genuinely moral argument, as opposed to merely pragmatic argument, presupposes the absolute value of every individual person. Consequently it presupposes that it is wrong to injure one person for the purpose of benefiting another. For that is what we mean by a crime. There is an inherent contradiction between utilitarianism as a total moral theory and the Principle of No Harm.

The Principle of No Harm is not a complete moral theory, however. Once the principle is acknowledged, there is legitimate room for utilitarian considerations in the remaining areas of moral life. Once deliberate harm is ruled out, and the question is only, what is the good or best thing to do in a positive sense, a case can be made that a decision which tries to maximize total or average happiness will be rational and good. Here the objection that utilitarianism sums happiness does not have the same devastating implications. While utilitarianism will not provide the basis for the Principle of No Harm, and cannot replace it as the most fundamental moral rule, it can be a fitting complement to it.

It is a commonplace observation among philosophers that the concept of justice is not a consequentialist one. Weighing benefits against harm is not what we mean by the idea of justice. Whether an action is just or not depends, not on what comes after the action, but on what took place before it. Justice is an "antecedentialist" concept. If you are a plumber, and I promise you $200 if you do some work, and you do the work, you are entitled to receive $200 from me. If I refuse to give you the money, I am acting unjustly. Suppose I could prove that the money would do more good in my hands than in yours, would that entitle me to withhold payment? Not at all. Whether my action is just or unjust has nothing to do with the consequences of my action in refusing to pay you; it is decided by what happened before, namely, by the fact that I promised you the money if you would do the work, and the fact that you did the work.

It may be felt that the example we have been discussing, of the Fat Man in the Cave, is not very helpful in regard to economic questions because in a democratic society no one proposes to kill innocent people in order to benefit others. There is a big difference, it may be felt, between killing people and inflicting a fine or other small harm on them. Supposing that by inflicting a small harm on some individuals, such as a small fine, we were able to confer a large benefit on many others, would that not be legitimate? At first sight this may seem a much more attractive prospect.

However, a number of questions must be asked. What constitutes a small harm? Typically laws affect large numbers of people. Is a small amount of harm inflicted on each of several million people still a small harm? What happens if the small fine is not paid? Will the individual have to go to jail? And is that a small harm? The fundamental principle is still objectionable, because it still treats the one person as a mere means or instrument for the purposes of the other. Admittedly, if truly only a small harm were done, then it could scarcely be considered a grave injustice; but it is still an injustice, and people who wish to have a sensitive conscience will refuse to support such laws. Furthermore, the question should be asked whether it is realistic to think that a large benefit can, in point of fact, be obtained for many people by imposing only a small harm on a few. (Which is not to suggest that it may be obtained by imposing a large one.)

If the criterion for laws were to be whether their benefits will outweigh their harm, then after every law has been passed legislatures should continue at the very least, as an essential part of their responsibility, to monitor the effects of the law and compare them with the effects anticipated from other alternatives, so that if it is discovered that the harm is excessive, it can be remedied. Most legislatures have no mechanism to carry out such a task, however. On the contrary, it is simply presumed that every law that is passed has only favorable effects. The burden of establishing that a law is doing harm and that the harm outweighs the benefits is left entirely on the shoulders of private citizens.

8

The Principle of
No Harm II

THE SECOND PRINCIPLE
*THOSE WHO DELIBERATELY CAUSE HARM TO THE INNOCENT
DESERVE TO BE PUNISHED PROPORTIONATELY.*

The reason for the Second Principle is that it is necessary to sustain the first. If those who have caused no harm ought not to be harmed, then those who harm them ought themselves to suffer harm. The First Principle is empty, a mere velleity, unless it is accompanied by the second.

Punishment

In the course of the twentieth century the idea of punishment has undergone a revolution. The traditional attitude in Western society emphasized that crime deserves punishment. During the Middle Ages, however, forms of punishment were developed which today are generally considered cruel and inhumane, a system which reached its peak in the eighteenth and early nineteenth centuries when it was possible for children to be sentenced to death for stealing a pair of shoes.[1] As we mentioned above, humanitarian feeling led to demands for reform, and imprisonment came to be generally accepted as a milder substitute for corporal punishment such as flogging and branding, while the scope of the death penalty was greatly reduced.

With the growth of the social and biological sciences an intensive effort was made to discover the causes of crime, in the hope that once these causes were known, it would be possible to remedy them, just as a physician cures a disease by removing its causes. For criminologists crime became a disease, psychological or sociological, and the criminal a patient to be treated. The idea of free will, that the criminal could have chosen to do other than commit the crime, was abandoned, and with it any genuine belief in personal responsibility. Prisons became "correction facilities." From this point of view the conception of punishment as retribution came to seem merely an irrational emotion, a form of sadism, a "primitive lust for revenge."[2] Instead the aim of punishment became deterrence, and then the rehabilitation of the criminal. In some quarters it has even been advocated that punishment for crime should be altogether abolished.[3]

It appears, however, that for the most part the high hopes of the social scientists have not been realized. Nothing has been found which could be considered a cause of crime in the strict and proper sense.[4] On the other hand some discoveries have been made. It seems that severe punishment does little to deter crime, while the certainty of a speedy arrest, trial and conviction, even with a relatively light sentence, has a much greater deterrent effect.[5]

While the deterrence of crime and the rehabilitation of the criminal are desirable goals, so far as it is possible to reach them, these are psychological or sociological purposes which leave the moral question, the question of justice, unanswered. No society can persist which does not believe in personal responsibility, and there can be no true personal responsibility without free will. The question of justice remains fundamental, and it remains what it has always been, the question of desert. What does the person deserve who has wilfully harmed others? There can only be one answer to this, though it is not a pleasant answer. And no doubt that answer has sometimes been understood in ways which were extremely and unnecessarily inhumane. But the concept of desert is not an irrational emotion. It is an elementary demand of moral reason, and there can be no justice without it.

If the idea of desert is abandoned, for example, there can no longer be any reason to insist that only those who are guilty of having committed crimes should be punished, for other goals such as deterrence can perhaps be better achieved by punishing persons who are not guilty, but whom the public believe to be guilty.[6]

The core forms of crime, those which represent what we have called the moral idea of crime, namely those which deliberately and of set purpose do serious harm to other human beings, such as murder and robbery, are not merely mistakes, the results of a lack of intelligence or education, or a psychological or social disease. They are *evil*. Our willingness to recognize this is a test of the genuineness of our conception of humanity. A true sense of humanity will affirm the sacredness of human life and will welcome whatever is of benefit to human beings. It is the logical and necessary counterpart of this to recognize that the willful causing of harm to innocent human beings is an abomination.

If we believe that those who do good deserve to receive good, we must be consistent enough to recognize that those who do evil deserve to suffer harm. It makes no sense to hold that those who do good should be praised, if we are not willing to admit that those who do evil should be blamed. It is surely no contribution to the cause of humanity to trivialize deliberate evil.[7]

As we shall argue, the idea of punishment as retribution is indispensable to the concept of human rights.

Innocence

It is reported that Will Rogers, on being told a story about an innocent bystander shot on a New York street, responded that he thought such a story highly improbable: it was hard to imagine a New York bystander being innocent.[8] This objection has been echoed by others in a more serious vein: who is innocent? Is this not a naive notion? Everyone in his life causes some harm to someone, it has been claimed. Even by the very fact of existing, it is sometimes maintained, we cause harm to others, since we use up resources that would otherwise be available for them. Not only philosophers but also theologians have objected to this notion. The Christian concept of original sin teaches that every human being is in a state of alienation from God, which suggests that a tendency to cause harm is an inescapable part of human nature.

These objections, however, are either misconceptions or exaggerations. The Christian concept of original sin refers to man's relationship to God and does not imply that every human being has caused harm to other human beings. If it did, the Christian Church would have to teach that all men should go to prison. Again, the mere fact that we breathe air and eat food does not automatically mean that we harm other people, so long as enough is left for them. Even this proviso may not be strictly necessary, as we shall see below.

To be innocent, in this context, means not to have caused substantial or notable harm to an individual or to society. The harm in question must be of sufficient significance to deserve punishment by the state. We have already observed in Chapters 2 and especially 5 that the conditions for the causation of harm are more stringent than is often assumed.

FORCE AND FRAUD

The Principle of Mutual Benefit, which we examined in Chapters 2 and 3, is that in the absence of force and fraud neither buyers and sellers nor competitors cause harm to one another, no matter what the terms of trade. It is part of this principle that force and fraud do cause harm. According to the Second Principle of No Harm those who engage in such practices deserve to be punished.

It has already been explained in previous chapters why force and fraud cause harm. Physical force used against a sane, conscious adult causes him harm because it deprives him of the power of free choice. (Force used with the insane, the unconscious, or children may cause them harm but does not necessarily do so, since they do not possess the power of free choice, or do not possess it fully.)[9] Fraud, or deliberate deception, causes harm because it causes a person to buy or sell something which he does not intend to buy or sell, so that the actual exchange is not freely chosen.

Force and fraud are the great enemies of the market. In every market transaction fraud especially is a possibility that must be guarded against. If the market is to function justly and effectively it is imperative that the legal system provide swift and easy remedies for it.

Rights, Human Rights, and the Principle of No Harm

To say that those who cause harm to the innocent deserve to be punished is equivalent to saying that persons have a right not to be harmed, unless they have caused harm. Since this is a right which all human beings have, it is a human right. We shall argue that it is, in fact, the only human right, that if it is properly understood, no more are needed.

The language of rights has come to play an ever more prominent role in the public discussion of ethical and social questions. But what is a right? This has been the subject of much debate among legal scholars and philosophers. Some, such as H. L. A. Hart, have felt that the concept of a right is too vague to admit of definition. Others have simply identified rights with claims. Joel Feinberg defines a right as a valid claim.

The key element in the concept of a right, however, and the element which is perhaps most frequently overlooked in discussions of it, is the idea of punishment. It is only in contexts where a possibility of punishment is at stake that we employ the notion of a right, either in the legal sense or in the moral sense. In the legal sense, we speak of a right where there is the possibility of enforcing a claim by means of a legal penalty. In the moral sense, we speak of a right where it is felt that there is an obligation to enforce the claim by means of a law, that is, a legal penalty. A right, then, is *a claim that can be enforced with punishment*. A legal right is a claim that can be enforced with a legal punishment. A moral right is a claim that *ought* to be enforced with legal punishment.[10] The only concept of punishment which fits this case is that of retribution.

What, then, is a human right? In itself the notion of a human right is that of a right possessed by all human beings. This is clearly a moral right, not a legal one, i.e., it is something which ought to be a legal right. A human right is understood to be a claim which all human beings have, and a claim which the legal system should ensure is satisfied.

Whether there actually are any rights which all human beings have, however, has also been a matter of dispute among philosophers. Some have held that there are no such things, since it has proved very difficult to provide a theoretical underpinning for them. "The truth is plain," writes Alasdair MacIntyre, in a widely acclaimed and otherwise stimulating book, "there are no such rights, and belief in them is one with belief in witches and in unicorns." His argument is that every attempt which philosophers have made to give a theoretical proof that such rights exist has failed.[11]

This is tantamount to saying that before we decide that robbery and murder are crimes, which ought to be punished, we should wait until philosophers are in agreement on some theory which proves that these activities are morally wrong. Now I argued above that before we condemn an activity as causing harm we should feel obliged to demonstrate that it does actually cause harm. But this is very different from what MacIntyre is saying. The implication of what MacIntyre is saying is that even when it is perfectly clear that an action causes harm, we are not entitled to hold that deliberately causing harm to an innocent person is wrong until we are agreed on a theoretical explanation as to why that must be so. With all due respect to MacIntyre, this is nonsense. As we pointed out above, it is sufficiently clear to most people that murder and robbery are wrong and ought to be punished, without waiting for philosophers to find a theoretical reason why that should be so. The remarks made above on p. 181 about the theoretical basis of the Principle of No Harm apply with equal force to human rights.

Those who accept the existence of human rights, however, are in profound disagreement as to what actual rights are covered by this concept. There are two main schools of thought. According to the tradition of classical liberalism, enshrined for example in the U. S. Declaration of Independence and the Bill of Rights, and in the French Declaration of the Rights of Man and the Citizen, human rights are essentially of a negative rather than of a positive sort, "liberty" rights rather than "performance" rights: they are rights that others should refrain from certain actions. The Declaration of Independence speaks of the right to life, liberty and the pursuit of happiness. The right to life here means, of course, not the right to be given life when one does not have it, which would involve some difficulties, but the right not to have one's life taken away. Similarly, the right to liberty is the right not to have that liberty violated, and the right to the pursuit of happiness is the right not to be hindered from pursuing happiness, not the right to be given happiness. The substantive rights recognized by the Bill of Rights (as opposed to the procedural rights, such as trial by jury) are essentially negative. Freedom of speech does not consist in possessing any positive means to express one's opinions, such as ownership of a newspaper, but in the absence of government hindrance to such expression. Freedom of religion does not consist in possessing any positive aids to the practice of religion, such as having a church or synagogue nearby, but in the fact that government does not prevent or hinder the practice of religion. The human rights recognized by the tradition of classical liberalism are asserted chiefly against government, since historically it is government which has been the chief violator of them.

Opposed to this view is that of modern liberalism, enshrined for example in the United Nations Declaration of Human Rights. In this document all human beings are said to have rights to such things as employment, housing, education, and health care. These are obviously positive performances, which it is thought ought to be provided by government. This view has attained very wide acceptance, and in the course of the twentieth century has been implemented to various extents by many governments.

It will be clear to the reader that human rights in the sense asserted by modern liberalism violate the Principle of No Harm, to the extent that they are positive benefits which can be given by government to some only by causing harm to others. Systems of public education, for example, exist only by the imposition of taxes for that purpose, which must be paid under penalty of the law by others than those who have children in the public schools.[12]

On the other hand the variety of human rights which traditionally have been recognized by classical liberals, such as freedom of religion and freedom of speech, and those mentioned in the Declaration of Independence, can be subsumed without difficulty under the umbrella of the right not to be harmed unless one has caused harm. The chief reason why it makes sense to recognize a right to freedom of religion is that, in Locke's words (quoted already), "If a Roman Catholic believe that to be really the body of Christ which another man calls bread, he does no injury thereby to his neighbour. If a Jew do not believe the New Testament to be the Word of God, he does not thereby alter anything in men's civil rights. If a heathen doubt of both Testaments, he is not therefore to be punished as a pernicious citizen. The power of the magistrate and the estates of the people may be equally secure whether any man believe these things or no."[13] Furthermore, the limits which have traditionally been placed on freedom of religion even in the United States can best be understood in this light. The courts, for example, have typically ruled that the freedom to practice one's religion does not extend to cases where it would cause harm to others, as in rulings that parents who are Jehovah's Witnesses and do not believe in various kinds of medical care are not entitled to leave their children's diseases untreated.[14]

Similarly, the right of free speech is best understood as an instance of the right not to be harmed unless one has caused harm. This again not only explains the right itself, but also the limits that classical liberals have traditionally been willing to place on it, by laws which forbid defamation, fraud, and incitement. A mere statement of a belief cannot in principle be harmful to anybody, even if it is mistaken, since it always rests within the power of the listener whether he is to believe it or not. But an incitement to action, such as crying "Fire!" in a crowded theater, may indeed cause harm. "An opinion that corn-dealers are starvers of the poor, or that private property is robbery, ought to be unmolested when simply circulated through the press," says Mill, "but may justly incur punishment when delivered orally to an excited mob assembled before the house of a corn-dealer, or when handed about among the same mob in the form of a placard."[15]

Again, the right to own property can be understood as one application of the right not to be harmed. We shall return to this question more fully below.

It may not be out of place to mention here that the idea of good manners is not entirely unrelated to the right not to be harmed, for it seems to be essentially the idea of avoiding behavior likely to cause others pain, rather than a set of positive prescriptions for giving them pleasure or doing them good. It is this aspect of good manners which leads people to feel that they have, if not a right in the strict sense of the term, nevertheless something very much like a right, to be treated with good manners, and which leads them to be offended when they are not.

Conflict of Rights

Where human rights are understood in the modern liberal sense, to include positive benefits which must be provided by government, it is possible for one right to conflict with another. On the one hand there are conflicts between positive rights, for since government has limited funds, it may easily happen that not all the positive benefits considered desirable can be afforded at one time, and hard choices must be made to fund some programs at the expense of others. On the other hand there are inherent conflicts between positive rights and negative rights, as pointed out above. When human rights are understood as consisting essentially in the right not to be harmed, however, conflicts between rights are eliminated, for it is always possible to refrain from causing harm. This is a factor of no small significance in the task of creating a harmonious society.

INNOCENT AGGRESSORS AND INNOCENT SHIELDS

Two kinds of case are sometimes felt to constitute special difficulties for the Principle of No Harm. Suppose that an infant gets hold of a revolver, and happens to point it in the direction of some other children while attempting to pull the trigger; and suppose further that the only way you could prevent him would be by some action which would harm him, perhaps even kill him. Would it not be contrary to the Principle of No Harm to take that action, when it will harm the infant, since the infant is not at fault?

The answer to this is No. Although the infant does not intend to do harm, he is, nonetheless, about to do it, and so he is not innocent in the sense relevant to the Principle of No Harm. In order to cause harm, it is not necessary to intend to cause it. According to the Principle of No Harm we are entitled to cause harm for two purposes: to prevent harm, and to punish harm. If we do harm in order to prevent harm, of course, it is a precondition that the harm which is prevented must be greater than the harm done to prevent it.

This does not mean that the infant deserves to be punished. To deserve punishment, it is necessary to intend to cause harm.

A somewhat similar case sometimes raised as an objection against the Principle of No Harm is that of an innocent person who is used as a shield, as for example when a terrorist takes a hostage. This question was discussed above, under the heading of the Principle of the Double Effect, p. 197, where we saw the conditions under which it is permissible to attempt to kill the terrorist.

HARM TO SOCIETY, UNFAIRNESS

So far we have been concerned with harm to individuals. However, in the discussion of economic questions mention is frequently made of public harm, or harm to society, and in fact this often predominates over the idea of harm to individuals.

The Second Principle, that those who cause harm to the innocent deserve to be punished, applies not only to those who cause harm to individuals, but also to those who truly cause harm to society. There are different opinions, however, as to what causes harm to society.

1) The most obvious way in which harm can be done to a society is by the use of armed force against a country or its legitimate government, as in the case of invasion by another country. Armed aggression usually causes harm not only to the society as such, but also to many individuals in it. The harm it causes is clear, and there is no significant dispute about this.

2) Another way is when harm is done, not to any individuals, but to the society as such. A judge who is trying a thief and accepts a bribe to let him off may not be causing harm directly to any individual, but he is causing harm to the society by subverting its system of justice. The harm done by such an action is also clear and not the subject of any dispute. Harm of this sort is social harm in the strict and proper sense, since harm is done, but not to any particular individual.

3) In a more controversial sense, harm is sometimes said to be caused to a society by anything which affects a large number of people disadvantageously. In this vein infectious diseases such as AIDS have sometimes been described by journalists not merely as harmful, but as harmful to society, simply in virtue of the fact that many people have contracted them; or, quite apart from any causation of harm in the strict sense, illiteracy has been described as harmful to society solely because it is prevalent. The description of some state of affairs as "social harm" or a "social problem" is often a prelude to a demand for government intervention to remedy it, for example by providing funds out of tax revenue to discover a cure for the disease, or to provide schooling.

   The fact that an individual cannot read or write does not mean that he causes any harm to other individuals, and the same is true of a million people who cannot read or write. Nor does the person who cannot read cause harm to his society; nor do a million illiterates cause harm to society. If they did, it would be permissible to fine or imprison them, which is not, so far, a common view.

   No doubt a society may be more capable of doing certain things if more of its members can read and write. But as we have seen earlier, failure to possess a benefit is not the same thing as suffering harm. No one has an obligation in justice to learn to read, or to avoid contracting a disease.

   Of course a person who communicates a disease to others causes those individuals harm. Justice in such cases can be done where appropriate by the normal courts of law. But there does not seem to be any justification for describing such a person as causing harm to society, except by a figure of speech.

In the case of what are usually called "social problems," there is no *causation* of harm to society analogous to that in the first two cases, of invasion and corruption. A social problem is a state of affairs, it is not an action causing harm distinct from itself. As a result there is an inherent problem with moralizing it.

Morality and immorality can be present only when there is a human action, that is, an action which is conscious and deliberate, performed by certain definite individuals. A state of affairs cannot be either moral or immoral, either just or unjust, it can only be good or bad. The mere fact that a state of affairs affects a large number of people, then, however much of a problem it may constitute for them or for some observers, does not warrant the use of law and punishment to remedy it. As we have seen, those who have not caused harm do not deserve to be punished.

To the extent that the condition of a society has deteriorated in some respect, it may be useful to speak of the society *suffering* harm even though no one has *caused* the harm, just as an individual may suffer harm without anyone having caused it. Yet it does not seem that numbers alone warrant us in speaking of a "social" problem. No doubt illiteracy is a problem, but is it precisely a social problem? If so, that cannot simply be the result of the fact that it affects many individuals, but it must be the result of the fact that in some way or other the society as a society is at stake in it. The illiteracy must stem from genuinely social influences, for example cultural ones, or must produce genuinely social effects, for example by altering the recognizable character of the society. A certain amount of caution is needed in using words which are so easily misused.

4) Modern liberals employ the idea of social or public harm in a related, controversial sense, to mean *arbitrary inequality*, or *unfairness*. What is thought of as unfair in this connection also need not be an action, but can just as well be a state of affairs, such as the existence of a monopoly, of an unequal balance of power between employers and employees, or the fact that some group in society such as blacks or women receive lower incomes or less education than some dominant group. Where such states of affairs appear to be particularly entrenched in a society they may be called "structural," a term intended to highlight the view that they are not necessarily the product of individual causation and responsibility, and also that the remedy for them will require legislation.

The usual argument given for this viewpoint is that inequality is arbitrary and unfair when it is not based on any morally relevant principle, as we saw above. If I hire two people to do the same work, say as accountants, and I pay one of them twice as much as the other because I like her appearance the reason for the different treatment I give them has nothing to do with the accuracy of their accounting. It is irrational, and so unjustifiable. And by the same token it is deficient in humanity, for a humane state of affairs seems to be one where equality prevails unless there is an overriding justification for inequality, since human beings all share a common nature.

In such cases it seems to some people that harm is being done, if not directly to the individual in question, at least in a broader sense of harm to the society. Even if the condition of the individual person has not actually been economically worsened from what it was previously, the unfairness seems to many inherently and automatically harmful to the society as such. It is not merely a private problem, but a social one. This social unfairness is typically referred to as a matter of distributive justice, or social justice. The most prominent theory of social justice in recent years has been that of John Rawls. Rawls identifies justice with fairness or equality, and the morally relevant principle which alone justifies inequalities in his view is that they improve the lot of the most disadvantaged.

Our essential reply to this is the overall thesis of this book, that legislation punishes individual human beings, not social structures or states of affairs, that only those individuals who have caused harm deserve to be punished, and that inequality alone is no indication that harm has been done. In previous chapters we have argued that individuals or corporations do not cause harm to their exchange partners or competitors by buying or selling under any terms so long as it is without force or fraud, or by refusing to buy or sell. The employer who hires two accountants and pays one twice as much as the other because he likes her appearance is doing neither of them any harm, but rather benefiting both of them, and is therefore doing nothing for which he can justifiably be punished, no matter how irrational his action may appear from the viewpoint of some onlookers.

Since economic states of affairs are created by the actions of individuals or corporations dealing with others, a special treatment here of societal inequality does not seem to be strictly necessary. However, since modern liberals typically place special emphasis on it, we will examine the thesis that inequality between significant groups, whether of employers and employees, of producers and consumers, or of different races and sexes, is harmful to the society.

Does Inequality Cause Harm to Society?

We pointed out in previous chapters two conditions that must be satisfied for harm to be caused. One is that there must be a deterioration in the condition of the person said to be harmed. The second is that the action of the alleged harm-doer must produce or bring about that deterioration: there must be causation. Both of these conditions apply equally as much when it is a question of causing of harm to society.

In the case of invasion by another nation, or the corruption of the system of justice, discussed above, p. 215, both conditions are fulfilled.

But the fact that the economic condition of the members of a society is unequal does not mean that there has been a deterioration in the condition of the society. On the contrary, as we pointed out in Chapter 3, it may indicate that there has been an improvement. When new inventions or discoveries are made, or new machines constructed, they may initially be available only to a few members of the society, and so to that extent inequality may increase. Yet the overall condition of the society has not deteriorated, but rather improved.

Even where inequality is arbitrary, it does not follow that it causes harm to the society. A person who leaves a large sum of money to a stranger solely on the grounds that he likes his appearance is causing no harm to any individual, nor to the society, even though the result is an arbitrary inequality.

Modern liberals reject both conditions, deterioration and causation, because they wish to maintain that inequality in itself is harmful, quite apart from any further consequences it may have. They reject the first condition, that deterioration must have taken place, because the inequalities they wish to abolish may have characterized a society from time immemorial. They reject the second because it implies individual responsibility, whereas modern liberals often must describe inequality as structural, a state of affairs rather than a deliberate action of some individuals. As we have just seen, however, states of affairs cannot be either moral or immoral, just or unjust. The view that inequality is harmful to the society, then, amounts simply to the feeling that it is regrettable and ought not to exist. But this is a far cry from showing that it ought to be prohibited by law.

Perhaps the paradigm case of economic inequality considered harmful to society in the United States is the racial discrimination which prevailed before the civil rights movement. There was an established pattern throughout the society of refusing to employ or otherwise trade with a large body of people, because of certain characteristics attributed to them. This seemed to many to be a perpetuation of slavery. We have discussed above, in Chapter 5, the question whether discrimination, that is, a refusal to trade, causes harm to the individual discriminated against. Here we address the question whether it causes harm to society.

In popular parlance discrimination sometimes appears to embrace more than mere refusal to trade, and the civil rights movement was certainly concerned with more than the unwillingness of private individuals to employ blacks, so perhaps for the sake of clarification something should be said about this. From the viewpoint of a supporter of free markets, the discrimination which was then practiced falls into some three different categories with significant differences between them.

On the one hand there was governmental or coercive discrimination, in the administration of justice, for example in the difficulty which blacks experienced in obtaining a fair trial and in exercising their right to vote; and in the various laws which prohibited blacks from engaging in numerous harmless activities on equal terms with whites, such as laws making it a penal offense for blacks to occupy certain seats in buses, the so-called Jim Crow laws. Someone who supports the idea of a free market will judge all coercive discrimination to be not only abhorrent, but strictly unjust and will welcome the fact that such laws and practices were outlawed by the Civil Rights Act.

A second species of activity sometimes classified under the heading of discrimination is the use of violence by private individuals against blacks and others, such as homosexuals, when they have done no harm, simply out of dislike. Examples of this are the cross-burnings and other damage to persons or property as expressions of hatred. Again, to a classical liberal all use of force against innocent persons is deplorable and criminal.

The third category is the peaceful discrimination practiced by individuals or corporations who simply did not wish to trade with blacks or others in various ways. While a free-marketer may feel that such discrimination is often inhumane, he will consider it should be protected by the law, just as the law protects the right of individuals to discriminate in their personal friendships, even though that can have very significant economic consequences; or as it protects the right of free speech, even though this sometimes results in speech or writing or works of art which many people dislike intensely. From the viewpoint of a supporter of free markets, the proper remedy for such discrimination is not the violent hand of the law, but the voice of persuasion and education. It is the churches, the synagogues, and the schools, not the police and the prisons, which should induce people to change their habits in such matters.

Does it harm society when private individuals refuse to trade with others? If so, then the same must be true of boycotts and strikes. We demonstrated in Chapter 5, as we believe, that none of these activities properly speaking causes harm to the individual, because it is impossible to cause harm by refusing to act—whether to buy, sell or work—unless there is a prior contractual agreement to act. For the same reason they do not cause harm to society. They simply leave it as they found it. On the other hand the very first principle of a humane society is not to punish those who do not deserve it. No society which systematically contravenes the principle of No Harm can be a just and fair society.

IS THERE A MORAL PRESUMPTION IN FAVOR OF SOCIAL EQUALITY?

Even if it should be granted that social inequalities do not cause harm in the proper sense of the term, and so that legislation ought not to be used to remedy them, nonetheless modern liberals typically feel that there is a moral obligation to bring about a more equal society by voluntary means. Societal equality is good, and therefore societal inequalities need to be specially justified, otherwise they are impermissible. Equality is compassionate and humane, it is indispensable if society is to be a place where human beings can flourish. Inequalities are allowable, therefore, only when it can be shown that they are necessary for the general welfare. Quite apart from legislative programs, modern liberals have been active in introducing affirmative action into institutions on a voluntary basis.

Now it is true that all things else being equal, a society in which human beings are treated equally will be in many ways a more humane society. All things else being equal, a society which is prepared to trade equally with all comers will be a more humane society than one which erects unnecessary barriers of inequality. It will also be economically a more successful society, because it will enjoy a larger market.

However, societal equality is not the only good. Humanity in this sense is not the only good. Many things are good for human beings, and some of those things are incompatible with other good things. If it can be good to have a relative equality of societal power, it can equally well be good for a society to have a strong family life, to have special respect for the aged, to have a voluntary division of labor between the sexes, to have a special sense of loyalty towards one's own nation, or race, or local community. Nothing is more natural than that people should like to be with their own kind, for example. All of these may be incompatible with societal equality as modern liberals typically understand it. The first consideration must always be that no harm is caused. Provided that no harm is caused, what is good for a society depends on the circumstances of the society, and opinions can legitimately differ. Whether a greater measure of equality will be good for a society will depend on what its consequences are for the society. For some societies in some circumstances it may be beneficial, for others it may threaten their existence.

There can be no general presumption in favor of any particular good, then, and especially there can be no such moral or absolute presumption. As we have seen, equality and inequality are not actions but states of affairs, and states of affairs cannot be either moral or immoral.

This is all the more true in that the concept of equality is itself ambiguous: there are different kinds of equality, and some kinds are incompatible with others. There is what may be called moral equality, the equality of human beings as human beings, also known as equality before God. It is this which provides the moral basis for the Principle of No Harm, which applies equally to all human beings. There is legal equality, which is the right to receive equal treatment at the hands of the law. This assumes that there is no legally privileged group such as an aristocracy in the society. There is political equality, which consists in the equal right to exercise political power, especially the power to vote. And there is economic equality, which is the possession of at least roughly equal economic power.

Economic equality can be maintained in a society (if it can) only by the use of force, that is, law, for in a free society the different initiatives undertaken by different individuals will bring them different degrees of economic power, as numerous other writers have pointed out. Laws to enforce economic equality must then take from some by force in order to give to others. But this offends against moral equality and destroys legal equality.

JUSTIFIED INEQUALITIES

What constitutes a morally relevant principle for allowing inequalities?

In order to be rational, modern liberals hold, justice must eliminate all arbitrary factors in the distribution of wealth. Differences of birth and talent are accidental and therefore arbitrary, it is maintained, and so must be considered irrelevant from a moral point of view. Natural inequality cannot be an ideal.

Now it is true that there is no particular merit in accomplishing something entirely by accident. A person who is given a valuable gift by another on a whim may have done nothing whatever to deserve it. But it does not follow from this that his possession of the gift is morally irrelevant. For that to follow, it would have to be shown that a person is entitled to possess only what he deserves to possess. But there are other kinds of moral relevance besides desert. The fact that one person freely chooses to give a gift to another person is a morally relevant principle on which that person may possess the object, and it is a morally relevant principle for allowing inequality between that person and others. The free choice of another person has just as much claim to count as a morally relevant principle of inequality as the possessor's deserts do.

If this is true in the case of a straightforward gift, why should it not be true in the case of a mutually conditioned gift, an exchange? For a person's free choice is not eliminated by the fact that he makes it conditional on receiving something from the other in return. And if a person is entitled to possess what some other person chooses to give him, why should it not be equally true that he is entitled to possess what nature gives him? As we routinely assume. For to deprive a person by force of some endowment which nature has given him, such as consciousness or muscular strength, is universally recognized as a crime.

As we pointed out in Chapter 3, the modern liberal thesis makes all human existence morally irrelevant, for all human existence arises to a large extent by chance. From the viewpoint of theoretical rationality it is an accident that I exist, because it was an accident that my parents met and married when they did. There is no individual human person who deserved to be brought into existence. If one were entitled to possess only what one deserved, there would be no right to life. If all arbitrary factors in the distribution of wealth must be eliminated, then all human beings must be eliminated.

Similarly, very many if not most political communities, whether cities or states, have arisen largely as the result of accidental factors.[16] To a considerable extent it is a historical accident that the United States exists because there was a great deal of good luck involved in the many steps that led to its founding: it was good luck that Columbus and his men did not go down in a storm at sea, it was good luck that the Pilgrims reached New England—there had to be good luck many thousands of times over, as well as a great deal of hard work on the part of many individuals, before the country we now know as the United States of America could come into existence. This is the case with every political community. If no accidental state of affairs can represent an ideal, then the ideal can never embrace any actual human person or political community.

The Ideal World

As we remarked in an earlier chapter, it is not uncommon to hear even persons who do not agree with socialism say that in the ideal world everybody would be equal. It is only a regrettable concession to the harshness of reality that leads them to conclude that socialism is mistaken.

But to say this is to say that it is not an ideal that individuals should be free to make their own choices, it is not an ideal that persons should have the astonishing power that they do have to initiate action and bear responsibility for what they do. If it is good that there should be individuals with the power of choice, and if it is good that they should have roots in particular communities, if it is good that improvements should take place in mankind's conditions of life, then it is good that there should be certain kinds of inequality, for it is good that there should be differences, and not all differences are commensurable.

It is good that there should be differences, significant differences, between people. One individual cannot exhaust all the possibilities of nature, for they are endless, and every human being is finite. There are many different kinds of intelligence, many different kinds of sensitivity, many different kinds of practical ability. This is not something that liberals disagree about; it is one of the great virtues of the liberal mind, even of the modern liberal mind, that it is generous to all those manifestations of humanity that are different from itself, and it readily admits that their existence is justified.

Is it or is it not an ideal, then, that these differences should make a difference? To desire that people should be different, yet to wish that these differences should have no effect on their welfare or their social condition, is inconsistent, and is merely daydreaming. To say that people have differences is to say that they have different kinds of well-being, and different kinds of well-being necessarily mean different degrees of well-being, for some kinds of well-being are not comparable to others.

Achievement

This can be brought out by considering the notion of achievement. All concrete achievement is relative to other achievement. When Roger Bannister broke the four-minute mile, or when Edmund Hilary conquered Everest, or when Einstein thought up the special theory of relativity, these were outstanding achievements only because no one else had done them previously. If running the mile in three minutes had been a common feat, Bannister's mile would scarcely have commanded our respect. Exactly the same is true, even if to a much lesser degree, of every product brought to the marketplace. It has exchange value only because it constitutes somebody's achievement, because it is not simply identical with what others have produced. But to say that is to say that producing it places its producer in a superior position in that respect to everyone else. To engage in any kind of economic activity is automatically and necessarily to attempt to achieve something special, something which is not being achieved by anyone else, and which therefore places that achiever in a superior position to others in that particular respect.

To see the desirability of factors that routinely cause inequality, it is not even necessary to focus on deliberate achievement. A person may discover a scientific truth or a remedy for a fatal disease by accident. To repeat what was said above, this immediately creates inequality. If it is unfair that one person should have more knowledge than others, then humanity will stay ignorant. That is scarcely a humane ideal.

Sometimes it is maintained that the ideal of equality can be met without sacrificing the ideal of achievement, because for example in hiring employees it is not advocated that incompetent persons should be hired, but only that among those who are competent preference should be given to members of disadvantaged groups. The effect of this, however, is to establish only minimum competency as the standard, which is certainly a sacrifice of the ideal of achievement.

Even granting that a particular gift or a particular agreement to trade or refusal to trade is irrational, should a person be punished for being irrational? No one believes that. People buy and sell every day on mere whim or fancy, and no one suggests jailing them. Some philosophers have argued that all morality is a form of rationality: moral choices are a species of rational choice, and immorality is irrational.[17] This may be true, but it will not suffice to establish the binding force of moral obligations, because it cannot establish a justification of punishment.

Social Structures

It may be objected that to focus on the individual in this fashion is to distort the picture. The social harm associated with economic inequality is not so much caused by the actions of individuals, but rather, as we have seen asserted, is structural in nature; it is not a matter of individual fault or guilt, but of the way in which the society is organized. The complaint of gender discrimination, for example, is typically not made because individual men are thought of as engaging in irrational behavior. Given the structure of the society, it may be rational for them to behave the way they do. The fault lies in the structure of the society, and it is that which must be remedied. The only way it can be remedied is by means of the law; since it is structural change which is needed, it cannot be left to voluntary action.

If the notion of a social structure is to imply anything more than a mere factuality, it suggests that there is some measure of necessity in the arrangements it refers to. But then it is ambiguous as between those arrangements which are imposed by law, and those which exist by the voluntary agreement of individuals. It is misleading to refer to voluntary behavior as if it were necessitated.

Even if the notion of a social structure as used in this connection were clear, however, the response suffers from the difficulty that laws do not penalize structures or societies, but individuals. Only individuals can be punished, only individuals can be sent to jail, only individuals suffer pain. "Structures" do not get sentenced to do five hundred hours of community service. (A corporation can be fined, of course, but that is a punishment of the shareholders or officers.) It is the innocent individual, the individual who has done no harm, and who does not deserve to be punished, who bears the entire brunt of the law.

Basic Needs

A common line of argument is that all human beings have certain basic needs, such as food, clothing, shelter, education, employment, health care, and an income in old age, and that therefore they have a right to these things, which should be provided by the state. When put in these terms, welfare laws are viewed not simply as laws which do harm to some in order to do good to others, but as a matter of justice, with the same claim upon the resources of the state (if not a stronger one) as its obligation to provide protection against crime and external aggression.

The considerations that have been given already tell also against this viewpoint. There are other difficulties with it too, however. One is that every adult has a moral obligation to support himself, an obligation not to be a burden on others. It seems fair to say that this obligation has been recognized by the vast majority of mankind. A person who becomes a burden on others is felt to have cause for shame. This obligation arises out of the fact that every adult is responsible for himself, for his own decisions, and for the consequences of those decisions, even consequences he did not intend. This is what distinguishes persons from animals: a person is a being capable of being responsible.

While most people recognize this obligation, modern liberals usually argue that it applies only to the extent that a person is able to support himself: the right to have one's basic needs provided for by society does not apply to the wealthy, only to the poor. The difficulty with this lies in ascertaining who is capable of supporting himself. The fact of having a low income is not sufficient by itself to show this, since there might be many other explanations for the low income.

Part of the problem in this area arises from the difficulty some people feel about pointing to defects of character as explanations of poverty. Many feel that it is inhumane and callous to say that Smith is poor because he is lazy. Since it is uncompassionate to blame the person himself, the cause must lie outside of him, in society. Now it can, of course, be difficult to know for certain in an individual case that laziness is really the cause of a person's problems. But such an explanation is not impossible. On the other hand, many social workers find by experience that the principal cause of poverty is not the difficulty people have in making an income, but the fact that they mismanage their expenses and as a result get into debt. Studies have shown, for example, that the single biggest item of expense for the poor is food, but that they typically do not shop around for the lowest prices but buy at the closest store; that they do little cooking, and instead buy expensive convenience foods; that they do not take much interest in the health aspects of diet, so that they and their children often suffer from vitamin and mineral deficiencies; that they do not plan their travel to take advantage of the cheapest fares; that they do not bother to find out the interest rate on their loans, and so on.[18] To say that they mismanage their expenses is not necessarily to blame them: they may never have been taught how to, they may come from a family or a culture where such behavior was not emphasized, they may suffer from chronic depression, there may be many good reasons why this happens to them. It is not only the poor who mismanage their expenses. It is by no means easy to help such people successfully, but in so far as anyone can help them, the best help consists in showing them how to become more competent in managing their affairs.

9

The Principle of No Harm III

THE THIRD PRINCIPLE
THOSE WHO DO NOT CAUSE HARM DELIBERATELY
OUGHT NOT TO BE PUNISHED.

This follows from the first and second principles. The first principle is that human beings ought not to be harmed unless they have caused harm to others. The second is that those who have caused harm to the innocent deserve to be punished. Since punishment is a form of harm, it follows that those who have not caused harm ought not to be punished.

Our thesis is that there are no grounds on which a person can deserve to be punished other than that he has caused harm to others, or to society, in the sense explained above. In earlier chapters we have argued that it does not make sense to believe that it is possible to cause harm to a person by trading with him, or by refusing to trade with him, in the absence of force and fraud, whatever the terms of the trade, and similarly that it does not cause harm to society.

It is often assumed that other grounds have historically been accepted for punishment than the causing of harm, notably those forms of immorality which do not cause harm, for example sexual immorality, and the paternalistic desire to protect individuals against themselves, as in the case of laws prohibiting gambling. There is reason to believe, however, that both of these have been made the subject of law primarily out of a belief that they are harmful to society.

The best-known argument in recent times for legislation against immorality has been that put forward by the British justice, Lord Patrick Devlin, in a work which otherwise merits high regard.[1] Devlin's argument

227

in brief is that any society in order to maintain itself presupposes a certain amount of agreement among its members on moral values. Since the existence of society depends on this agreement on moral values, government is entitled to use its force of arms to maintain the agreement. "An established morality is as necessary as good government to the welfare of society,"[2] and therefore "society may use the law to preserve morality in the same way as it uses it to safeguard anything else that is essential to its existence."[3]

The form of this argument is that society is entitled to do whatever is necessary to maintain itself in existence. But does society actually need agreement on morality beyond the Principle of No Harm in order to maintain itself in existence? And even if it did, is it true that society is entitled to do whatever is necessary to maintain itself in existence?

Devlin considers monogamy a good example for his purpose. "Marriage is part of the structure of society," and monogamy "is built into the house in which we live and could not be removed without bringing it down."[4] But how essential is monogamy to the survival of society? It is estimated that in the western states of the United States there are some tens of thousands of polygamous marriages. From time to time in the past attempts were made to enforce laws against them, but these were spiritedly resisted not only by the polygamists themselves but also by their neighbors, on the grounds that the polygamists cause no harm to anyone. As a result the attempts at enforcement have now been discontinued. There is no evidence to suggest that the polygamists are worse citizens than others, if anything rather the contrary. Although it is often assumed by monogamists that polygamy exploits women, some of the most animated defenses of polygamy have come from women, who have found the society of other women in the marriage supportive.[5]

Even if it were the case that monogamy was necessary for the survival of a society, is it true that a society is entitled to do anything whatever in order to keep itself in existence? Suppose that a nation has depleted its supply of some essential item, say water, and the only way it can discover to survive is by invading a neighboring country and taking whatever it needs, would that be morally justifiable? This is the case of the Fat Man in the Cave which we discussed above, and we concluded there that such action cannot be justified. The reason why it cannot be justified is that it causes harm to others who have themselves caused no harm. The Germans and the Japanese may well have believed in 1940 that the survival of their nations demanded that they have more territory, as Saddam Hussein may have believed that it was necessary for the survival of Iraq to occupy the oilfields of Kuwait; but if they did, the international community disagreed that that gave them the right to invade other nations. The criterion for legislation and governmental action must be, not what a society believes is pragmatically necessary for its survival, but what is just.

The second main candidate usually mentioned as grounds for punishment other than the causing of harm has been the paternalistic desire to protect individuals against themselves, as evidenced in laws which restrict gambling and the sale of alcohol, or which require car drivers to wear safety belts. According to Devlin, however, the driving force behind such laws is not in the first instance a desire to protect individuals against themselves, but a desire to protect society. "You may argue that if a man's sins affect only himself it cannot be the concern of society. If he chooses to get drunk every night in the privacy of his own home, is any one except himself the worse for it? But suppose a quarter or a half of the population got drunk every night, what sort of society would it be? You cannot set a theoretical limit to the number of people who can get drunk before society is entitled to legislate against drunkenness. The same may be said of gambling." He quotes the Royal Commission on Betting, Lotteries and Gaming, "Our concern with the ethical significance of gambling is confined to the effect which it may have on the gambler as a member of society."[6] Similarly, the arguments in the United States for laws requiring drivers to wear safety belts have pointed to the costs to society of caring for accident victims.

Our question here is the same as with monogamy: is it actually the case that drunkenness in the privacy of one's own home causes harm to society? Is it antecedently impossible, for example, that societies in which there is no prohibition against drunkenness may prove to be more contented, to have fewer psychological problems, and to work harder during the day, even if there is drunkenness at night, while other societies in which private drunkenness is prohibited are discontented, suffer from low morale, and are more inclined to revolution? Instead of simply assuming that societies with laws against drunkenness are better and happier than those without, there is surely an obligation incumbent on legislators to discover the facts of the case. And even if societies which have laws against drunkenness should prove to be better and happier, would it follow that those who get drunk privately deserve to be punished?

The paternalistic argument is that it is permissible to threaten a person with a smaller evil in order to prevent him from suffering a greater one. This is essentially a species of consequentialist argument, that the end justifies the means, and our response to that has already been indicated.

WHEN IT IS PERMISSIBLE TO CAUSE HARM

It may possibly be helpful to summarize when it is permissible to cause harm, according to the view being advocated here. There are two such situations:

1) *When it is necessary to punish harm*. If a person has deliberately caused harm to another, it is permissible and necessary to cause him a proportionate harm in return. If Smith has robbed Brown, it is not sufficient to persuade Smith not to do such things again, nor is it sufficient to compel him to make restitution to Brown. Smith deserves to be punished, albeit with moderation and humanity. Punishment here is not some primitive expression of sadism, but a rational and necessary consequence of esteem for human life. What constitutes proportionate punishment, however, is often a difficult decision. The question has been much discussed whether only the death penalty can be a proportionate punishment for murder, and it is not intended to settle that question here.

2) It is permissible to cause harm *when it is necessary to prevent harm*. If Jones is threatening to shoot Robinson, and the only way that Green can prevent him is by shooting Jones, it is permissible for him to do so. If there is a danger that in attempting to shoot Jones, Green may possibly injure Black, the Principle of the Double Effect will apply.

JUSTICE AND THE PRINCIPLE OF NO HARM

What is the relationship of the Principle of No Harm to the idea of justice? The relationship can be formulated in this way, that the Principle of No Harm provides the foundation of the idea of justice.

It is generally believed that justice means a certain kind of equality, or at least proportionality. But what kind? About this there is much dispute. According to the view we have explained above, all human beings share a common nature as human beings, which bestows on them a moral equality, equality before God. The result of this is that each one owns himself and is bound to respect others' ownership of themselves. Each is therefore bound not to cause harm to others, for to cause them harm is to violate their ownership of themselves. If justice is a certain kind of inequality, then it seems plausible to take it as the inequality implicit in the act of causing harm to others; that is, injustice is a doing of harm viewed from the aspect of the inequality implied in it.

Although the Principle of No Harm is in the first instance simply the expression of the fundamental obligation not to cause harm and does not directly denote equality, as justice is taken to denote equality, it implies it indirectly. The First Principle gives expression to the moral equality which exists between human beings as human beings sharing the same nature, an equality which forbids them to harm one another unless the other has done something to deserve harm. Crime violates that equality, as Aristotle points out.[7] The Second Principle points to the necessity of attempting to restore that equality by inflicting punishment for the crime.

By injustice, then, we typically mean a doing of harm viewed from the aspect of the inequality implied in it. By the same token, we mean by injustice not any inequality, but that inequality which is implied in the doing of harm. I employ a carpenter to install a door in my home, at an agreed price, and he installs the door as agreed, but I do not pay him. I am causing him harm, and by that fact I violate the moral equality which exists between us as human beings sharing the same human nature.

Although we typically use the term injustice when referring to an instance of harm when it is thought of from the aspect of inequality, when pressed we are usually ready to agree that there is no significant difference. For whenever harm is caused to a person who has done no harm, inequality is also created. We do not usually call a murder a case of injustice because the element of inequality is not emphasized (and also perhaps because of a feeling that injustice is too weak a word), but if we are pressed we will usually agree that it is, in point of fact, an injustice. It is an injustice because by the very fact that this harm is done to an innocent person, the harm-doer, the murderer, who is of an equal nature with the murdered person, and who has no moral entitlement to dispose of his life, treats him as if he were an essentially inferior being in killing him.

The Principle of No Harm and the idea of justice in effect are interchangeable, then. To do an injustice is to cause harm. To cause harm to an innocent person is to do an injustice. There is no injustice, however, unless harm is done. An inequality does not constitute injustice unless it causes harm.

Although in practice the Principle of No Harm is interchangeable with the idea of justice, then, it is also true to say that the Principle of No Harm underlies the idea of justice, and has priority over it. For the idea of justice adds to the Principle an emphasis on the element of equality. The socialist and modern liberal misunderstanding lies in assuming that inequality by itself automatically causes harm, without stopping to investigate what harm actually is done.

FAIRNESS

How does justice relate to fairness? These two ideas are not simply interchangeable, because the idea of unfairness does not seem necessarily to include the idea of causing harm. Unfairness means inequality, and an inequality which from some viewpoint ought not to be present, but in common parlance there can be unfairness without harm. A father who has two sons, both well-to-do, and who leaves everything he possesses to the one, but nothing to the other, might well be accused of treating the second son unfairly, but has not caused him harm.

The crucial question so far as social policy is concerned is whether punishment should be inflicted as a remedy for unfairness. To maintain that it should be is to eliminate any significant distinction between unfairness and injustice.

The relationship between justice, fairness and harm-doing is brought out well in the parable of the wine grower told in the Gospel of Matthew, Chapter 20, which we may take the liberty of giving here:

"The Kingdom of Heaven is like this. There was once a landowner who went out early one morning to hire laborers for his vineyard; and after agreeing to pay them the usual day's wage he sent them off to work. Going out three hours later he saw some more men standing idle in the marketplace. 'Go and join the others in the vineyard,' he said, 'and I will pay you a just wage,'[8] so off they went. At noon he went out again, and at three in the afternoon, and made the same arrangement as before. An hour before sunset he went out and found another group standing there; so he said to them, 'Why are you standing about like this all day with nothing to do?' 'Because no one has hired us,' they replied; so he told them, 'Go and join the others in the vineyard.'

"When evening fell, the owner of the vineyard said to his steward, 'Call the laborers and give them their pay, beginning with those who came last and ending with the first.' Those who had started work an hour before sunset came forward, and were paid the full day's wage. When it was the turn of the men who had come first, they expected something extra, but were paid the same amount as the others. As they took it, they grumbled at their employer: 'These late-comers have done only one hour's work, yet you have put them on a level with us, who have sweated the whole day long in the blazing sun!' The owner turned to one of them and said, 'My friend, I am not doing you an injustice.[9] You agreed on the usual wage for the day, did you not? Take your pay and go home. I choose to pay the last man the same as you. Surely I am free to do what I like with my own money. Why be jealous because I am kind?' Thus will the last be first, and the first last."[10]

From the viewpoint of the laborers the landowner was unfair because he did not pay them proportionately to their labor. But the landowner's response is that he is not acting unjustly, because he is not doing them any harm: he is paying them the full wage they agreed on.

THE PRINCIPLE OF NO HARM AND THE POLITICAL SYSTEM

What is the relationship of economic justice to the political constitution of a society? Modern liberals and market socialists typically view the two as very closely linked. They tend to see the political constitution as a matter of justice, and political justice as paramount, with economic justice a subspecies of that. Economics is inherently political, and economic activity should be constantly subject to political control, they believe. The only acceptable form of government in this view is a representative democracy.

According to the view defended in these pages, the situation is very different. The Principle of No Harm indicates that economic activity should be entirely free from political control. Relationships between buyers and sellers, between employers and employees, should be regulated by the standard of justice, of No Harm. But of itself the Principle of No Harm does not directly specify any particular political system. No doubt there is in general a special affinity between market freedom and the Principle of No Harm on the one hand, and democratic or representative government on the other. In the long run a democratic or representative system is likely to be much more favorable to the Principle of No Harm. But this is not guaranteed. In the course of the twentieth century, as representative systems of government became more widespread in the wake of the First and Second World Wars, they have rarely supported total market freedom, being generally inclined to some form of semi-socialism. On the other hand it is not impossible that other forms of government may rule on the basis of the Principle of No Harm and support market freedom. The colonial British government of Hong Kong has not been democratic or representative, but has steadfastly maintained what may with some fairness be described as a scrupulously just regime, with full respect for human rights, and a far larger degree of market freedom than most democratic regimes, to the great benefit of its population. I am not inclined to think that the Principle of No-Harm dictates any particular form of government, or political system, though of course it must dictate its policies. The Principle of No Harm says nothing directly about how the members of the government come to hold office, or what offices there should be, and so although it implies human rights, and so economic rights, it does not imply political rights, such as a right to vote. In other words it is a matter of political wisdom and prudence, rather than of justice, to have a democratic or representative form of government, and the power to vote is not a human right.

If the example of Hong Kong is any guide, the principal reason why people desire to have a voice in the government is that otherwise they fear for their freedom, especially their economic freedom. A minimal government which guarantees its people total freedom, including total economic freedom, in accordance with the Principle of No Harm, may experience little or no opposition, even if it is not constituted democratically. This may be important for nations which for historical or cultural reasons find it difficult to implement a democratic regime.

Some recent writers have taken issue with the view that any one system of political justice can be universal, in the sense of being obligatory for all societies. John Gray maintains that it is a fundamental defect in liberalism that it tries to found itself on universally valid principles. The notions of universal humanity and abstract personhood, he claims, are "spurious." The ideal of a liberal society can apply only to certain particular societies which have developed ideas and traditions related to representative democracy. On a similar note John Rawls, after developing a theory of justice which appeared to be intended to possess universal significance, now seems to restrict its application to those societies which have developed democratic forms of government. His theory of justice is essentially a political theory, he says, that is, one which aims at securing the largest measure of agreement possible in the society, and it is only applicable to societies which have developed the values and conceptions that would support it.[11]

From the point of view developed in this book, both these approaches make the mistake of identifying too closely the moral and the political. Political systems, that is, systems for deciding which offices there will be, and which persons will occupy them, must inevitably vary from culture to culture. And no doubt these will enshrine certain values at the expense of others. But there is not the same difficulty about holding for the universality of the basic principle of justice which forbids such crimes as slavery, murder and robbery, namely the principle of No Harm. Whether the kingship should be hereditary or elective is a question of a fundamentally different kind from whether slavery should be permitted. If I am not mistaken, both Gray and Rawls would disapprove of slavery, wherever it may be found. The argument for the universal validity of the Principle of No Harm, which is arguably the very essence of liberalism, does not necessarily entail any particular form of government. Although I have no doubt that representative democracy is the best and wisest form of government where it is capable of existing, I also do not doubt that other forms of government are compatible with the principle, as just explained. The arguments to be made for representative democracy are prudential arguments, not moral ones: the reason for having it is that, all things else being equal, it is the one likely to come the closest to implementing the principle of No Harm. But the principle of No Harm is just the formalization of the reason why we rule out slavery, murder and robbery universally.

The Principle of No Harm is put forward here as in the first instance a universally valid moral principle which rests on the most obvious moral intuitions that human beings possess, and which requires only clarification, not a theoretical underpinning. In the second place, however, it also has a claim as the fundamental principle of a sound *political* philosophy. The aim of political thought is not so much to arrive at truth, but to work out a system which will secure the largest measure of support in the society. To do this it must be as compatible as possible with the most diverse views, it must be, so to speak, a "lowest common denominator" between the extremes of left and right. The Principle of No Harm would seem to be in the best position to fulfill that function. To indicate its force in this regard we may compare it briefly to another approach which has been suggested, that of John Rawls.

If a group of people were to meet for the purpose of setting the ground rules of the society, each individual being ignorant of his own position, and so unaware of whether he is rich or poor, talented or not, to ensure impartiality, what sort of system would they be most likely to favor? Rawls, as is well known, in posing this question suggests that the system most likely to secure agreement will be one that enforces equality, both political and economic, except where it can be demonstrated that an inequality is for the benefit of the least advantaged.

But a system where it must be *demonstrated* that a particular inequality is for the benefit of the least advantaged *before* that inequality can be allowed, will prove to be inherently inferior, in the benefits it brings to *all* the members of the society, to a system where each individual is free to do as he wishes providing he causes no harm to others. In the first case there is a heavy burden of proof which is entirely absent in the second. This burden of proof presupposes that we possess a theory which will enable us to predict successfully what results will follow from what particular situations. But it is a notorious fact that we do not possess any such theory: our ability is extremely limited, almost nonexistent, to make successful particular predictions about human society. Many activities turn out to be beneficial which could not be demonstrated in advance to be such on the basis of any theory.[12] We have already seen, in Chapters 2 and 3, that there are grounds, both historical and economic, for believing that overall a free market will benefit the disadvantaged in the long run more than any regulated market, because it maximizes employment and minimizes prices. But to prove in advance that a particular inequality by itself will benefit the least advantaged would be difficult, if not impossible.

In a free market, for example, there would be no laws imposing a certain number of years of schooling, and given the diversity of human nature it must be assumed that there would be considerable inequality in regard to education, though probably less than there is now, since the long-term effect of a free market is to increase equality. Such a society might well be happier than ours, where large numbers of students who detest school are forced to endure it nonetheless. It would probably on balance be better educated than ours, since competition between schools would be increased, and so the quality of education would be improved; and education would almost certainly come to be held in higher esteem, since it would be a free choice. The society would probably be more productive than ours, and so the standard of living would be higher, especially for the less advantaged, since prices would be lower and jobs would be more plentiful. But could it be demonstrated that precisely the inequality between the well-educated and the uneducated redounded to the benefit of the uneducated? Scarcely. It is not the inequality as such which is beneficial, but the freedom of the market from governmental restrictions.[13]

Similarly, particular scientific discoveries and inventions cannot be predicted before they occur, for to predict them would be to make them. The benefits to be obtained from them also therefore cannot be predicted. Yet history gives us good grounds for thinking that societies which allow freedom of scientific research are more beneficial than those which attempt to restrict freedom of research for the sake of equality, as we observed previously. If we receive the benefits, then, we shall know them. But if we are prevented from receiving them, we shall never know what we missed. There is no way to calculate the number of people who have died as the result of not having a drug which was never discovered.

In other words, there are grounds for believing that it would be reasonable for people who were placed in Rawls's "original position" to choose, not his second principle of justice, which requires inequalities to be of demonstrated benefit to the least advantaged, but the Principle of No Harm.

If we were to hold a referendum giving a choice between a Rawlsian society and a free market, which one would be chosen? This is of course as impossible to predict as any other human decision. Yet we are not lacking in evidence as to people's inclinations when they have a choice between a redistributive society and a free market. Every year millions of people attempt to enter the United States from other countries which have more extensive welfare programs, not because of the welfare programs it makes available, but because they believe it offers economic freedom.

The Autonomy of Professor Raz

Joseph Raz has developed a political theory which places at its center the idea of personal autonomy, which he understands in the positive sense we have discussed earlier, the freedom of the individual to choose from among a wide range of options (rather than the concept of autonomy assumed in this book, which is a power to originate action, a power understood to be given automatically in the case of sane, conscious adults who are not suffering coercion). This positive personal autonomy is the prime value. Governments are justified, in Raz's view, because they have the task of fostering this autonomy, and for this purpose they are entitled to engage in coercion, including such coercive policies as the redistribution of resources. Raz accepts what he terms a widened version of the principle of No Harm, that the only justifiable ground for coercive interference with a person is the prevention of harm to anyone, including himself.[14]

Since coercion diminishes or removes a person's autonomy, however, to say that we are justified in coercing Smith in order to foster Brown's autonomy, is to say that we are justified in diminishing Smith's autonomy in order to increase Brown's autonomy. It is difficult to see that in such a view autonomy is the prime value. The prime value is rather a particular form of equality, namely equality of autonomy.

As for the view that we may be justified in diminishing Brown's autonomy for the purpose of increasing Brown's autonomy, how can this be anything but a contradiction in terms? As Dicey remarked, and as can be witnessed by any unbiased observer of our welfare systems, State help kills self-help.

TAXATION

Any theory which purports entirely to reject the causing of harm to the innocent must give some consistent account of taxation. Since taxes are coercive, they are by their very nature harmful, though this harm is usually defended by pointing to the benefits alleged to follow from them. Does a strict interpretation of the Principle of No Harm require the drastic conclusion that taxation must be ruled out? If so, how will the various justifiable activities of government in promoting defense and justice be carried out? Or is there some way of understanding taxation according to which it can be compatible with the principle of No Harm? And if it does so prove to be compatible with it, must we not then allow other similar activities on the part of government which also cause harm, provided that they bring corresponding benefits?

Locke argues that taxation is justified because it is fitting that those who enjoy their share of the protection afforded by government should contribute towards its support, on condition that they, that is, a majority of them, consent to the tax. There are two elements in this analysis, neither of which by itself could provide a justification: the idea that those who benefit from the tax should contribute to it, and the consent of the majority.

It is the consent of the people which legitimizes a tax, just as it is the consent of the people which legitimizes a government. As we have seen, government is not something good in itself, but a necessary evil: evil because every act of government involves the causing of harm, since every law is accompanied by the threat of physical punishment; but necessary, because in the ordinary course of events the disadvantages of having no government at all are even greater than those of having a government. For a government to be legitimate, then, it must enjoy the support and consent of the governed. Only their willing acceptance of the harm it unavoidably involves can justify it.

Similarly, for a tax to be legitimate, the people must consent to it. Taxes imposed without the consent of the people are tyranny. But what constitutes the consent of the people? If a direct vote of the citizenry were taken on each tax or tax increase before it is introduced, that would be plain enough. Under the current customs of representative government, however, where this practice is not typically followed, the question is not always easy to answer. Where a political party has made it clear before an election that if elected they will impose a particular tax, the people can perhaps justifiably be understood to consent to the tax by the fact that they elect that party to government. But this does not always happen. The necessity of a tax may become apparent only between scheduled elections. Sometimes, knowing that taxes are unpopular, candidates for office even conceal their intention to impose or raise taxes until after the election. It may then become plain, however, that the tax does not enjoy the consent of the people. Representative government as generally constituted at present has not devised any effective method of obtaining the explicit approval of the citizens for particular taxes or tax increases, or of declaring unpopular taxes illegitimate.

If the consent of the people is required before a government with its laws and taxes is legitimate, how does it come about that the consent of the majority will suffice? Why is it not necessary that all those who suffer from the laws and taxes must give their consent? The reason why this is so has two main elements in it.

One is that each individual must indeed consent voluntarily to be a citizen of his state, and this individual consent must be presupposed by any tax. No doubt in the ordinary case, where an individual grows up in a society, there is often no single step by which he makes an explicit decision to become a citizen. Rather, being the child of his parents, he initially becomes a member of the political community through them, even as a child, and acquires certain rights and privileges through them which are characteristic of that society. But as he comes of age and becomes an independent person, able to make decisions for himself in his own right, he assumes the mantle of citizenship, at least implicitly, by making use of the benefits which the protection afforded by the society places at his disposal. Does he wish to be a member of this community or not? He does, even though he may dislike many of its features. Anyone may at any time disown his citizenship.

But can we truly say that for most people citizenship is a voluntary action? Is it not rather the case that the person usually has no genuine choice in the matter? This is a question about what we take to be the criteria for a voluntary choice. If we believe that a choice is voluntary only when it is made in the absence of pressure and with a range of options available with relative ease, then this will not be a voluntary choice. We have argued above, however, that this is an inadequate notion of voluntariness and is rather a notion of ability. We saw that an adult's decisions concerning life in society must be considered voluntary choices so long as they are not deliberately impeded by others through willful deception or the use of physical force.

A second and even more crucial element in the reason why the consent of the majority can suffice to legitimize a government, and so a law, including a tax, is that the purpose of it is to protect everyone equally from harm. It is true that everyone will be harmed by having to pay the tax. But the only purpose of the tax, in the Lockean view, is to ward off from everybody a greater harm by supporting the justice and defense system, which is the sole justifiable reason for having a government, and from which the individual has already decided to benefit by being a citizen.

Our conclusion is, then, with Locke, that in order to have a legitimate tax, it is not necessary that it be approved unanimously, but only by a majority of the society, since *in matters like this* a majority can speak for the whole.

Since some taxes can be justified, then, does it follow that a government is entitled to impose any taxes on its citizens which it may consider to be for the good of the society, and which a majority may approve of? In the light of our reasoning the answer to this is clearly, no. The only taxes which can be imposed legitimately are those *to support the system of defense and justice*, because only these are for the purpose of warding harm off equally from all the citizens. In particular, this argumentation cannot be used to justify the transfer payments characteristic of the redistributive state. Robin Hood, and the government which takes it upon itself to act like him, is not protecting everyone equally from harm, but deliberately causing harm to some in order to provide a positive benefit to others. This is not only contrary to the basic principle of justice, but it also undermines the foundation of government, for it weakens or even entirely eliminates the principal motive which leads people to live under government, namely to be protected from harm. The redistributive state is a step back towards anarchy.

Do any rules follow, from the Lockean argument, for the apportionment of taxes among the citizens? The rule that would seem to follow would be that just as the protection from harm must be provided equally for all, so also the harm involved in that protection should fall so far as possible equally on all. This, of course, is a difficult thing to measure in detail, because of the many subjective elements, but a flat percentage tax would seem to be a fair approximation. It is sometimes objected that the protection which government affords does not fall equally on all, since the rich, having more possessions, receive more protection, and the poor less. The protection provided by the law is not quantifiable in this way, however. It is not as if the police employed more men to guard the lives, liberties and possessions of the rich than those of the poor. (In point of fact the costs of the police force are often higher for poorer neighborhoods.) The law protects by punishing those who cause injury. The punishment for the murder of a rich man is the same as that for the murder of a poor one; and the penalty for robbing the wealthy is the same as that for robbing the needy. A flat percentage tax is of course not an equal tax, but a proportionate one, yet historically it has often been looked at as if it were equal, and this has led to the introduction of what is called progressive taxation, which imposes a higher percentage on those who have more. The intent of this system is usually explicitly redistributive.

The validity of the Lockean argumentation must prevent us from ruling taxes out altogether on moral grounds. Yet considering the harm they do, it would certainly be for the benefit of mankind if other means could be devised to finance the legitimate tasks of government, for instance participation of some sort by the treasury in the market, since, as we have seen, market exchanges do not harm their participants.[15]

PRIVATE PROPERTY

The right to private property is an application of the principle of No Harm. Harm can be done to a person not only by violating his bodily integrity, but also by depriving him forcibly of the fruits of his labor. To rob a person is to harm him. And this is true whether he is poor or wealthy.

The reason why robbery is harmful is not far to seek. Locke's argument on this is essentially sound, despite the objections that have been raised against it. It derives from our ownership of our own persons. As we saw earlier in this book, to be a person is to possess the power of free choice, and with it the power of self-government, or autonomy. This brings with it the moral necessity not to use force to deprive another person of his power of free choice and self-government. The realm of free choice and autonomy is the person's entire self, including his body and his actions.

Human action is capable of being productive, that is, of fashioning the material of the universe into forms which serve human purposes. The physical and mental activity by which an individual labors to produce things is part of his existence as a person, his personal and bodily integrity, and falls most intimately within the realm of his power of self-government. To deprive a person by force of the goods which he has produced is to violate his power of self-government, and so to violate the primary moral necessity. As John Gray writes, "For anyone to have a property in his person means, in the first place and at the least, that he has disposition over his talents, abilities and labor. Unless this requirement of selfownership be satisfied, human beings are chattels – the property of another (as in the institution of slavery) or a resource of the community (as in a socialist state). This is because, if I lack the right to control my own body and labor, I cannot act to achieve my own goals and realize my own values: I must submit my ends to those of another, or to the requirements of a collective decision-procedure."[16]

Locke argues that we come to own property by "mixing our labor" with natural objects: we find an acorn, perhaps, or we catch a fish, and appropriate it as food. When, he asks, does it become ours? It is plain, he replies, that unless that first taking made it ours, no subsequent event could.

Critics profess to find this argument unsatisfying. What does it mean, they ask, to "mix our labor" with a natural object? – as if this were some profound puzzle. Jeremy Waldron asserts that it is a "category mistake," because labor is not an object, and the only things that can be mixed with objects are other objects.[17] Robert Nozick asks why mixing one's labor with something should make one the owner of it. When I mix my labor with something, why shouldn't it follow that I lose my labor rather than gain the thing? If I own a can of tomato juice and spill it in the sea, I don't come to own the sea, I merely lose my tomato juice, he objects. John Gray asserts on the basis of such objections that although it is clear that people have a right to dispose of their own labor, no adequate theory can be built on this as to how it is possible to acquire property initially.

Ownership means that an individual has a right against all the world to use an object as he wishes. That is, no one else is justified in using force to prevent him from doing with it as he wishes, provided that he causes no harm to others. The key question is the use of force. As we have seen, the use of force on a human being is always harmful. Sometimes that harm can be justified, namely when it is necessary to prevent or to punish harm. But otherwise the use of force is not justified. To say that Smith owns a watch is to say that if someone else tries to use that watch in a way that Smith does not consent to, it is permissible for Smith or the government to use force to prevent him; and that it is impermissible for anyone else to use force to prevent Smith from doing what he wants with the watch.

The least difficulty in this idea is presented by the case of creation. The poet who creates a poem, or the carpenter who creates a chair out of driftwood, clearly has an exclusive right to dispose of what he has created. If they wish to destroy their creations, or exchange them, no one else can have any right to prevent them. As Nozick concedes, "anyone is entitled to own a thing whose value he has created."

The case of an object which already exists, however, appears initially to be very different. When a fisherman catches a fish, his role may seem to be much less than that of a creator. Nozick asks why his entitlement should extend to the whole fish rather than just to the *added value* his labor has produced. And he remarks that "no workable or coherent value-added property scheme has yet been devised."

Despite the doubts harbored by philosophers, however, in the eyes of most people the fish becomes the property of him who catches it, and anyone who takes it from him is a thief. Let us analyze, then, what happens conceptually when we catch a fish, to see if there is any basis for this common view. Before the fish is caught it belongs to no one. Locke, it is true, basing himself on a literal reading of Genesis, felt obliged to assume that God gave the world to mankind, and that therefore everything in the world belonged to the human race in common until it was appropriated by individuals. This idea, however, seems somewhat far-fetched, that the squirrels on my front lawn and the flounder in the Atlantic belong to mankind in general. It seems truer to the actual state of affairs to say that they do not belong to anybody.

When Smith catches the fish, what has his labor accomplished, that it should have the result that Smith becomes the exclusive owner of the fish? The answer is surely that it has made the fish available for human consumption. When Smith catches the fish, he establishes a special relationship between himself and the fish, such that this-fish-lying-here-on-this-rock-and-available-for-human-consumption now constitutes the fruit of his labor, just as the portrait produced by the painter and the manuscript produced by the writer constitute the fruit of their labor.

Nozick assumes that the fish already has economic value before it is caught, and that the fisherman only adds to its value. But this is a mistake.

The uncaught fish swimming in the ocean has no economic value. Economic value, as we saw in Chapter 4, is created by the proportion of demand to supply. Just as a gadget which no one wants has no economic value, no matter how much work may have gone into it, and no matter what other values it may possess, such as beauty or sentimental value, so an object which is not somehow in the possession of a human being has no economic value. No doubt it has something which we could call potential for economic value, but not economic value itself. Economic value is always easy to measure (in a free market): it is the price which a buyer and a seller agree on. There is no way to measure the economic value of an uncaught fish, or of any unappropriated object. There is no way to measure even its use-value, since that can become apparent only after taking into account the labor of acquisition, which cannot be known before acquisition.[18] The economic value of an unappropriated object is like the sound of one hand clapping.

At the present time there is widespread understanding of the desirability of preserving endangered species of wildlife. This is not based on their present economic value, which we have no idea how to estimate, but on the assumption that in virtue of their genetic characteristics they may some day prove to be of value in ways that we are now unaware of. How would that future value, if it should exist, become available for human beings? Only by reason of the fact that someone possesses them, or possesses other forms of life on which they have a beneficent influence.

But isn't it possible for something to have value even though no one owns it, such as the sunlight and the air?

Value is always the value of some definite thing for some definite person or persons. We must ask: what is the value of what particular sunlight for what particular person? The sunlight that falls on my lawn has the value (if that is the right term in the middle of summer) that it makes the grass grow. The sunlight that falls on a particular person may increase his store of vitamin D or give him skin cancer. The sunlight that falls on his solar heating collector warms his house. Each of these potential values becomes an actual value by coming into the possession of an actual person.

There is some sense in which even the most ardent collectivist will grant a right to private property. The principal problems arise not so much in regard to the idea of personal ownership as such, but in regard to the extent or the limits of that ownership. Granted that at some point and in some sense individual persons can own the food that they eat and the clothes that they wear, can this ownership be absolute and unconditional, or is it always subject to conditions arising out of the community, so that at least in some circumstances others can have a right to them? If Jones is starving, does the community not have the right to take the fish that Smith has caught and give it to Jones?

Locke recognizes a twofold limit on the right of an individual to catch fish (and so, by extension, to acquire any property). One is that he must catch only as much as he can use, there must be no spoilage, otherwise the equal rights of others to catch the fish and benefit from them are infringed upon. This limitation is removed, however, by the invention of money, says Locke, since all goods can be exchanged for money, and money does not spoil. With the invention of money, then, there are no limits in principle to the amount of wealth a person may own.

The second limitation which Locke places on the right to catch fish is that there must be "enough and as good" left for others. This limitation is widely accepted even by defenders of free markets. In Nozick's view it casts a "shadow" over all subsequent acquisition of property in the market, to rule out all monopolies of things necessary for life.

But this also is a mistake. Suppose that there is only one fish left in the ocean: is there then an obligation to leave it there for others to catch? As Nozick seems to recognize, if everyone has the same obligation, it will never be permissible to catch the fish. And if there are two fish left, it will not be permissible to catch one, since that would leave only one. And if there are three, it will not be permissible to catch one, since that will leave only two. And so on *ad infinitum*.

A group of people are trapped in a bank vault. Eventually their supply of oxygen will run out. Each one, just by the fact of breathing, is eventually going to bring it about that not enough and as good air is left for the others. Does this mean that each one has an obligation in justice to stop breathing? Presumably not. The same will hold good for their supply of food and water. If this is the case, then there cannot be a general principle which requires us always to leave enough and as good for others.

The true limit on the quantity of property that one may initially appropriate out of the "state of nature" is set, not by whether one leaves enough for others, but by whether what one appropriates is being used, or is intended to be used, for human purposes. A farmer who moves onto unclaimed land and begins growing crops on it, even if only for himself, acquires title to that land because he is making it productive for human consumption. And if he stakes out a further piece of land next to it for the purpose of growing crops on it in the near future, he acquires title to that land also. On the other hand, if he intends to grow crops on it only in fifty years' time, his position is much less secure. This means that title to property can come in varying degrees. In order to exchange property, one must have full title.

Nozick, who accepted "the Lockean proviso," concluded that it rules out certain kinds of monopolies, such as ownership of all the drinkable water in the world, or of the only water-hole in a desert, or at least that it rules out such an owner's charging whatever he likes. Nozick allowed, by contrast, that this limitation does not prevent a medical researcher who invents a new drug from refusing to sell except on his terms. The difference between the two cases in Nozick's view is that in the second the owner is not worsening the condition of others because the substance did not previously exist, or at least its properties were not known, and so no one has suffered a loss by his discovery; but in the case of the water monopoly the condition of the others is being worsened because the water existed previously. The crucial question, he maintained, is whether one worsens the condition of others. (He also seems willing to allow a monopoly of a water-hole where the water would have dried up but for the action of the owner.)

But, as we have seen, not all worsening of a person's condition constitutes causing him harm. To repeat the example given earlier, if I have a close friend whose companionship I cherish, and he goes to live in India, while I remain in the United States, my condition is worsened because I lose his companionship, but it would not be correct to say that he has caused me harm.

Floating in the middle of the Atlantic ocean is an unusual piece of seaweed, which happens to have the property that it cures cancer. Brown, who has cancer, and is sailing by, notices it and uses it. It is true that he does not leave enough and as good for others. But has he caused them harm? No. Suppose that others know that it is there (it has been sighted from a plane), but they have been slow to get there. Is he causing them harm? Still, no. Suppose that instead of using it himself, he sells it to the highest bidder. Has he now caused harm to the others? Again, no.

If a person already has clear and full title to a water-hole and prohibits a person dying of thirst from drinking at it, or charges a very high price for it, he may be behaving with immense inhumanity, but we are not entitled to say that he is causing his death. If the traveler had brought a water-bottle with him, and he stole it, he would be causing his death.

WIDER IMPLICATIONS OF THE PRINCIPLE OF NO HARM

Some commentators have felt that one of the chief objections to the Principle of No Harm arises from the consequences that would follow from it in other fields than the economic. In particular it seems that sexual morality as sanctioned by the law would have to undergo a revolution. If market exchanges take place only because both parties expect to benefit and should therefore not be regulated by any special laws, it would seem that the same principle should apply to sexual behavior between consenting adults. In that case adult incest, prostitution, polygamy and polyandry should be allowed by the law. The free marketer is then impaled on the horns of a dilemma: either he must reject this conclusion, in which case he will be guilty of an impossible inconsistency, or he must allow it, in which case he takes a position which appears to be thoroughly repugnant to most Americans and which has no practical chance of being enacted into law.

Sexual behavior undoubtedly occupies a special place among human concerns, since it has to do with the procreation of human life and touches on the most intimate aspects of human personality. If human life is sacred, arguably that sacredness extends to the process by which individual persons come into existence. It seems reasonable, then, to believe that sexual behavior ought to be governed by certain moral principles and that some kinds of sexual behavior should be rejected as immoral. But it does not follow from this that sexual immorality ought to be punished by the law. There is an analogy here between sexual immorality and other forms of immorality. The person who could easily help someone in distress but callously refuses to do so violates a moral principle and is behaving immorally. But we have argued that he ought not to be punished by the law because he has not caused harm. Behavior can be justly prohibited by the civil law only if it causes harm, and not merely because it offends against other canons of morality. But the mere fact that an action (or a failure to act) is immoral does not mean that it causes harm. Whether an action causes harm is a factual question, to be decided by the evidence.

Although in the case of certain kinds of sexual behavior between consenting adults it is possible for a person to cause harm to himself or herself, we must rule out the possibility that one may cause harm to the other, for reasons we have already seen. But it remains possible that harm may be caused to third parties. The third parties who are most obviously candidates for being harmed are children and spouses. Since this book is concerned in the first instance with the market, and not with sexual behavior, it would be out of place to investigate this question in the detail it deserves, but we can indicate perhaps some broad outlines.

It is well established that incest may cause genetic harm to children. This presupposes of course that the incestuous act is not effectively contraceptive, a condition now easily avoided by most people in societies with advanced economies. But even where a defective child is born from an incestuous union, and even though there can be no doubt that the parents are responsible for the condition of the child, it is not automatically clear that they can properly be said to have caused harm to the child in the sense required by the Principle of No Harm. The only alternative in this case to being born with a genetic defect is not to be born at all, but those who are born with disabilities do not typically believe that they would have been better off if they had never been born.[19] The principle that persons ought not to be harmed assumes that those persons already exist, and conceiving and giving birth to a deformed child is not the same thing as causing harm to an already existing person. A woman who smokes, and as a result gives birth to a child suffering from a deformity, although she has acted in a regrettable and irresponsible fashion, is not widely thought to have committed a crime, even if she realized that there was a danger of such an outcome, whereas if she had caused comparable harm to the child after its birth, that would certainly be the case.

Does polygamy cause harm to women? Here the chief question for us is that of consent. If a man has one wife, and wishes to take another, there cannot be any objection if both women give genuine consent. The first wife must consent not only in principle, but to the particular person of the second wife. Polygamy has often been practiced, however, on the assumption that the existing wife or wives have no voice in the matter, an arrangement which violates their contractual rights. Where this assumption prevails, polygamy will rightly be felt to be demeaning to women. But where the existing wives have absolute power of veto, it is difficult to see how it could be demeaning to them.

The same considerations will apply to polyandry. An additional objection sometimes made to polyandry is that it harms the children, or society, by making it impossible to identify their father. But the need to identify the father arises chiefly from the necessity of making him responsible for his children. This can be taken care of in a polyandrous family by making both or all the husbands fully responsible for all the children.

In the case of prostitution the question of harm arises chiefly in relation to public decency. Solicitation for prostitution can be carried on in such a way as to constitute a public nuisance, and in that case can justifiably be regulated by law like any other nuisance, but it is the manner of the solicitation, not the prostitution, which causes the harm. Something similar can be said in regard to homosexual practices, which do not deserve to be prohibited by law, since consenting homosexuals cannot be viewed as causing harm to one another. The public flaunting of homosexuality, however, can raise legitimate problems of offensiveness, analogous to that of a public nuisance.

There is reason to believe that the American public is by no means so opposed to the legalization of these victimless "crimes" as is widely supposed, and also that the catastrophic effects commonly expected from such legalization are not actually to be feared. Homosexual practices, once punishable by death, have now been generally legalized. Anglo-American common law does not make incest a criminal offense. In England, although the Puritan government of Cromwell made it punishable by death in 1650, from the time of the Restoration the statute was long not strictly enforced, and numerous attempts to make it a crime were unsuccessful until the Punishment of Incest act of 1908. In the United States there are still some states where it is not a crime, and even where it is, it is not widely enforced. Yet it is not clear that this has produced any widespread practice of it. It seems safe to say that nature has made it sufficiently repugnant that it will never be practiced to any great extent.

Prostitution as such is not penalized by the law in Great Britain, which focuses chiefly on public decency, and on procurers.[20] In the United States the law on prostitution allows more freedom in some states than others, Nevada being perhaps especially noteworthy, since the state government there became itself the owner, if reluctantly, of a house of prostitution.[21] In the Middle Ages prostitutes had in effect their own guild, and enjoyed special legal protection, as they still do in parts of Europe.[22] A person of liberal mind should be open to the possibility that at least for some people under some circumstances this kind of sexual outlet may serve a positive function. For example, for some disabled persons who are cut off from the possibility of marriage by their physical condition this may be the only viable form in which they can experience sexual intimacy. There is general agreement among those who have studied the question closely that more harm is caused by driving prostitution underground than by permitting it, subject to regulation as regards public decency.[23]

In Utah and neighboring states it is estimated that there are some tens of thousands of polygamous families, as mentioned above.[24] Periodic attempts have been made to enforce the law against them, but these attempts have generally encountered so much opposition from their neighbors that they have been quickly abandoned. The neighbors apparently feel that they should be let alone since they are not causing harm.[25] Even St. Augustine of Hippo considered that a plurality of wives (as contrasted with a plurality of husbands) was not against the nature of marriage.[26]

CONCLUSION

The temptation to use the ferocious penalties of the law against those who have done no harm, in order to achieve ends deemed noble, seems to be endemic to even the highest-minded idealists. Despite the great and undoubtedly often selfless contributions of organized religion to the human enterprise, for example, there is scarcely any major form of it which has not leapt to enforce its beliefs by the sword when that opportunity became available to it. The Inquisition, though a particularly notorious instance of this, was only one. When Calvin's Geneva burnt the Basque scholar Michael Servetus at the stake because he had written a heretical book, many Protestant intellectuals rushed to defend the action against criticism. Cried the prominent theologian Theodore Beza on the subject of heresy, "What greater, more abominable crime could one find among men? . . . It would seem impossible to find a torture big enough to fit the enormity of such a misdeed."[27] As late as 1766, in a France esteemed the crown of European enlightenment, when the young Chevalier de la Barre failed to doff his hat in respect while a Capuchin procession passed through the streets of Abbeville, since it was raining, he was charged and convicted of blasphemy and sentenced to "the torture ordinary and extraordinary," his hands to be cut off, his tongue torn out with pincers, and to be burned alive.[28]

We look on such events with horror. How could a civilized people, let alone a religious one, we ask, condone such barbarity? *We* would never dream of doing such things. We believe in fairness. We believe in sensitivity. If we sentence people to life imprisonment without parole for possessing a pound and a half of cocaine,[29] or confiscate their cars, boats, and houses,[30] or bomb people in Columbia for growing the drug, that is altogether different. If we are prepared to allow people to die of AIDS or heart disease rather than let them be "exploited" by buying an experimental medicine, that bears no resemblance to the religious inhumanity of the Middle Ages. If we deprive seamstresses of their livelihood for no other reason than that they use machines at home;[31] if we threaten to put employers out of business who create jobs at "only" $4 an hour; or who employ only members of their own sex, or sell only to their own race; if we tear buildings down without compensation because they do not have ramps for the disabled; if we imprison managers whose workers are injured on the job;[32] if we fine those who offer rides in their car for a fee without special governmental permission—all of these penalties are sensitive and humane, promote fairness, and should not be mentioned in the same breath with the absurdities of past ages.

In the meantime, we complain about the state of our economy. If our productivity is declining, if we are ever less competitive against other nations, if we suffer wracking recessions, that must be the fault of our managers, or our workers, or our spendthrift consumers, and could not possibly be the fault of our laws. This is like the man who hobbled his horse, then whipped it because it would not gallop.

Those who cause harm to others should be punished. Gangsters who demand protection money should go to prison, cheaters and frauds should feel the heavy hand of the law. But no one should be penalized for providing jobs that other people willingly apply for, for offering goods or services for sale that others are willing to buy, or for refusing to do business with anyone they have not contracted to do business with, whatever their reasons.

Notes

Introduction

1. The cost of labor includes not only wages and benefits but also the costs imposed by union work rules and job classifications, and by the inefficiencies of hiring and firing rules. See: Peter Drucker, "Workers' Hands Bound by Tradition," *Wall Street Journal*, Aug. 2, 1988; id. "The Danger of Excessive Labor Income," *Wall St. J.*, Jan. 6, 1981; Arthur Neef and Christopher Kask, "Manufacturing Productivity and Labor Costs in 14 Economies," *Monthly Labor Review*, 114: 12 (Dec. 1991), 24–37; Richard Epstein, *Forbidden Grounds: The Case Against Employment Discrimination Legislation* (Cambridge: Harvard Univ. Press, 1992); Clyde V. Prestowitz Jr., *Trading Places* (New York: Basic Books, 1988); Steve H. Hanke and Stephen J. K. Walters, *Social Regulation, a Report Card* (Washington, DC: National Chamber Foundation, 1990); "Preserving Jobs and Productivity," *Business Week*, 78 (Sept. 1990) 27–28.

2. See, for example, Beryl Sprinkel, "An Anti-Recession Agenda," *Wall St. J.*, Jan. 25, 1991, sec. A; David Wessel, "As Banks Get Tough with Borrowers, Fears of a Recession Rise," *Wall St. J.*, Mar. 22, 1990, sec. A; Alan Murray, "Fed's Stinginess Aggravates the Threat of a Long Recession, Economists Say," *Wall St. J.*, Sept. 25, 1990, sec. A; Paul Craig Roberts, "How To Wreck An Economy," *National Review*, 44 (1992) Mar. 30, 32–33.

3. See Andrew S. Carron, *The Plight of the Thrift Institutions* (Washington, DC: Brookings Institution, 1982); James R. Barth, *The Great Savings and Loan Debacle* (Washington, DC: AEI Press, 1991); Edward J. Kane, *The S & L Insurance Mess: How Did It Happen?* (Washington, DC: Urban Institute Press, 1989).

4. See John Chubb and Terry M. Moe, *Politics, Markets, and America's Schools* (Washington, DC: Brookings Institution, 1990); id., *Politics, Markets, and the Organization of Schools* (Washington, DC: Brookings Institution, 1989); Chester E. Finn, *Education Reform in the 90s* (New York: Macmillan, 1992); id., *Scholars, Dollars and Bureaucrats* (Washington, DC: Brookings Institution, 1978); Diane Ravitch, *The Schools We Deserve* (New York: Basic Books, 1985).

5. Charles Murray, *Losing Ground,* American Social Policy 1950–1980 (New York: Basic Books, 1984).

6. See the study by Melinda Warren, *Government Regulation and American Business,* Center for the Study of American Business (St. Louis: Washington University, 1992). Since 1990 alone, the Clean Air, Americans with Disabilities, Nutrition Labeling and Education, Workers Right to Know, and Family Leave Acts have been passed.

7. See also the statement of Pope John Paul II on the deficiencies of capitalism: *New York Times,* May 10, 1990, sec. A, a view repeated in his encyclical letter *On the Hundredth Anniversary of Rerum Novarum (Centesimus Annus),* par. 42.

8. Socialism can be defined in a variety of ways, but the description given here is perhaps the one most relevant to the twentieth century.

9. Fred Mannering and Clifford Winston, "Economic Effects of Voluntary Export Restrictions," in Clifford Winston and Associates, *Blind Intersection: Policy and the Automobile Industry,* Washington, DC: The Brookings Institution, 1987), Chap. 4, pp. 61ff.

10. See Robert DeFina, *Public and Private Expenditures for Federal Regulation of Business,* Working Paper No. 22, Center for the Study of American Business (St. Louis: Washing Univ., 1977); Murray Weidenbaum, *The Future of Business Regulation* (New York: American Management Association, 1979); Milton and Rose Friedman, *Free To Choose* (New York: Avon Books, 1980); Steve H. Hanke and Stephen J. K. Walters, *Social Regulation: A Report Card* (Washington, DC: National Chamber Foundation, 1990); Stephen J. K. Walters, *Enterprise, Government, and the Public* (New York: McGraw-Hill, 1992); Steven Landsburg, *Price Theory and Applications* (Fort Worth: Dryden Press, 1992); Edward F. Denison, "Effects of Selected Changes in the Institutional and Human Environment upon Output per Unit of Input," *Survey of Current Business,* Washington, DC: Brookings Institution, Jan. 1978. A short, easily readable article is that by Richard Vedder and Lowell Gallaway, "How To Increase Unemployment," *National Review,* 44, no. 22 (Nov. 16, 1992). The economic effects of government regulation of market activities are examined to some extent in most standard textbooks of economics.

11. Also a good deal of moral pressure is applied: the U.S. Catholic bishops, for example, who have advocated heavy regulation of the economy in the name of fairness, concede that Catholics may disagree with their position about the means of the economic transformation of society, but not about the "basic moral objectives." These appear to include "economic rights": rights to food, clothing, shelter, rest, medical care, basic education, employment and social security. The U.S. Catholic Bishops, *Economic Justice for All: Catholic Social Teaching and the U.S. Economy* (Washington, DC: Origins, 1986): no. 84.

12. Some laws, of course, provide exemptions from penalties, but they are parasitic upon those that impose the penalties. This topic is discussed further in Chapter 6.

13. Peter Berger, *The Capitalist Revolution* (New York: Basic Books, 1986), 19.

14. Michael Novak, in his book *The Spirit of Democratic Capitalism* (New York: American Enterprise Institute, Simon and Schuster, 1982), makes an argument for capitalism as a tripartite system, economic, moral and political, but as contrasted with market freedom.

15. Albert Einstein, "Ueber den Einfluss der Schwerkraft auf die Ausbreitung des Lichtes," *Annalen der Physik*, Ser. 4, vol. 35 (1911); "Die Grundlage der allgemeinen Relativitaetstheorie," *Annalen der Physik*, Ser. 4, vol. 49 (1916) 769–822. Described by A. P. French in "The Story of General Relativity," *Einstein, A Centenary Volume* (Cambridge: Harvard Univ. Press, 1979) 98ff; by Ronald W. Clark, *Einstein, The Life and Times* (London: Hodder & Stoughton, 1973) Chap. 8; and by Leopold Infeld, *Albert Einstein, His Work and Its Influence on Our World* (New York: Scribner's, 1950) Chap. IV. It seems, however, that Einstein was supremely confident that his theory was correct.

16. I accept Lakatos's thesis that it may take a long time and a complex effort before it becomes generally clear in the natural sciences that a theory should be abandoned. See his "Falsification and the Methodology of Scientific Research Programmes" in Imre Lakatos and Alan Musgrave, eds., *Criticism and the Growth of Knowledge* (New York: Cambridge Univ. Press, 1970) 91–196. As a general rule it seems to be true that theories are not so much proven to be true as shown to warrant reasonable assent. However, it seems to me to be an exaggeration to think, as many philosophers of science now apparently take for granted, that no theory whatsoever can be finally refuted. The phlogiston theory would appear to be a clear example of a theory which has no chance of being resurrected. Nor does it seem to be correct to believe that no theory whatsoever can be unquestionably confirmed. The Law of Fixed Proportions in chemistry would seem to be a clear example of a theory which will not be falsified. Besides this there is surely an important difference between disproving a theory and showing that it applies only to a narrower range of phenomena than was previously supposed.

17. As even some philosophers have acknowledged; see Richard Rorty, *Philosophy and the Mirror of Nature* (Princeton, NJ: Princeton Univ. Press) 1979.

18. In an earlier publication I remarked that "the movement for social justice . . . must be regarded as the most significant event of the modern age," and that "the legal, economic and even linguistic structures of society must be transformed to confer equality on disadvantaged minorities and the underprivileged of every sort." *The Fragile Universe, An Essay in the Philosophy of Religions* (London: Macmillan, 1979) 106.

Chapter One: The Liberal Society

1. Patrick Devlin's argument for the protection of morality by legislation is not dissimilar to this in *The Enforcement of Morals* (Oxford: Oxford Univ. Press,

1965). The idea of "shared meanings" derives from George Herbert Mead. For a history of English law relating to heretics, see Pollock and Maitland, *History of English Law*, 2d ed. (Cambridge: Cambridge Univ. Press 1898) 2:543–557.

2. Initially the amendment was understood to apply only to federal legislation, so that restrictive state laws could still be maintained.

3. This development did not come out of the blue. It had been preceded in England by the Act of Toleration in 1689, which guaranteed freedom of religion to those who dissented from the Church of England, although the Church of England remained, as it does to this day, the established church of that country, and although Catholics remained under certain civil disabilities. In Boston more moderate Puritans had gained the ascendancy, and in the colonies in general a spirit of tolerance had become prevalent. It seems clear, however, that the scope of the First Amendment, as it was understood by the members of the First Congress, was more restricted than it has subsequently been interpreted to be. See Chester James Antieau, Arthur T. Downey, and Edward C. Roberts, *Freedom from Federal Establishment, Formation and Early History of the First Amendment Religion Clauses* (Milwaukee: Bruce Publishing Co., 1964).

4. Roger Williams, *Bloudy Tenent of Persecution for Cause of Conscience* (1644). This is with reference to organized religion. No doubt there are certain minimal convictions about ethical and moral principles which need to undergird a society, in order to uphold the rule of law. It remains to be seen to what extent these can be maintained in the general absence of private religion.

5. G. P. Thomson, article "Censorship," *Encyclopedia Britannica*, 14th ed. (1961): 5:119.

6. Text of the rules handed to travelers at the Austrian border, quoted in George R.Marek, *Beethoven, Biography of a Genius* (New York: Funk and Wagnalls, 1969) 355.

7. This was the Roman doctrine of "concession," "under which no group or association, however deeply rooted in history and tradition, however profoundly structured in human allegiances, could claim to have legal existence, legal reality, indeed, except insofar as this existence and reality had been conceded by the sovereign." Robert Nisbet, *Twilight of Authority* (New York: Oxford Univ. Press, 1970) 170; quoted in N. Rosenberg and L. E. Birdzell, Jr: *How The West Grew Rich* (New York: Basic Books, 1986) 196. One of the obstacles to the creation of the modern commercial corporation was "the assumption, which runs through the whole of continental public law, that associations of any kind must not be formed without being authorised by the State" (Sir Frederick Pollock, *A First Book of Jurisprudence* 5th ed. (London: Macmillan, 1923] 115–116; also quoted in Rosenberg and Birdzell).

8. John Locke, *A Letter Concerning Toleration*, vol. 35, *Great Books of the Western World* (Chicago: Encyclopedia Britannica, 1952).

9. Historically, the growth of respect for the individual person and the emergence of freedom of religion, of speech, and of association accompanied the growth and development of the middle class.

10. Locke, *Toleration*.
11. While the liberal society did not blossom until the nineteenth century in Great Britain, aspects of it were already well developed by the time of the Glorious Revolution, and paradoxically even earlier under Cromwell. French and German society were also in the process of liberalizing, if somewhat more tardily. One example of this is the principle of the freedom of teaching and learning (*Lehrfreiheit* and *Lernfreiheit*) at the German universities.
12. John Gray, *Liberalisms: Essays in Political Philosophy* (London: Routledge Press, 1989) 241.
13. Ibid., 243.
14. See Harry Elmer Barnes, *The Story of Punishment* (1930, Stratford Co.; reprint, Montclair NJ: Patterson Smith, 1972) Chaps. 5, 6.
15. Ibid., Chap. 3.
16. Ibid., Chap. 1.
17. Concern for health and economic efficiency played a large role in enacting the Prohibition laws, as well as explicitly religious and moral concerns. The Report of the Federal Council of Churches mentions some negative effects of Prohibition. See Ernest H. Cherrington, *The Evolution of Prohibition in the USA*, 1920; D. L. Colvin, *Prohibition in the US: A History of the Prohibition Party & Movement*, 1926; P. H. Odegard, *Pressure Politics: the Story of the Anti-Saloon League*, 1928.
18. L. T. Hobhouse, *Liberalism* (New York; Oxford Univ. Press, 1911).
19. A thorough analysis of the various meanings of "freedom" is given by Friedrich von Hayek in his classic work *The Constitution of Liberty* (Chicago: Univ. of Chicago Press, 1960) Chap. 1.
20. However, it may be permissible not to enforce certain kinds of contract. See "The Enforcement of Contracts," Chapter 2, 70–73.
21. As a political term in English it is derived from the "Liberales," a Spanish political party of the early nineteenth century.
22. John Stuart Mill, *On Liberty*, Ch. 1. ed. Alburey Castell, (Arlington Heights, ILL: Harlan Davidson, 1947).
23. As we shall see in Chapter 2, the threat of force may not always be sufficient to remove freedom in the case of the commission of a crime.
24. Nathan Rosenberg and L. E. Birdzell, Jr., *How The West Grew Rich* (New York: Basic Books, 1986) 37ff.
25. R. H. Tawney, *Religion and the Rise Of Capitalism* (West Drayton, U.K.:Penguin, 1926; New York: Harcourt, Brace and Co, 1937) 58.
26. Gray, *Liberalism*, 33.
27. Lawrence M. Friedman, *A History of American Law* (New York: Simon and Schuster, 1973) 296.
28. Ibid., 384–408.
29. Ibid.
30. Editorial in the July 20, 1991, issue of *The Economist*.
31. In an incident which has been the subject of much comment, the Scripps-Howard News Service reported in September 1990 that an undergraduate at the University of Pennsylvania was corrected by an instructor for using the

word "individual" because it was bound up in the "dominant culture."
Montgomery County Record, Sept. 1990.
32. "Human Sacrifice," editorial in the *Wall St. J.*, June 2, 1987
33. The case of the Living Well Lady fitness centers; see *Philadelphia Inquirer*, Nov. 27, 1990.
34. See Don R. Pember, *Mass Media Law* (Dubuque, Iowa: William C. Brown Co., 1977) 452ff.
35. See Milton Friedman, "The Economics of Free Speech," in Bernard H. Siegan, ed., *Regulation, Economics, and the Law* (Lexington: MA: D. C. Heath and Co., 1979) 111–117. R. H. Coase has an excellent treatment of this question in *The Market for Goods and the Market for Ideas* (Washington, DC: American Enterprise Institute, 1975).
36. A particularly egregious example is the recent furor at Harvard over a book classifying blacks and women together with low-risk-takers as having a high "interpersonal orientation." See "Harvard Memo Ignites Debate on Race, Sex," *Wall St. J.*, Oct. 30, 1992. The chief question a university should be concerned about is surely whether such conclusions are true.
37. Adam Smith, *Wealth of Nations*.
38. See Henry Brod, "Philosophy Teaching as Intellectual Affirmative Action," in *Teaching Philosophy* (March 1986).

Chapter Two: The Principle of Mutual Benefit

1. See "New Rules Unravel Careers for Home Knitters," *Philadelphia Inquirer*, Oct. 22, 1990, sec. D. See also "Beware of Ads for At-Home Workers," ibid., Nov. 8, 1990, sec. C.
2. Ibid.
3. F. H. Bradley, *Ethical Studies*, 2d ed. (Oxford Clarendon Press, 1927) 26–27. It is true that Bradley seems later to distance himself somewhat from this view, but the present author considers it a valid statement.
4. "Mistake" in the sense, for example, of buying something one did not intend to buy: as when you order a book with a certain title, but get sent one with a similar but different title by mistake.
5. Plato, *Republic*, Book 2. Friedman points out: "Adam Smith's key insight was that both parties to an exchange can benefit and that, *so long as cooperation is strictly voluntary*, no exchange will take place unless both parties do benefit." *Free To Choose*, xv.
6. This formulation I owe to Prof. John Hasnas.
7. Smith, *Wealth of Nations*, Bk. 4, Chap. 2.
8. Joel Feinberg, *Harmless Wrongdoing* (New York: Oxford Univ. Press, 1988) 184.
9. Joel Feinberg, *Harm to Self* (New York: Oxford Univ. Press, 1986) 226. Feinberg is dealing directly with the question whether an action is an offer or a threat. Since the difference is that an offer is beneficial, while a threat is harmful, it seems clear that the same criteria apply to the question of benefit and harm.

Robert Nozick takes a similar position to Feinberg's in this respect, that the baseline should be "what would have been in the normal and expected course of events," whereby "expected" is meant to straddle "predicted" and "morally required." "Coercion," *Philosophy, Science and Method*, ed. S. Morgenbesser et al., (New York: St. Martin's Press, 1969) 447.

10. Feinberg, *Harm to Self*, and Harm To Others (New York: Oxford Univ. Press, 1984) Chap. 4.

11. Franz Hinkelammert, *The Ideological Weapons of Death, A Theological Critique of Capitalism* trans. Phillip Berryman (Maryknoll, NY: Orbis Books, 1986) esp. 28ff.

12. Aristotle, *Nichomachean Ethics*, 1110a and b.

13. Alan Wertheimer, *Coercion* (Princeton: Princeton Univ. Press, 1987), summarizes on p. 172.

14. Wertheimer, *Coercion*, Part 2, esp. 307ff. In Wertheimer's view, whether a situation is to be interpreted as coercive depends, and should depend, on our independent moral judgement as to whether the person is entitled to do what he is under pressure to do. Feinberg, however, rejects a moralized concept of coercion.

15. David A. Hoekema, in his otherwise excellent book *Rights and Wrongs, Coercion, Punishment and the State* (Cranbury, NJ: Associated University Presses, 1986), seems to adopt two contradictory positions on this. On the one hand he clearly makes a distinction between ability and freedom: "Lack of freedom should not be confused with inability. Everyone is free to play the *Hammerklavier* sonata on the piano, or for that matter on the accordion. . . . A person who studies the piano until he can play the Beethoven sonatas gains an ability he lacked but does not increase his freedom" (p. 65). But a few pages later he seems to forget this, when he allows the possibility that a mountain range may make the residents of a valley unfree, and remarks that an airline pass or a check for $100,000 can greatly increase a person's freedom. What these things increase is surely a person's ability to accomplish something.

16. Information about this Soviet law, which is a law against exploitation, was obtained largely in conversation with Soviet economist Yuri Kochevrin, of the Institute of World Economy and International Relations (USSR), May 19, 1990.

17. Richard Norman, *Free and Equal, A Philosophical Examination of Political Values* (Oxford: Oxford Univ. Press, 1987) 47.

18. See Harry Frankfurt, "Coercion and Moral Responsibility," in *Essays on Freedom of Action*, ed. Ted Honderich; Virginia Held, "Coercion and Coercive Offers," in *Coercion Nomos* 14: 49–62; ed. Pennock and Chapman; Hoekema, *Rights and Wrongs*, 48f.; Robert Stevens, "Coercive Offers," *Australian Journal of Philosophy*, 66 (1988):83–95; Wertheimer, *Coercion*, Chap. 12 and esp. 13; Vinti Hiksar, "Coercive Proposals," *Political Theory* 65 (1976):4; Bernard Gert, "Coercion and Freedom" in *Nomos* 14; Feinberg, "Non-coercive Exploitation," *Paternalism*, ed. Rolf Sartorius (Minneapolis: Univ. of Minnesota Press 1983) 208–9; Theodore Bendit, "Threats and Offers," *The Personalist* 58 (1977):382, 384; David Zimmerman, "Coercive Wage Offers," *Philosophy and Public Affairs*, 10 (1981).

Nozick however rejects the view that an offer of a benefit can be coercive. Similarly Richard Epstein, "A Common Law for Labor Relations: A Critique of the New Deal Labor Legislation," *Yale Law Journal* 92 (1982):1357, 1372 (a prospective employer does not coerce anyone if he decides not to start the business).

Feinberg has an amusing paragraph on the difference between threats and offers. He considers the case (given by Nozick) of a man B whose boat has capsized and who has been swimming for hours and is now near exhaustion when A's boat approaches. A says that he will rescue B if B promises to pay $10,000 within three days. "Suppose we ask whether B would be worse off . . . if the projected consequence occurred than he would be in the normal course of events that could have been expected had A never even chanced upon the scene." Feinberg follows the argument through carefully and finds that he has come to the conclusion that A was *not* threatening B in saying that he would not rescue him unless he promised to pay the money. But, says Feinberg, this conclusion is too counterintuitive to be true (*Harm To Self*, 220).

19. For example Hoekema, *Rights and Wrongs*, 48.
20. Feinberg, *Harm To Self*, 233. Frankfurt, in his article "Coercion and Moral Responsibility," says that an offer of a benefit is coercive when the person is "incapable" of resisting his desire for the benefit, and when he would over-come this desire if he could. The effect of this, however, is to make a person who is merely weak-willed not responsible for his actions.
21. *Harm To Self*, 234f.
22. *Harm To Self*, 254. Feinberg makes this remark comparing two different but related cases. In the first case a woman has a baby who will die without expensive surgery, and a "lecherous millionaire" offers to provide the neces-sary money if the woman will sleep with him. In the second case, a gunman kidnaps the child and threatens to kill it unless the woman sleeps with him. Feinberg had previously, p. 234, given as a similar instance to the first, the case of the executive choosing between the jobs in New York and Houston.
23. Robert Nozick, in his article "Coercion," gives a good explanation of why the hold-up is wrong. It is not simply that the victim is harmed by giving up his money, because in a certain sense that is not true, since giving up his money saves him from the threatened harm, but that he has been placed against his will in a situation where he must choose between only two alternatives, giving up his money and suffering harm.
24. Jeffrie G. Murphy asks this question in: "Blackmail: A Preliminary Inquiry," *The Monist*, 63, no. 2 (1980):156–171. Murray N. Rothbard, a noted Liber-tarian, takes this position in *Man, Economy, and State*, (Princeton: Van Nos-trand, 1962) 1:443, n.49.
25. The Crimes Code of Pennsylvania, which may be taken as representative, defines theft by extortion as follows (3922):

A person is guilty of theft if he intentionally obtains or withholds property of another by threatening to:
1. commit another criminal offense;

2. accuse anyone of a criminal offense;

3. expose any secret tending to subject any person to hatred, contempt or ridicule;

4. take or withhold action as an official, or cause an official to take or withhold action;

5. bring about or continue a strike, boycott or other collective unofficial action, if the property is not demanded or received for the benefit of the group in whose interest the actor purports to act;

6. testify or provide information or withhold testimony or information with rspect to the legal claim or defense of another; or

7. inflict any other harm which would not benefit the actor.

It seems clear from the final clause that in the minds of the authors all of these were instances of harm.

26. Cf. Nozick, "Coercion."

27. See for example James J. White and Robert S. Summers, Uniform Commercial Code, Sec. 2–608(2).

28. More accurately, the award is computed by the party's "expectation interest," namely, the dollar amount of damages sufficient to place the plaintiff in the position he would have been in had the contract been performed. See Gordon D. Schaber and Claude D. Rohwer, *Contracts*, (St. Paul, MN: West Publishing Co., 1990), 247.

29. E. Allan Farnsworth, *Contracts* (Boston: Little Brown & Company, 1982) 813.

30. Peter Drucker, "Workers' Hands Bound By Tradition," *Wall St. J.*, Aug. 2, 1988.

31. Sometimes it is argued that the cure for this imbalance between manufacturing in the United States and in East Asia lies in a stronger union movement in East Asia. This may very well happen, but its consequence will be that American consumers will pay higher prices – something which the wealthy can no doubt afford, but which will make life that much more difficult for the poor.

At the present time the U.S. government has secured an international agreement to keep the value of the dollar below its market level apparently for the principal purpose of preserving jobs in the manufacturing sector. This may effectively prevent the union contracts from causing jobs to be eliminated, but only at a very high price to the rest of the country.

32. White and Summers, Uniform Commercial Code, #2–312, 314, 315, 316.

33. Ibid.

34. The warranty of title is not deemed by the Code to be an "implied" warranty for certain technical reasons, but since it is binding even though not mentioned expressly, it can be treated as an implied warranty in other respects. See Official Comment 6 to #2–312.

35. The case of TPA. See *Wall St. J.* Sept. 8, 1987.

36. Uniform Commercial Code; p. 188.

37. Ibid., 181–210.

Chapter Three: Is the Market Imperfect?

1. *Wall St. J.*, Jan. 4, 1991, sec. B6.
2. *Wall St. J.*, May 23, 1991, sec. A16.
3. *Wall St. J.*, May 20, 1991, sec. B6B.
4. *Wall St., J.*, August 20, 1991, sec. C13.
5. *Works and Days*, 11; from Richmond Lattimore, *Hesiod*, (Ann Arbor: University of Michigan Press, 1959).
6. Smith, *Wealth of Nations*, Bk. 4, Chap. 2.
7. For an account of the idea of perfect competition, see any textbook of economics. The present account is taken largely from Richard G. Lipsey, Peter O. Steiner, and Douglas D. Purvis, *Economics*, 8th ed. (New York: Harper and Row, 1987) 214ff.
8. Adam Smith, however, argues for a free market knowing well that it is not perfect competition. David Gauthier is clearly mistaken in supposing that "Smith envisaged the 'system of natural liberty' as a perfectly competitive market" (*Morals by Agreement*, Chap. 4.).
9. Galbraith, John Kenneth, *American Capitalism: The Concept of Countervailing Power* (White Plains, NY: M.E. Sharpe, 1980) 13ff.
10. This was the force of the guild system, about which romantic notions are sometimes harbored.
11. Galbraith, *American Capitalism*. A reader of this manuscript advanced the following problem: theoretically it would be possible in a totally free market for one individual to buy up all the land on the globe, and since new land does not get created, there would be no possibility of substitute products, and the monopoly could not be broken by competition.

    But this overlooks a number of things. First, the remedy proposed for this is law, that is, government, which is itself a monopoly, and one far more powerful than any monopoly of mere ownership. Some people advocate establishing a single world government, which would be a world monopoly. Second, the only way that anyone could buy up all the land on the globe in a free market would be by others selling to him voluntarily, which means that the sellers as a group would become extremely wealthy. What would they do with their wealth? If they wished to obtain back some land, they could invest their wealth in producing some product which the monopolist would want, such as a protection against some disease, and for which he would be willing to sell some land. Third, even if we concede that there are no substitutes for land, there are substitutes for owning land: if those who had sold their land to the monopolist continued to live on the planet, it would presumably be by means of leases, which would give them contractual rights which could be exchanged. Fourth, since we are speaking theoretically, given sufficient incentives, it could not be ruled out that substitutes for land might be developed, such as floating sea platforms, moon or space stations and space ships. (Such a scenario was developed by Arthur C. Clarke in his short story "Rescue.")
12. Natural monopolies are usually defined by economists as industries in which only one firm can operate at the minimum efficient scale.

13. Joseph Schumpeter, *Capitalism, Socialism, and Democracy*, 3d ed., (New York: Harper and Row, 1950) 106.

14. Cf. Lipsey, Steiner, Purvis, et al., *Economics*, 257ff.

15. Some questions related to this are examined in other places in this book. The question whether it causes harm to a person to fail to provide him with help will be a principal topic of Chapter 5. The question whether persons who are in need have a special right to be helped will be examined in Chapter 8, pp. 316ff. Some related questions about the right to private property in life-threatening monopoly situations will be discussed in Chapter 9, pp. 339ff.

16. Although the protests made by victims of AIDS when a pharmaceutical company recently put on the market a new drug of its own discovery and manufacture at what they considered a high price may now make this statement questionable.

17. For a discussion of Japanese trading practices, see for example Clyde V. Prestowitz, *Trading Places: How We Allowed Japan to Take the Lead* (New York: Basic Books, 1988). Prestowitz does not seem to see U.S. antitrust law as a major problem, however.

18. Message of April 29, 1938, quoted in J. K. Galbraith, *American Capitalism*, 57.

19. Ibid., 51.

20. Some writers have discussed whether it is appropriate to employ the idea of "threatening" in describing such a situation. To issue a threat, they argue, means to express a determination to cause harm, and since we commonly speak of someone threatening to withhold a donation, we must assume that withholding a donation causes harm. But the use of the term "threat" is governed by other considerations than harmfulness; in particular it is governed by whether the action was customary. We can speak of someone threatening to withhold something which we recognize to be a benefit, in cases where it was customary for him to confer the benefit. In general we describe as a threat any announcement of an intention to do something that we dislike. That does not necessarily mean that it causes harm.

21. Andrew Schotter, *Free Market Economics: A Critical Appraisal* (New York: St. Martin's Press, 1985) 52. In addition to the examples of alleged market failure which we discuss here, Schotter gives several others, which however manifest such a basic misunderstanding of the idea of a free market that they are not seriously worth discussing, in the view of this writer, and are in any event sufficiently covered by other observations and arguments in this book.

22. Cf. Lipsey, Steiner, Purvis, *Economics*, 412.

23. Milton Friedman and Anna Schwartz, *A Monetary History of the United States, 1967–1960* (Princeton, NJ: Princeton Univ. Press, 1963).

24. John Rawls, *A Theory of Justice*, (Cambridge: Harvard Univ. Press, Belknap Press, 1971) 15, 72ff, 100ff.

25. See for example Max Weber, *The Protestant Ethic and the Spirit of Capitalism*, trans. Talcott Parsons, (New York: Charles Scribner's Sons, 1958) 75, 180. It is true that Weber in this book is interested chiefly in what he calls the "irrational element" in capitalism, the idea of a calling; but this is for the purpose of discovering the specific *kind* of rationality that characterizes capitalism and

does not prevent him from recognizing that "one of the fundamental elements of the spirit of modern capitalism [is] rational conduct on the basis of the idea of the calling" (p. 180.).

26. For the theory, see Steven E. Rhoads, *The Economist's View of the World* (New York: Cambridge Univ. Press, 1985) 44. For the current U.S. system, see the *Christian Science Monitor*, Nov. 23, 1992, v. 84, n. 252, p. 9.

27. See Randy T. Simmons and Urs P. Kreuter, "Herd Mentality," *Policy Review* (Washington, DC: Heritage Foundation, Fall 1989); and *Executive Alert*, (Dallas: National Center for Policy Analysis, vol. 4, no.1, 1990. See also Raymond Bonner, *At the Hand of Man, Peril and Hope for Africa's Wildlife* (Alfred A. Knopf, 1993).

28. Kenneth J. Arrow, *Social Choice and Individual Values* (New York: John Wiley and Sons, 1951) 2f.

29. Ibid., 59.

30. It is a matter of debate whether the use of armed force by government to protect the members of the society against aggression can be considered wealth-producing. It is more properly seen as a precondition for the production of wealth than itself a productive enterprise. However it is apparently possible to attribute an economic value to it.

It is of course possible for government to use tax revenue to employ workers to produce goods and services. For further discussion of this see the discussion of productivity, Chapter 4, pp. 163ff.

31. Schumpeter, *Capitalism, Socialism, and Democracy*, Chap. 5. Milton and Rose Friedman, *Free To Choose*, Chap. 5, p. 138.

32. André Armengaud, "Population in Europe 1700–1914: in Carlo M. Cipolla, ed., *The Fontana Economic History of Europe, The Industrial Revolution* (Glasgow: Fontana/Collins, 1973) 47.

33. Kuznets gives the following figures for income before direct taxes:

"In the United States, in the distribution of income among families (excluding single individuals), the shares of the two lowest quintiles rise from 13½ percent in 1929 to 18 percent in the years after the second world war (average of 1944, 1946, 1947, and 1950); whereas the share of the top quintile declines from 55 to 44 percent, and that of the top 5 percent from 31 to 20 per cent.

In the United Kingdom, the share of the top 5 percent of units declines from 46 percent in 1880 to 43 percent in 1910 or 1913, to 33 percent in 1929, to 31 percent in 1938, and to 24 percent in 1947; the share of the lower 85 percent remains fairly constant between 1880 and 1913, between 41 and 43 percent, but then rises to 46 percent in 1929 and 55 percent in 1947." "Economic Growth and Income Inequality" in Economic Growth and Structure, (New York: Norton, 1965) 260.

Kuznets points to two stages in economic growth, an early one, when inequality increases, and a later one, when it declines, and then perhaps levels off. While his remarks about the later stage are based directly on the historical data, this is not true of his observations about the initial stage, for which essentially we do not possess useful data in regard to the countries he studies. Kuznets arrives at his conclusions about the initial stage by analyzing the data available, which indicate decline in inequality, and postulating a number of explanations for that, then arguing that these explanatory factors were not present in the initial stage. On this basis he hypothesizes that equality must have increased in the initial stage. But this is no longer a direct empirical argument.

34. Peter Berger, in his otherwise outstanding book *The Capitalist Revolution*, accepts Kuznets's conclusions about both stages as if they were equally based on empirical evidence (p. 44ff).
35. See Peter Berger, op.cit.
36. Cf. T. W. Ferguson, in the *Wall St. J.*, March 27, 1990, sec. A.
37. Ernest L. Bogart, *Economic History of Europe, 1760-1939* (New York: Longmans, Green and Co., 1942) 196.
38. Melvin M. Knight, Harry Elmer Barnes, Felix Flügel, *Economic History of Europe* (New York: Houghton Mifflin, 1928) 395.
39. Ibid.
40. *The Life of William Hutton*, ed. Ll. Jewitt, 1872; quoted in Arthur Redford, *The Economic History of England 1750-1860* (Westport, CN: Greenwood Press, 1960).
41. *Factory Inspectors' Reports*, December 1838, Appendix V, p. 98; quoted in Redford, op.cit.
42. Redford, op.cit.
43. Redford, op.cit.
44. *History of the English Poor Law*, Vol II (1854), pp. 18, 58; quoted in Redford, p. 65.
45. T. S. Ashton, *An Economic History of England: The 18th Century* (London: Methuen, 1955) 204.
46. Ashton, op. cit., p. 212.

Chapter Four: Economic Value

1. Karl Marx, *Capital*, Chap. 1.
2. Thomas Aquinas, *Summa Theologica*, II-II, q. 77, art. 1.
3. Duns Scotus, *Qaestiones in Quartum Librum Sententiarum*, dist. XV, q. 2a, nn. 22-23, quoted in Alejandro Chafuen, *Christians for Freedom: Late-Scholastic Economics* (San Francisco: Ignatius Press, 1986) 107, n. 46.
4. Chafuen, Chap. 7.
5. *Rerum novarum* (On the Condition of the Working Classes). Leo argues in support of the just wage that human labor is not merely personal in character, which would allow it to be given in exchange for any or no wage, but is Necessary for life. From which it follows, he says, that each one has a natural right to procure what is required in order to live.
6. *Quadragesimo anno* (On Social Reconstruction), (Boston: the Daughters of St. Paul, no date).
7. Encyclical *Laborem Exercens* (On Human Work), (Boston: the Daughters of St. Paul, no date), Chap. 7.

8. Thomas Hobbes, *Leviathan*, Part I, Chap. 15. (Chicago, Encyclopedia Britannica, Great Books, ed. Nelle Fuller, 1952, Vol. 23, p. 93.)
9. David N. Laband, "In Hugo's Path, A Man-made Disaster," *Wall St. J.*, Sept. 27, 1989, p. A22, and the author's personal inspection of Charleston in 1990.
10. Chafuen, *Christians for Freedom*, chap. 7.
11. See for example Lipsey, Steiner, Purvis, *Economics* p. 488.
12. It is surely legitimate to see this as one of the principal reasons for the failure of the communist economies, for the very notion of economic value is meaningless in such a system.

Chapter Five: Causing Harm

1. *Philadelphia Inquirer*, July 25, 1992.
2. *Philadelphia Inquirer*, July 25, 1992.
3. Subsequently the award was voided by the court as excessive. *New York Times*, July 23, 1992.
4. Mill, *On Liberty*.
5. Ibid., Chap. 1.
6. This is Nozick's position, among others.
7. το εδεος (Luke 10:37).
8. "My own intuition is that bad samaritan statutes are morally legitimate in principle, though there may be some practical difficulties in their implementation. Therefore, if the harm principle does not place its stamp of certification on them, we shall have to amend that principle . . . so that preventing as well as not-doing harm may be required by the criminal law." Feinberg, *Harm to Others*, 128.
9. Ibid. p. 129.
10. An interesting technical question arises here about the identity of a light wave, but we can pass over that here.
11. An excellent book on causation is Richard Taylor's *Action and Purpose*, (Englewood Cliffs, NJ: Prentice-Hall, 1966; reprinted 1973 by Humanities Press.).
12. It is sometimes maintained that there is no significant difference between action and inaction, in that any positive action can be described negatively, and any negative action can be described positively. Bentham answers this sufficiently: "It is to be observed, that the nature of the act, whether positive or negative, is not to be determined immediately by the form of the discourse made use of to express it. An act which is positive in its nature may be characterized by a negative expression: thus, not to be at rest, is as much as to say to move. So also an act, which is negative in its nature, may be characterized by a positive expression: thus, to forbear or omit to bring food to a person in certain circumstances, is signified by the single and positive term *to starve*." *An Introduction to the Principles of Morals and Legislation*, ed. J. H. Burns and H. L. A. Hart (London: The University of London, Athlone Press, 1970) p. 76.
13. March 13, 1964. Her assailant, one Winston Moseley, confessed to the murder and was sentenced to death, but the sentence was commuted to life imprisonment.

14. "Bad Samaritanism and the Causation of Harm," *Philosophy and Public Affairs*, 9 (1980):241.

15. Feinberg, *Harm to Others*, 184. Feinberg does not seem to be familiar with the use of the term *conditio sine qua non* to refer to a nonproductive necessary condition, for in speaking of a wind which causes a barn to collapse, he refers to the wind as a *conditio sine qua non*.

16. Ibid., 167. The case is given by Thomas C. Grey, *The Legal Enforcement of Morality*, (New York: Random House, 1983), 159–160.

17. Lance K. Stell, "Dueling and the Right to Life," *Ethics* 90 (1979):12; quoted in Joel Feinberg, *Harm to Others*, p. 132.

18. Some boycotts are illegal: for example, secondary strikes by trade unions, against employers not directly connected to the employer who is the primary object of a strike.

19. At the time of writing two Korean–owned stores in Brooklyn are being boycotted by the black community, a boycott which Mayor David Dinkins has protested as unjustified and mistaken, but which no one has suggested should be prohibited by law. See *New York Times* September 28, 1990.

20. Edward J. Kionka, *Torts*, (St Paul, MN: 1977) 265ff.

21. Peter Huber, *Liability, The Legal Revolution and its Consequences* (New York: Basic Books, 1988) 81.

22. Ibid., 156.

23. There are now cases where children are born addicts, since their mothers were addicts. But even there, unless there has been some genetic change which would render them essentially insane, they retain the genetic ability to become masters of themselves.

Chapter Six: The Individual and the Community

1. Galbraith, *American Capitalism*, 29.

2. Robert N. Bellah, Richard Madsen, William M. Sullivan, Ann Swidler, and Steven M. Tipton; *Habits of the Heart, Individualism and Commitment in American Life* (Berkeley, CA: Univ. of California Press 1985., *passim*, but especially pages 35–36, 262–270, and the concluding chapter.

3. Ibid., 23–24

4. This does not mean, of course, that a government must actually impose the death penalty, but that it must have that power, otherwise it is no government.

5. It is true that there is a theory held by some philosophers that only just laws are genuine laws. This seems to have been the view of Aquinas, who stated: "If in any point [human law] is not in harmony with the law of nature, it is no longer a law but a corruption of law." (*Summa Theologica*, Ia IIae, Q. 95, Art. 2). Aquinas defined law as *ordinatio rationis ad bonum commune* (Ia IIae Q. 90, Art. 4): a law is a law only if it is reasonable. If you try telling this to the judge, however, your last state is likely to be worse than your first. And with good reason, for since the justice of any law can be questioned, all law enforcement becomes impossible on such a view. In other places, however, Aquinas speaks of some laws as

being unjust (e.g., Ia IIa Q.96, Art. 4), which seems to indicate that perhaps in some sense they are, after all, genuine laws in his opinion.

6. *Second Treatise of Government*, #3.

7. Jeremy Bentham, *An Introduction to the Principles of Morals and Legislation*.

8. Joel Feinberg's opinion.

9. To speak of the use of force on a person is to speak of something which is done to the person against his will. Where a person approves of what is being done to him, we are not entitled to speak of the use of force. A surgeon making an incision is damaging the integrity of the patient's body, but so long as it is with his consent, we do not say that force is being used.

10. Historically, it has long been taken for granted that it can be necessary and permissible to confine the insane by force to an asylum so that they may receive proper care, or to carry an unconscious person out of a fire, or to compel a child to take medicine that he does not like, and in what follows we will take these exceptions for granted without repeating them. Our thesis concerns only sane, conscious adults. In recent years, of course, courts appear to have taken the position that the insane have a right not to be so confined unless they are dangerous—which seems to be a misunderstanding of the implications of insanity and the notion of human rights.

11. Whoever owns a road is entitled to say how it should be used, and so is within his rights in requiring cyclists to wear helmets. But this is true properly speaking only where ownership of roads exists in a free market. In our current system road ownership is a government monopoly, and so the normal rights of ownership need to be modified.

12. See H. L. A. Hart, *The Concept of Law* (Oxford: Clarendon Press, 1961).

13. Bentham: "Every law, when complete, is either of a coercive or uncoercive nature. A coercive law is a command. An uncoercive, or rather a discoercive, law is the revocation, in whole or in part, of a coercive law." *Introduction*, 302.

14. *The Concept of Law*.

15. Ronald Dworkin, *Taking Rights Seriously* (Cambridge: Harvard Univ. Press. 1977).

16. Taken from Lipsey, Steiner, Purvis, *Economics* 253, 254.

17. There is no way to measure the efficiency of government in its exercise of the police power, that is, in the national defense and the justice system, and so we must exclude that from this statement. I owe this observation to my colleague Michael Leeds.

18. No doubt in some industries there are obstacles to entry, but experience with the deregulation of industries previously thought to be natural monopolies, such as the telephone companies, together with the truth pointed out below, that there can be substitutes for any product, indicates that the importance of obstacles to entry should not be exaggerated.

19. W. L. Letwin, article "Monopoly," *Encyclopedia Britannica*, 14th ed., (1961):15:730.

20. This does not mean that there can be no substitute for force, for example in settling disputes, but that there can be no substitute for the *right* to use force. Force must always be available to protect against aggressors and to punish criminals.

21. Some philosophers, such as Robert Nozick, discuss the possibility of private or voluntary protective organizations, which would be in competition with one another. But we are not lacking in experience with these, and it has not been reassuring.
22. See especially the writings of James M. Buchanan. The implications of Buchanan's theory are explained in Henri Lepage, *Tomorrow Capitalism*, trans. Sheilagh Ogilvie (La Salle, IL: Open Court Publishing Co., 1982).
23. Peter Bachrach, *The Theory of Democratic Elites, a Critique* (Washington, DC, Univ. Press of America, 1980) 101.
24. Ibid.
25. "Prominent Doctor Assails Profit-Oriented Health System," *Philadelphia Inquirer*, June 1990.
26. These remarks are not meant to prejudge the question of Aristotle's overall views about justice and society.
27. Bellah *et al.*, *Habits of the Heart*.
28. The Americans with Disabilities Act giving special rights to the disabled is the latest instance.

Chapter Seven: Justice and the Principle of No Harm

1. See Chapters 2 and 6. As was pointed out there, some laws exempt from punishment.
2. To threaten to cause harm is already to cause harm of a certain sort, just by the fact of the threat itself, though of course not the harm which is threatened.
3. J. Locke, *Second Treatise of Government*, Chap. 2, par. 6.
4. Thorsten Sellin, "Crime," *Encyclopedia Britannica*, 14th ed. (1961):6:703.
5. Devlin, *Enforcement of Morals*, 33.
6. It is sometimes objected to statements of this kind that they are not helpful since murder is wrong by definition, and a more neutral term such as homicide should be used. But the point here is that there is a good *reason* why some homicides are crimes.
7. Mill, *On Liberty*, Chap. 1.
8. Rule utilitarianism is the view that what is moral is ultimately a question of what is useful, but that what is useful is to have certain rules, rather than to have usefulness judged on the basis of individual actions.
9. The notion of morality is understood here as relating in the first instance to the idea of freedom of choice: actions are immoral because they violate a person's freedom of choice. It may be objected that there are areas of morality where this does not appear to be the case, for example sexual morality. Sexual intercourse outside of marriage has often been considered the paradigm of immorality, yet it does not seem to represent any infringement of freedom of choice.

    It can be argued, however, that the canons of sexual morality have grown up out of concern to preserve the sanctity of human life, and therefore the sanctity of the procreative procedure by which new life emerges into the world. That is, sexual morality is meant to protect children, and because of them, women, from harm.

    Much of the conception of morality prevalent among Western peoples stems from a religious inheritance according to which the fundamental immorality is to disobey God. In this case the whole world is seen as the realm which is subject to God's power of free choice and government.

10. Locke, *Second Treatise of Government*, Chap. 2.

11. David B. Wong, *Moral Relativity* (Berkeley, CA: Univ. of California Press, 1984).

12. A cross-cultural survey of people in India, Indonesia, Iran, Italy (Sardinia), Yugoslavia, and the United States conducted by Graeme Newman showed that 98.8 percent said that robbery should be illegal. Murder was not among the activities mentioned. *Comparative Deviance: Perception and Law in Six Cultures* (New York: Elsevier, 1976). Quoted in James Q. Wilson and Richard J. Herrenstein, *Crime and Human Nature* (New York: Simon and Schuster, 1985) 448.

13. G. K. Chesterton, "The Blue Cross: in *The Innocence of Father Brown* (London: Dodd Mead and Co., 1911).

14. According to Joel Feinberg we should not speak of harm in such cases, for the notion of harm implies a lack of consent. But this is because he restricts harm to the infringement of rights.

15. The blackmailer says: Pay me money, or be disgraced; the challenger to a duel says: Fight with me to the death, or be disgraced. A challenge to a duel imposes on the challenged a choice of life and death which he does not wish, but cannot escape. We argued in a previous chapter that the legal system of a free market cannot condone blackmail, contrary to the opinion of writers such as Murray Rothbard (with whom I am otherwise to a large extent in agreement), because the intention of the blackmailer is to harm his victim. The goal of the challenger to a duel is to kill his opponent. Only, in order to create a semblance of fairness and make the harm feasible, he gives his opponent the right to make a similar attempt on his own life. No doubt the challenger typically believes that his opponent has insulted him, but there is, or should be, a normal legal remedy for that. Duelling usurps the function of government which is to protect its citizens against harm.

    What makes duelling particularly repulsive is the disproportion between the cause and the remedy. The cause is usually a personal insult, or something which is felt to be a personal insult, but may in point of fact be relatively trivial. The remedy, however, is a battle to the death. If the remedy were a fistfight or boxing match carried out under proper supervision to prevent serious injury, much of the opprobrium attached to it would perhaps be dispelled.

16. Feinberg, *Harm to Others*, 34.

17. Ibid., Chap. 1, sec. 4, p. 45ff.

18. Ibid., Chap. 1, par. 4.

19. Feinberg, *Offense to Others* (New York: Oxford Univ. Press, 1985) Chap. 9.

20. Robert H. Bork, *The Tempting of America* (New York: the Free Press, 1990) 80.

21. A consequentialist position is one that justifies an action by its consequences. Utilitarianism is one kind of consequentialism, but not the only possible kind.
22. A similar point is made by Nicolai Hartmann in his *Ethics*. See on this John Findlay, *Axiological Ethics*.
23. See Bernard Williams, "Persons, Character and Morality," in Amelie Oksenberg Rorty, ed., *The Identities of Persons* (Berkeley, CA: Univ. of California Press, 1976) 199.

Chapter Eight: The Principle of No Harm II

1. "In 1814 three boys—aged eight, nine, and eleven—were sentenced to death for stealing a pair of shoes." Quoted from "Punishment of Death," *Philanthropist* 4: 190, 1814, in Edwin H. Sutherland and Donald R. Cressey, *Principles of Criminology*, 7th ed. (Philadelphia: Lippincott, 1966) 315.
2. Ledger Wood, "Responsibility and Punishment," *Journal of Criminal Law and Criminology*, 28 (1938)635.
3. "Our modern knowledge of the nature of criminal conduct renders the whole conception of punishment archaic. It is as futile and foolish to punish a criminal as it is to punish a person suffering from a physical or mental disease." Harry Elmer Barnes, *The Story of Punishment* (Montclair, NJ: Patterson Smith, 1972) 265.
4. "The student of criminology wants to know, 'What cause delinquency and crime?' The realistic answer is, we don't know. Not all of our investigations, taken together, have yielded up a single *cause* of delinquency and crime, if we define cause as an invariant relationship. . . ." D. Dressler, *Readings in Criminology and Penology* 2d ed. (New York: Columbia Univ. Press, 1972) 245.
5. "It appears that the certainty of discovery and punishment is a more significant element in general prevention than the severity of penalties." Paul W. Tappan, *Crime, Justice and Correction* (New York: McGraw–Hill Book Co., 1960) 251.
6. This has come to be referred to as desert or retribution in distribution, following H. L. A. Hart, who maintains that accepting it does not necessarily entail accepting any further role for desert, for example as the goal of punishment. But if the concept of desert is valid in specifying that only those who have offended should be punished, why should it not be a valid motive for punishment? See Hart, *Punishment and Responsibility, Essays in the Philosophy of Law* (Oxford: Clarendon Press, 1978).
7. For a defense of the retributive theory of punishment, see: Morris R. Cohen, in Leon Radzinowicz and Marvin C. Wolfgang, eds., *Crime and Justice*, Vol. 2 (New York: Basic Books, 1971) 27–29. Also, C. S. Lewis, "The Humanitarian Theory of Punishment," *Res Judicatae* 6(1953)224–230, given in *Crime and Justice* 2:43–48.
8. Quoted by Russell Baker, *New York Times*.
9. See Chapter 6, pp. 216f above.
10. The inherent connection of rights with punishment was seen already by Bentham. "Without the notion of punishment, . . . no notion could we have

of either right or duty." *Fragment on Government*, 1776. But in subsequent discussion it became submerged beneath his view that rights are correlative to duties, and that duties exist only where they can be enforced by legal punishment.

11. *After Virtue* (Notre Dame, IN: Univ. of Notre Dame Press, 1981) 67.
12. Of course, if other, voluntary ways could be discovered to finance such programs, for example by means of a state lottery held not as a monopoly but in open market competition, there could scarcely be any objection to them from a classical liberal standpoint.
13. Locke, *Letter Concerning Toleration*.
14. Parents, on the view defended here, by the fact that they have engaged in marital intercourse, have taken on themselves the obligation of caring for their children.
15. Mill, *On Liberty*.
16. This has been argued by Loren E. Lomasky, *Persons, Rights and the Moral Community* (New York and Oxford: Oxford Univ. Press, 1987) 135–141.
17. David Gauthier, *Morals By Agreement*; Alan Gewirth, *Reason and Morality*. Gauthier's argument, to summarize it briefly, is that in a perfectly competitive market there would be no need of morality, for each person's private interest would coincide with the interest of society, as Adam Smith pointed out with his doctrine of the invisible hand. Morality is needed only because in many respects life is not a perfectly competitive market, but one which suffers from deficiencies or failures, called externalities in market theory—for example the fact that we often do not know in advance all the consequences of our actions. In such cases of market failure, the rational thing is to cooperate with others, instead of merely seeking to maximize our own private benefit, making certain concessions in return for the greater long-term good that will result from the cooperation. Morality, therefore, is rational, a form of rational choice.
18. Digby Anderson, *The Unmentionable Face of Poverty in the Nineties* (Altrincham, Cheshire, U.K.: The Social Affairs Unit, no date).

Chapter Nine: The Principle of No Harm III

1. Devlin, *The Enforcement of Morals*.
2. Ibid., 13.
3. Ibid., 11.
4. Ibid., 9
5. See, for example, the column by Elizabeth Joseph, a lawyer, "My Husband's Nine Wives," in the *New York Times*, May 23, 1991, sec. A.
6. Devlin, *Enforcement of Morals*, 14.
7. Aristotle, *Nicomachean Ethics*, Bk. V, Chap. 4.
8. Ηο εαν ε δικαιον δοσο ηξμιν.
9. Ουκ αδιχο σε.
10. Translation taken mainly from the *New English Bible*, with author's translation of certain portions.

11. John Rawls, "Justice as Fairness: Political not Metaphysical" in *Philosophy and Public Affairs 14* (1985):223–251.
12. A point emphasized by economists of the Austrian school.
13. It might be objected that the impossibility of predicting the future applies with equal force to the claims made for the free market. If it is so difficult to predict what will be beneficial, how can we be sure that the free market will prove to be beneficial?

    The claim made for the free market is that societies which adopt it will be better off, all things else being equal. In the concrete, however, all things else may not be equal. Some natural disaster may overtake a society which practices market freedom, while some accidental good fortune may come to a highly regulated one.
14. Joseph Raz, *The Morality of Freedom* (Oxford: Clarendon Press, 1986) esp. Part V.
15. During the Middle Ages European monarchs had to finance government out of their own pockets, that is, out of the rents they received from the royal lands. The modern equivalent would seem to be participation in the market.
16. Gray, *Liberalism*, 1986.
17. Jeremy Waldron, *The Right To Private Property*, (Oxford: Clarendon Press, 1988) 184ff.
18. Perhaps, to be fully accurate, we should say that while the *abstract* use-value can be known before acquisition (*if* I possessed that fish, it would keep me alive for the next two days), the *concrete* or *actual* use-value, or the balance of use-value over the costs of acquisition, can only be known after acquisition. What would the use-value of the fish be, if it took me three days' work to catch it?
19. See for example "Abortion Issue Divides Advocates for Disabled," *New York Times*, July 4, 1991, sec. A.
20. T. E. James, "Prostitution," 14th ed., *Encyclopedia Britannica*, 1961.
21. The case of the Mustang Ranch.
22. James, op. cit.
23. See T. E. James, *Prostitution and the Law*, 1951.
24. P.335.
25. See, for example, *New York Times*, April 9, 1991, sec. A.
26. *De Bono Coniugali.*
27. Paul Johnson, A History of Christianity (New York: Atheneum, 1976) 290.
28. Ibid., 353.
29. Ronald Hermelin was arrested in Oak Park, Michigan, on May 12, 1986, and sentenced to life imprisonment without parole for possessing 672 grams of cocaine. *Philadelphia Inquirer*, November 5, 1990, 2a.

    Trena Canada, the mother of five children aged 2 to 7, was sentenced to six to 23 months in prison for delivering a $20 bag of cocaine to an undercover state trooper in Montgomery County, Pennsylvania. Montgomery County Record, October 28, 1990.
30. *Philadelphia Inquirer*, February 18, 1990, 8A.

31. Ibid., October 21, 1990.
32. Howard Elliott was sentenced to prison in Chicago on September 14, 1989, because a trench caved in and killed two workmen. *New York Times*, September 20, 1989.

Bibliography

Note: The letter F after an item indicates that the work is generally sympathetic to free markets.

Abell, Aaron I., ed. *American Catholic Thought on Social Questions*. Indianapolis: Bobbs-Merrill, 1968.

American Law Institute. *Selected Commercial Statutes*. St. Paul, Minn.: West Publishing Co., 1990.

Anderson, Digby. *The Unmentionable Face of Poverty in the Nineties*. Altrincham, Cheshire, England: The Social Affairs Unit, no date. F.

Anscombe, Elizabeth. *Ethics, Religion and Politics*. Minneapolis: University of Minnesota Press, 1981.

Antieau, Chester James, Arther T. Downey, and Edward C. Roberts. *Freedom from Federal Establishment: Formation and Early History of the First Amendment Religion Clauses*. Milwaukee: Bruce, 1964.

Aristotle. *Nicomachean Ethics*. Translated by W. D. Ross. Chicago: Encyclopedia Britannica, 1952. Vol. 9 of *Great Books of the Western World*.

———. *Politics*. Translated by W. D. Ross. Chicago: Encyclopedia Britannica, 1952. Vol. 9 of *Great Books of the Western World*.

Arrow, Kenneth J. *Social Choice and Individual Values*. New York: John Wiley & Sons, 1951.

Arrow, Kenneth J., and Hervé Raynaud. *Social Choice and Multicriterion Decision-Making*. Cambridge, Mass.: The M.I.T. Press, 1986.

Ashton, T. S. *Economic History of England: The Eighteenth Century*. London: Methuen, 1955.

———. "The Treatment of Capitalism by Historians." In *Capitalism and the Historians*, edited by F. A. Hayek. Chicago: University of Chicago Press, 1974.

———. "The Standard of Life of the Workers in England, 1790-1830." In *Capitalism and the Historians*, edited by F. A. Hayek. Chicago: University of Chicago Press, 1974.

Austin, John. *The Province of Jurisprudence Determined*. New York: Humanities Press, 1965. Reprint.

Bachrach, Peter. *The Theory of Democratic Elitism*. Washington D. C.: University Press of America, 1980.

Baker, C. Edwin. *Human Liberty and Freedom of Speech*. New York: Oxford University Press, 1989.

Barnes, Harry Elmer. *The Story of Punishment*. Montclair, N. J.: Patterson Smith, 1930. Reissued 1972.

Barnes, Harry Elmer, and Negley K. Teeters. *New Horizons in Criminology*. Englewood Cliffs, N. J.: Prentice-Hall, 1959. 3rd ed.

Bastiat, Frederic. *The Law*. Translated by Dean Russell. Irvington-on-Hudson, N. Y.: The Foundation for Economic Education, 1950. French original published 1850. F.

Benn, Stanley I. *A Theory of Freedom*. Cambridge, England: Cambridge University Press, 1988.

Benne, Robert. *The Ethic of Democratic Capitalism*. Philadelphia: Fortress Press, 1981. F.

Bentham, Jeremy. *An Introduction to the Principles of Morals and Legislation*. Edited by J. H. Burns and H. L. A. Hart. London: University of London, The Athlone Press, 1970. F.

Berger, Peter. *The Capitalist Revolution*. New York: Basic Books, 1986. F.

Berns, Walter. *The First Amendment and the Future of American Democracy*. New York: Basic Books, 1976. F.

Block, Walter. *The U. S. Bishops and Their Critics*. Vancouver: Fraser Institute, 1986. F.

Bogart, Ernest L. *Economic History of Europe 1760–1939*. New York: Longmans, Green and Co., 1942.

Bork, Robert H. *The Tempting of America*. New York: The Free Press, 1990.

Bowden, Witt, Michael Karpovich, and Abbott Payson Usher. *An Economic History of Europe Since 1750*. New York: American Book Company, 1937.

Bradley, F. H. *Ethical Studies*. 2d ed. rev. Oxford: Clarendon Press, 1927.

Bronfenbrenner, Martin. *Income Distribution Theory*. Chicago: Aldine Atherton, 1971.

Buchanan, James M. and Robert D. Tollison, eds. *The Theory of Public Choice: Political Applications of Economics*. Ann Arbor: University of Michigan Press, 1972. F.

Buchanan, James M. *The Demand and Suppy of Public Goods*. Chicago: Rand McNally, 1968. F.

———. "Rawls on Justice as Fairness." *Public Choice* 13 (1972). F.

———. "A Hobbesian Interpretation of the Rawlsian Difference Principle." *Kyklos* 29 (1976). F.

———. *Liberty, Market and State: Political Economy in the 1980s.* Brighton, Sussex, England: Wheatsheaf Books, distributed by Harvester Press, 1986. F.

———. *Essays on the Political Economy.* Honolulu: University of Hawaii Press, 1989. F.

———. *The Limits of Liberty.* Chicago: University of Chicago Press, 1975. F.

———. "The Inconsistencies of the National Health Service." *Occasional Paper 7* (1965). London: Institute for Economic Affairs. F.

———. *Cost and Choice: an Inquiry in Economic Theory.* Chicago: Markham Publishing Co., 1969. F.

Cameron, Rondo. *A Concise Economic History of the World.* New York: Oxford University Press, 1989.

Cave, Roy C., and Herbert H. Coulson. *A Sourcebook for Medieval Economic History.* New York: Biblo and Tannen, 1965.

Chafuen, Alejandro. *Christians For Freedom.* San Francisco: Ignatius Press, 1986. F.

Chelsea House, publishers. *The Economic Regulation of Business and Industry: A Legislative History of U. S. Regulatory Agencies.* Statutory History of the United States. New York, 1973.

Cipolla, Carlo M., ed. *The Industrial Revolution.* Vol. 3 of *The Fontana Economic History of Europe.* Glasgow: William Collins Sons & Co. Ltd., 1973.

Coase, R. H. "The Problem of Social Cost." *Journal of Law and Economics* 3 (1960). F.

———. *The Market for Goods and the Market for Ideas* Washington, D.C.: American Enterprise Institute, 1975. F.

Coleman, D. C. *History and the Economic Past: An Account of the Rise and Decline of Economic History in Britain.* Oxford: Clarendon Press, 1987.

Detlev Rahmsdorf, and Hans-Bernd Schaefer, eds. *Ethische Grundfragen der Wirtschafts-und Rechtsordnung.* Hamburg: Dietrich Reimer Verlag, 1988.

Devlin, Patrick. *The Enforcement of Morals.* Oxford: Oxford University Press, 1965.

Duncan-Jones, Richard. *The Economy of the Roman Empire.* Cambridge, England: Cambridge University Press, 1974.

Dworkin, Ronald. *Taking Rights Seriously.* Cambridge, Mass.: Harvard University Press, 1978.

Etzioni, Amitai. *The Moral Dimension: Toward a New Economics.* New York: The Free Press, 1988.

Feinberg, Joel. *Harm to Self.* The Moral Limits of the Criminal Law. New York: Oxford University Press, 1986.

———. *Offense to Others.* The Moral Limits of the Criminal Law. New York: Oxford University Press, 1985.

———. *The Idea of the Obscene.* Lawrence, Kansas: University of Kansas, 1979.

————. *Harm to Others*. The Moral Limits of the Criminal Law. New York: Oxford University Press, 1984.

————. *Harmless Wrongdoing*. The Moral Limits of the Criminal Law. New York: Oxford University Press, 1988.

————. *Social Philosophy*. Englewook Cliffs, N.J.: Prentice-Hall, 1973.

Fellman, David. *The Constitutional Right of Association*. Chicago: University of Chicago Press, 1963.

Finnis, John. *Natural Law and Natural Rights*. Oxford: Clarendon Press, 1980.

Friedman, David D. *The Machinery of Freedom*. La Salle, Ill.: Open Court Press, 1989. F.

Friedman, Milton and Rose. *Free To Choose*. New York: Avon Books, 1979. F.

Friedman, Milton. *Capitalism and Freedom*. Reissued. Chicago: University of Chicago Press, 1982. F.

Friedman, Lawrence M. *A History of American Law*. New York: Simon & Schuster, 1973.

Fuller, Lon L. *The Morality of Law*. New Haven: Yale University Press, 1964.

Galbraith, John Kenneth. *Economics in Perspective: A Critical History*. Boston: Houghton Mifflin Co., 1987.

————. *The Affluent Society*. Houghton Mifflin Co. Cambridge, Mass.: The Riverside Press, 1960. Originally published 1958.

————. *The Nature of Mass Poverty*. Cambridge, Mass. and London: Harvard University Press, 1979.

————. *The New Industrial State*. 2d ed., revised. Boston: Houghton Mifflin Co., 1971.

————. *American Capitalism: The Concept of Countervailing Power*. Houghton Mifflin Co. White Plains, N.Y.: M. E. Sharpe, 1980. Originally published 1952.

Gewirth, Alan. "There Are Absolute Rights." *Philosophical Quarterly* 32 (1982): 348–353.

Gilder, George. *Wealth and Poverty*. New York: Basic Books, 1984. F.

————. *The Spirit of Enterprise*. New York: Simon & Schuster, 1984. F.

Gray, John Chipman. *The Nature and Sources of the Law*. 2d ed. Edited by Roland Gray. Gloucester, Mass.: Peter Smith, 1972. reprint of 1921 edition.

Gray, John. *Liberalisms: Essays in Political Philosophy*. London: Routledge, 1989.

————. *Liberalism*. Milton Keynes: Open University Press, 1986. F.

Grey, Thomas C. *The Legal Enforcement of Morality*. New York: Alfred A. Knopf, 1983.

Gross, Hyman. *A Theory of Criminal Justice*. New York: Oxford University Press, 1979.

Hall, Kermit L., ed. *The Law of Business and Commerce: Major Historical Interpretations*. New York: Garland Publishing, 1987.

Hampshire, Stuart. *Morality and Conflict*. Oxford: Basil Blackwell, 1983.

Hart, H. L. A. *Law, Liberty, and Morality*. Stanford, Calif.: Stanford University Press, 1963.

————. *The Concept of Law*. Oxford: Clarendon Press, 1961.

————. *Punishment and Responsibility: Essays in the Philosophy of Law*. Oxford: Clarendon Press, 1978.

Hart, H. L. A., and A. M. Honoré. *Causation in the Law*. Oxford: Clarendon Press, 1959.

Hayek, F. A., ed. *Capitalism and the Historians*. Chicago: University of Chicago Press, 1974. F.

Hayek, Friedrich A. *The Constitution of Liberty*. Chicago: University of Chicago Press, 1960. F.

Henderson, Ernest F., trans. and ed. *Select Historical Documents of the Middle Ages*. New York: Biblo and Tannen, 1965.

Hoekema, David A. *Rights and Wrongs: Coercion, Punishment and the State*. Cranbury, N.J.: Associated University Presses, 1986.

Huber, Peter W. *Liability*. New York: Basic Books, 1988. F.

Hunt, E. K. *Property and Prophets: The Evolution of Economic Institutions and Ideologies*. 4th ed. New York: Harper & Row, 1981.

Husak, Douglas N. *Philosophy of Criminal Law*. Totowa, N.J.: Rowman & Littlefield, 1987.

Johnson, Paul. *A History of Christianity*. New York: Atheneum, 1976.

Johnson, Elmer Hubert. *Crime, Correction and Society*. rev. Homewood, Ill.: The Dorsey Press, 1968.

Jones, A. H. M. *The Roman Economy*. Edited by P. A. Brunt. Totowa, N.J.: Rowman & Littlefield, 1974.

Katz, Michael L., and Harvey S. Rosen, *Microeconomics*. Homewood, Ill.: Irwin, 1991.

Knight, Melvin M., Harry Elmer Barnes, and Felix Fluegel. *Economic History of Europe*. Boston: Houghton Mifflin, 1928.

Koslowski, Peter. *Ethik des Kapitalismus*. Walter Eucken Institut, Vortraege und Aufsaetze. Tuebingen: J. C. B. Mohr (Paul Siebeck), 1982. F.

Kristol, Irving. *Two Cheers for Capitalism*. New York: Basic Books, 1978. F.

Kuznets, Simon S. "Economic Growth and Income Equality" in *Economic Growth and Structure*. New York: Norton, 1965.

Landsburg, Steven E. *Price Theory and Applications*. Fort Worth: Dryden Press, 1992, 2d ed.

Lay Commission on Catholic Social Teaching. *Toward the Future*. New York: Lay Commission, 1984. F.

Lepage, Henri. *Tomorrow Capitalism*. Translated by Sheilagh Ogilvie. La Salle, Ill.: Open Court Publishing Co., 1982. F.

Lindley, Richard. *Autonomy*. Atlantic Highlands, N.J.: Humanities Press International, 1986.

Lipsey, Richard G., Peter O. Steiner, and Douglas D. Purvis. *Economics*. 8th ed. New York: Harper & Row, 1987.

Locke, John. *Second Treatise of Government*. Edited by R. Cox. Arlington Heights, Ill.: Harlan Davidson Inc., 1982. F.

———. *A Letter Concerning Toleration*. Trans. by William Popple. Chicago: Encyclopedia Britannica, 1952. Vol. 35 of *Great Books of the Western World*.

Lomasky, Loren. *Persons, Rights and the Moral Community*. New York and Oxford: Oxford University Press, 1987. F.

Lopatka, Adam. "The Right to Live in Peace as the Human Right." *Dialectical Humanism* (1982).

Lyons, D. "Liberty and Harm to Others." *Canadian Journal of Philosophy* 5 (1979): 1•d19.

Macedo, Stephen. *Liberal Virtues: Citizenship, Virtue, and Community in Liberal Constitutionalism*. Oxford: Clarendon Press, 1990.

Machan, Tibor R. *Capitalism and Individualism*. Hemel Hampstead, England: Harvester-Wheatsheaf, Ltd., 1989. F.

———. *Individuals and Their Rights*. La Salle, Ill.: Open Court Press, 1989. F.

———. *Human Rights and Human Liberties*. Chicago: Nelson Hall, 1975. F.

———. *The Moral Case for the Free Market Economy*. Lewiston, NY: Mellen Press, 1988. F.

MacIntyre, Alasdair. *After Virtue*. Notre Dame, Ind.: University of Notre Dame Press, 1981.

Mack, Eric. "Bad Samaritanism and the Causation of Harm." *Philosophy and Public Affairs* 9 (1980): 230–260. F.

Marx, Karl and Engels, Friedrich. *Manifesto of the Communist Party*. Translated by Samuel Moore. Chicago: Encyclopedia Britannica, 1952. Vol. 50 of *Great Books of the Western World*.

Marx, Karl. *Capital*. Translated by Samuel Moore and Edward Aveling. Chicago: Encyclopedia Britannica, 1952. Translated from the third German edition, edited by Friedrich Engels. Revised, with additional translation from the fourth German edition, by Marie Sachey and Herbert Lamm. Vol. 50 of *Great Books of the Western World*.

McCloskey, Donald N. *Applied Theory of Price*. New York: Macmillan Pub. Co., 1982.

Milne, A. J. M. *Human Rights and Human Diversity*. London: The Macmillan Press, 1986.

Murray, Charles. *Losing Ground: American Social Policy 1950–1980*. New York: Basic Books, 1984. F.

Murray, John Courtney. *We Hold These Truths*. London: Sheed & Ward, 1960.

Narveson, Jan. *The Libertarian Idea*. Philadelphia: Temple University Press, 1988. F.

Nell, Edward J., ed. *Free Market Conservatism*. London: George Allen & Unwin, 1984.

Norman, Richard. *Free and Equal*. Oxford: Oxford University Press, 1987.

Novak, Michael. *The Spirit of Democratic Capitalism*. New York: Simon & Schuster, 1982. F.

———. *Freedom with Justice*. San Francisco: Harper & Row, 1984. F.

———. *Will It Liberate?* Mahwah, N.J., 1986. F.

Nozick, Robert. "Coercion." In *Philosophy, Science and Method*, edited by S. Morgenbesser et al., 440–472. New York: St. Martin's Press, 1969. F.

———. *Anarchy, State and Utopia*. New York: Basic Books, 1974. F.

O'Connell, Jeffrey, and C. Brian Kelly. *The Blame Game: Injuries, Insurance and Injustice*. Lexington, Mass.: D. C. Heath and Company, 1987.

Oakeshott, Michael. *On Human Conduct*. Oxford: Clarendon Press, 1975.

Pope John Paul II. *On the Hundredth Anniversary of Rerum Novarum (Centesimus Annus)*. Boston: Daughters of St Paul, 1991.

Pope Leo XIII. *On the Condition of the Working Classes (Rerum Novarum)*. Boston: Daughters of St. Paul, no date. Original 1891.

Radzinowicz, Leon. *Ideology and Crime*. New York: Columbia University Press, 1966.

Rawls, John. "Justice as Fairness: Political Not Metaphysical." *Philosophy and Public Affairs* 14 (1985): 223–251.

———. *A Theory of Justice*. Cambridge, Mass.: Belknap Press of Harvard University Press, 1971.

Raz, Joseph. *The Morality of Freedom*. Oxford: Clarendon Press, 1986.

———. *The Concept of a Legal System*. Oxford: Clarendon Press, 1970.

Redford, Arthur. *The Economic History of England 1760–1860*. 2d ed. Westport, Conn.: Greenwood Press, 1974. Original published 1960 by Longmans, London.

Rhoads, Steven E. *The Economist's View of the World*. Cambridge: Cambridge University Press, 1985. F.

Rosenberg, N., and L. E. Birdzell, Jr. *How the West Grew Rich*. New York: Basic Books, 1986. F.

Ross, W. D. *The Right and the Good*. London: Oxford University Press, 1930.

Rothbard, Murray N. *Individualism and the Philosophy of the Social Sciences*. Cato Paper No. 4. San Francisco: Cato Institute, 1979. F.

———. *For A New Liberty*. New York: Macmillan, 1973. F.

Rutland, Robert Allen. *The Birth of the Bill of Rights 1776–1791*. Chapel Hill, N.C.: University of North Carolina Press, 1955.

Schall, James V. *Religion, Wealth and Poverty*. Vancouver: Fraser Institute, 1990. F.

Schumpeter, Joseph. *Capitalism, Socialism and Democracy*. New York: Harper & Brothers, 1942.

Shuman, Samuel I. *Legal Positivism*. Detroit: Wayne State University Press, 1963.

Siegan, Bernard H., ed. *Regulation, Economics and the Law*. Lexington, Mass.: D. C. Heath and Co., 1979.

Smith, Adam. *An Inquiry into the Nature and Causes of the Wealth of Nations*. Chicago: Encyclopedia Britannica, 1952. Originally published 1776. F.

Smith, J. C. *Legal Obligation*. Toronto: University of Toronto Press, 1976.

Sterba, James, P. *The Demands of Justice*. Notre Dame, Ind.: University of Notre Dame Press, 1980.

Strauss, Leo. *Liberalism Ancient and Modern*. New York: Basic Books, 1968.

Tappan, Paul W. *Crime, Justice and Correction*. New York: McGraw-Hill, 1960.

Tawney, R. H. *Religion and the Rise of Capitalism*. West Drayton, England: Penguin, 1926.

Taylor, Richard. *Action and Purpose*. Englewood Cliffs, NJ: Prentice-Hall, 1966, re-issued 1973 by Humanities Press.

Thomas, D. A. Lloyd. *In Defence of Liberalism*. Oxford: Basil Blackwell, 1988.

Thomson, Judith Jarvis. "Remarks on Causation and Liability." *Philosophy and Public Affairs* 13: 2 (1984): 102–103.

Tinbergen, Jan. *Income Distribution*. New York: American Elsevier Publishing Co., 1975.

U.S. Catholic Bishops. *Economic Justice For All: Catholic Social Teaching and the U.S. Economy*. Washington, D.C.: Origins, 1986.

Van Den Haag, Ernest, editor. *Capitalism, Sources of Hostility*. Epoch Books. New Rochelle, N.Y.: Heritage Foundation, 1979. F.

Waldron, Jeremy. *The Right to Private Property*. Oxford: Clarendon Press, 1988.

Waligorski, Conrad P. *The Political Theory of Conservative Economists*. Lawrence, Kan.: University Press of Kansas, 1990.

Walzer, Michael. *Spheres of Justice: A Defense of Pluralism and Equity*. New York: Basic Books, 1983.

Warren, Melinda. *Government Regulation and American Business*. St. Louis: Center for the Study of American Business, Washington University, 1992. F.

Wasserstrom, Richard A., ed. *Morality and the Law*. Belmont, California: Wadsworth, 1971.

Weber, Max. *The Protestant Ethic and the Spirit of Capitalism*. Translated by Talcott Parsons. New York: Charles Scribner's Sons, 1976.

Weidenbaum, Murray. *The Future of Business Regulation*. New York: American Management Association, 1979. F.

Weigel, George, and Robert Royal, eds. *A Century of Catholic Social Thought*. Washington D.C.: Ethics and Public Policy Center, 1991. F.

Wellbank, J. H., Dennis Snook, and David T. Mason. *John Rawls and His Critics*. New York: Garland Publishing, 1982.

Wertheimer, Alan. *Coercion*. Princeton, N.J.: Princeton University Press, 1987.

White, James J. and Summers, Robert S. *Uniform Commercial Code*. 3d. Hornbook Series. St. Paul, Minn.: West Publishing Co., 1988.

Wilson, James Q., and Richard J. Herrenstein. *Crime and Human Nature*. New York: Simon & Schuster, 1985.

Wolfe, Alan. *Whose Keeper? Social Science and Moral Obligation*. Berkeley: University of California Press, 1989.

Wong, David. *Moral Relativity*. Berkeley: University of California Press, 1984.

Index